PRAISE FOR CLIVE VERONI AND *SPIN*:

"Elegantly written, smart, and substantive."　　— *Hill Times*

"Delightfully captivating and riveting, this is a must-read."
　　　　　　　　　　　　　　　　　　— *Publishers Weekly*

"Clive Veroni recasts the rules for marketing and branding in the digital age — a smart, entertaining romp lush with insight and example. Read it and reap."
　　　　　　　　　— William Thorsell, Editor-in-chief,
　　　　　　　　　　　　　Globe and Mail 1989–1999

"In an approachable, entertaining, highly readable manner, Clive Veroni takes us into the world of tribal consumers, big data, open branding, permission marketing, and the rise of individualized targeting. As such he takes us into the world of the future in political and commercial marketing campaigns. Enjoy the read, but ponder the implications!"
　　　　　　　— Dr. Alan C. Middleton, Executive Director,
　　　　　　　　Schulich Executive Education Centre (SEEC)

SPIN

POLITICS AND MARKETING IN A DIVIDED AGE

CLIVE VERONI

ANANSI

First published in Canada in 2014 by House of Anansi Press Inc.
This edition published in Canada in 2018 and the USA in 2018
by House of Anansi Press Inc.
www.houseofanansi.com

House of Anansi Press is committed to protecting our natural environment.
As part of our efforts, the interior of this book is printed on paper that contains
100% post-consumer recycled fibres, is acid-free, and is processed chlorine-free.

22 21 20 19 18   1 2 3 4 5

Library and Archives Canada Cataloguing in Publication

Veroni, Clive, 1956–, author
Spin : politics and marketing in a divided age / Clive Veroni.

Orginally published: Toronto, ON : House of Anansi Press Inc., 2014.
Includes bibliographical references and index.
ISBN 978-1-4870-0544-3 (softcover)

1. Marketing--Political aspects. 2. Communication in politics.
3. Campaign management. 4. Marketing. I. Title.

HF5415.123.V47 2018   658.8'02   C2018-901989-1

Library of Congress Control Number: 2018940371

Cover design: WAX
Text design and typesetting: Alysia Shewchuk

 Canada Council   Conseil des Arts
for the Arts   du Canada

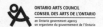 ONTARIO ARTS COUNCIL
CONSEIL DES ARTS DE L'ONTARIO
an Ontario government agency
un organisme du gouvernement de l'Ontario

*We acknowledge for their financial support of our publishing program the Canada
Council for the Arts, the Ontario Arts Council, and the Government of Canada
through the Canada Book Fund.*

Printed and bound in Canada

RECYCLED
Paper made from
recycled material
FSC® C103567
FSC
www.fsc.org

To my mother, Estelle Weynman, who constantly inspires
with her open heart and curious mind.

CONTENTS

INTRODUCTION TO THE NEW EDITION

FAST FORWARD

The original edition of this book opens with a description of election night 2008, Barack Obama's historic first election as president of the United States of America. I watched that event unfold at a raucous viewing party at the Albany Club, Canada's oldest private members club for those of the conservative political persuasion. Founded in 1882, it was named in honour of Queen Victoria's youngest son, Prince Leopold, the Duke of Albany — a descendant of George III, against whose rule the American colonies had revolted. Its greatest claim to fame is that the club's founding president was Sir John A. Macdonald, Canada's first prime minister and a prodigious boozer. Sir John A. would have felt quite at home that night in the midst of a crowd buoyed by a river of free-flowing liquor. To add to the festive atmosphere, the usual dark oak panelling and dun-coloured walls of the club were papered over with red, white, and blue bunting, American flags, and star-spangled balloons.

The evening was hosted by a Canadian public affairs firm, and the guests — including politicians, business and media

types, political junkies, and assorted hangers-on — represented the full spectrum of political allegiances. Even the U.S.
ambassador to Canada was in attendance. Despite the diversity
of political views in the room, it was clear that everyone was
united in rooting for only one candidate in the race.

The party was spread over two floors and multiple rooms,
and several large television screens were scattered throughout. CNN called the election for Obama at approximately
11 p.m. Eastern time. Wild cheers broke out as the crowd
applauded the election of the first Black president of the
United States. One wonders what the Duke of Albany or Sir
John A. would have made of it all. The jubilation that rose up
inside the venerable club was echoed around the world. The
news skipped across the globe like a glittering stone, igniting,
wherever it landed, joyful outbursts of shouting and dancing
in the streets. For many it was a stunning moment, a moment
beyond belief.

Fast forward eight years to election night November 8,
2016, and the world was once again stunned into disbelief. But
this time it received the news largely in confounded silence.
Donald Trump had been elected the forty-fifth president of
the United States. This time I viewed the results from inside
the belly of the beast, so to speak — I was inside a television
news studio. I had been invited to be a panellist on election
night coverage for the CTV News Channel, part of Canada's
leading private television network.

Arriving at the sprawling studios on the outskirts of
Toronto, I am ushered first into the makeup department. Then
I'm led down the hall to the cramped green room, where most
of the other on-air guests have already gathered. The first

person I see, occupying a substantial corner of the only sofa in the room, is Conrad Black. I'm not surprised to find him here. Black, a disgraced former media mogul with a taste for pomp and circumstance and comically obtuse language, is what passes for a star. He is, by far, the biggest name in the room. Sitting on the coffee table in front of him are a couple of delivery pizzas in their bright orange boxes. Next to them is a grocery store pound cake, peeking out of its cellophane wrapper. There is a mini-fridge with cold beverages, and an overworked coffee machine is sighing in the corner.

On this night, there is no unity of opinion among Canadians watching the election results unfold. And none on the studio panel, which has a distinct rightward tilt — thanks to Black and his tag-team partner for the evening, Adrienne Batra, editor-in-chief of the *Toronto Sun*. The *Sun* is Toronto's answer to the ignoble tradition of British red-top tabloids. Famous for its Page Three "Sunshine Girl," it's a defiantly conservative newspaper that offers its readers an intoxicating cocktail of outrage, salaciousness, and sentimentality. And, like a volatile drunk at the local pub, it always seems to be spoiling for a fight.

Prior to assuming the editorial role at the *Sun*, Batra had been press secretary to the man who single-handedly put Canadian municipal politics on the global stage, for all the wrong reasons — former Toronto mayor Rob Ford. International media and late-night talk show hosts were momentarily transfixed by reports and videos of his alleged drug and alcohol use. Ford had campaigned on a simple slogan aimed at disaffected working-class voters: "Stop the Gravy Train!" A message, in other words, aimed squarely at the average reader of the *Sun*. He was a skilled practitioner of the Trumpian politics of resentment before Trumpian politics was even a thing. It was not surprising, then, that Batra spent much of election night joining Black in defending Trump's outrageous behaviour on the campaign trail.

As an example of a typical back-and-forth between Black and Batra, someone mentioned Trump's race-baiting tactics, to which Black replied: "[Trump] did not say that Latinos in general were rapists and murderers; he was talking about about illegal immigration." Like a student eager to please her mentor, Batra jumped in with, "That's how it was spun, that he just gave it as a blanket statement. But Conrad's right, he wasn't talking about all of them."

Like many defenders of Trump's more outrageous comments, Batra and Black were making a distinction without a difference. Trump's comments about Mexican rapists came at his now famous campaign launch announcement at Trump Tower in June 2015. He began by saying that America was in serious trouble. The Chinese and Japanese were beating America on trade. The Mexicans, too, were beating the U.S. "at the border....And now they are beating us economically....The U.S. has become a dumping ground for everybody else's problems."

Then he delivered the comment that would dog him for the rest of the campaign: "When Mexico sends its people, they're not sending their best....They're sending people that have lots of problems, and they're bringing those problems with us [*sic*]. They're bringing drugs. They're bringing crime. They're rapists. And some, I assume, are good people."

Is he referring to all immigrants from Mexico, or just illegal immigrants, as Black would have us believe? It's not clear. What is clear is that, either way, he's branding Mexican immigrants as rapists, while acknowledging that some, presumably, may be "good people."

Even so, the distinction Black is making is immaterial. To broadly label illegal Mexican immigrants as rapists remains one of the most extraordinary acts of race-baiting ever to issue forth from a modern American presidential candidate. More importantly, this parsing of Trump's often confusing language also serves to distract from the larger issue. By repeatedly connecting immigrants with criminals, Trump was clearly intent on stirring up the long-suppressed racial anger among many of his supporters, some of whom were still seething over having a Black man in the White House for eight years. Trump, let us recall, began his political ascent by promulgating a racist lie: that Obama was born in Africa. A claim he only abandoned in the final weeks of the campaign. This was but one small sign of what was to come from Trump apologists, not just on election night, but in the months and years to follow.

As Canadians we are sometimes reluctant to talk directly about race and racism — our own, as well as that of others. This might explain why, almost three hours into the election night broadcast, as we sat around the studio desk baffled by why Trump was doing so well, the subject still hadn't come up. Where were all these Trump voters coming from? the panellists wondered. Who made up this silent Trump majority? Which prompted me to eventually say, "One of things we haven't talked about, and might be contributing to this, is the question of race." Trump, I went on to suggest, was tapping into the deep anxiety many Americans were feeling about the country moving inexorably toward being a majority-minority state, in which racial minorities would become the largest segment of the population.

Later in the evening, Conrad Black would return to this subject, and to Trump's defence, saying, "I think he would actually be surprisingly moderate." And later adding, "He isn't racist. He's just politically incorrect."

Of course, little more than six months into his presidency, Trump's political incorrectness would achieve new heights following protests in Charlottesville, Virginia, in which white nationalists spouting Nazi slogans clashed with counter-protesters. A white nationalist sympathizer ploughed his vehicle into the crowd, killing a young woman. Standing in the lobby of Trump Tower, the president drew a moral equivalency between the two sides, saying, "I think there is blame on both sides," then adding that there were "very fine people on both sides." His comments would prompt howls of outrage, even from within the Republican Party. But race forms only one piece of the puzzle that led to Trump's unlikely rise to power.

As election night unfolds, the guests in the green room rotate in and out, taking turns in front of the cameras to try to explain and analyze an event that seems increasingly beyond the reach of explanation or analysis. As Trump breaks through the "blue wall" states of Wisconsin, Michigan, and Pennsylvania that were supposed to insulate Hillary Clinton from defeat, it becomes clear that things are not going as anyone had anticipated. And certainly not as the polls had predicted. The electoral map starts to look like one of those slow-motion demolition videos of a building imploding. It is both riveting and stomach-churning. It will be hours before the dust settles. Arguably, it still hasn't.

Stunned by what we are seeing unfolding on the screens in front of us, the first words out of my mouth are, "It's a remarkable event in American political history, because you have a man who is basically a vulgar, puerile man-boy who's running for president and might in fact make it to the White House." In the moment, I am struck by how far the Republican Party has sunk from the lofty and cerebral aspirations of William F. Buckley, Jr. I am appalled at how a man who is so unfit for high office now has the presidency within reach. And so I continue: "I think his campaign is really an insult to the great tradition of intellectualism in the Republican Party. It's an insult to the American democratic process. And frankly, it's an insult to basic human decency."

Later, back in the green room, I think to myself that my spontaneous outburst may have been too harsh. But then the weeks and months roll by, and the shape of the Trump presidency comes into focus: his haranguing of the press as purveyors of fake news; the outbursts against his own justice department; an erratic management style that leads to unprecedented turnover among White House staff; the scandals involving *Playboy* models and porn stars; his attacks on football players who kneel during the national anthem, with calls to "get that son of a bitch off the field right now!"

Nothing, it seems, has prepared us for this moment. The two halves of American society, left and right, are farther apart than they have ever been, and are now shouting at each other across a great divide. And their political leaders are leading the braying chorus. Former vice-president Joe Biden and Donald Trump threaten to beat each other up in a schoolyard brawl. In the U.K., the emergence of a new grassroots political movement, called Momentum, pulls the Labour Party sharply to the left, even as the Brexiteers in Prime Minister Theresa May's cabinet drag the Tories further to the right. In Italy, France, and Germany, populist parties are resurgent, and in Eastern Europe nationalism is on the rise.

As the results move inexorably toward a Trump victory, and the mood in the green room turns to bewildered silence, Conrad Black becomes more and more animated. Happily digging into the pound cake in front of him, he says, "Try the cake. It's quite good, actually."

It's clear that this night will stand as a demarcation point, a before-and-after moment against which everything to follow will be measured. For decades to come, any analysis of Western politics in general and American politics in particular will be viewed through the distorting lens of the Trump presidency. This book is no exception. It's not possible to contemplate some of the major themes of this book — the widening gulf between the two halves of American society; the hollowing out of the traditional middle ground; the emergence of a hostile new tribalism; the willingness of politicians to piss people off — without seeing how they are playing out in real time all around us. The only thing that has changed is that all of these trends have been thrown into greater relief by Trump. And they're being exploited in ways never before anticipated thanks to a president, cabinet, White House staff, and GOP leadership who have elevated shamelessness to an art form.

To understand how America reached this pivotal point in its history, we must consider whether Trump is an aberration — an errant comet that flares, then fades as quickly as it came — or whether he is part of something larger, a sudden manifestation after a long, slow evolution.

Long before election night, during the extraordinary nomination campaign, Republican intellectuals were already distancing themselves from Trump. Conservatives who had been weaned on the high-minded musings of the *National Review* and its founder William F. Buckley, Jr., were horrified by Trump's steady march toward victory. It was an outrage! they harrumphed. The party had been hijacked by a vulgar interloper! they sputtered. He most certainly did *not* represent the party of Lincoln! Goddammit, he wasn't even a Republican, he was a lifelong Democrat! Long think pieces appeared in the *National Review*, all trying to explain why Trump was not a Republican, and certainly not a conservative.

The magazine dedicated its entire January 2016 issue to the case against a Trump presidency. On the cover were the words "Against Trump" in large gold lettering, set against a royal blue background and crowned with a curlicue of acanthus leaves imitating a crest. The editorial that accompanies the issue observes that "Trump is a philosophically unmoored political opportunist who would trash the broad conservative ideological consensus within the GOP." Baffled by Trump's surging popularity among Republican voters, the editors make the usual defensive and unpersuasive noises about the legitimate concerns of blue-collar workers and the working-class agenda. And they conclude with a statement about how Trump is out of step with the long history of conservative thinking: "Donald Trump is a menace to American conservatism who would take the work of generations and trample it underfoot on behalf of a populism as heedless and crude as the Donald himself."

All of this impotent outrage mattered not, as a long list of Republican candidates — from party royalty like Jeb Bush, to bright young things like Marco Rubio, to comedy acts like Ben Carson — were felled by Trump's inexorable advance. Right-wing urban sophisticates chose to call themselves conservatives, not Republicans, as a way of distinguishing themselves from a party that had devolved into something they saw as bizarre and unrecognizable. But they, along with the editors of the *National Review*, were wrong.

Trump was not a usurper from a foreign land. He was a creature of their own making. His emergence as the party frontrunner was the natural outcome of decades of Republican missteps — anti-science and anti-intellectual rhetoric, pandering to evangelical religious extremism and bigotry, race-baiting and anti-immigrant sentiment, and simplistic anti-government, anti-tax policies — that had come not from the lunatic fringes of the party but from its messy mainstream.

The Republican Party has stitched together these ideas to consolidate the various factions of modern American conservatism: home-schooled evangelicals who dismiss evolution as sham science; anti-government libertarians who think the only mission of bureaucrats is to curtail their freedoms; NRA fanatics who are determined to hold onto their AR-15s even if only in their cold, dead hands; the House Freedom Caucus, composed of peevish Tea Party holdovers; rabid Focus-on-the-Family homophobes; angry working-class whites ready to blame immigrants and minorities for all their woes; a moneyed class willing to starve governments of tax revenue in order to fill their overstuffed pockets with more cash. All these groups have found a home in the Republican Party, in a grand coalition of the dispossessed. And now the GOP is horrified to find that it's created a monster that is alive and kicking and has a mind of its own. Like Dr. Frankenstein, they will have to face the prospect of being driven mad by their own creation.

Donald Trump was not an anomaly in Republican politics. He was not an infectious bacterium that had jumped species from Democrat to Republican. After years of pressure from these conservative factions, he was simply a final coalescence into the most obdurate substance known to man. He was an idea whose time had come.

And his elevation to the highest office in the land exposed the unseen flaw at the heart of the American Dream: the idea that every American has an equal opportunity to achieve success, an idea that finds its most popular expression in the notion that "anyone can grow up to be president of the United States." With Trump, this mantra has reached its *reductio ad absurdum* and now must be expanded to say, "Anyone can grow up to be president of the United States, no matter how unfit they are for the job." In the words of Republican strategist Steve Schmidt, "The country has never before now elected somebody who is so manifestly unfit intellectually, morally, temperamentally, for the office of president of the United States."

What unsettled the conservative elite most about Trump was his witlessness. They could tolerate his infidelities and even his boorish behaviour, but his breathtaking stupidity was simply embarrassing. A leader who could absorb information only if it was presented to him in short bursts and with lots of pictures did not reflect back at them the image of conservatism they wanted to see. Behind his back, two of the most senior members of his administration were widely reported to have called him "an idiot" and "a moron." But as much as it shocked the intellectual wing of the party, it served as an energizing jolt to the great mass of Republican voters. Indeed, one of the most significant consequences of the Trump era is the mainstreaming of anti-intellectualism.

It's a phenomenon that was certainly not evident during the Obama years — the Harvard graduate and professor of constitutional law in Chicago who could speak extemporaneously in perfectly formed paragraphs. And not even during the time of George W. Bush, who, despite his Yale degree and Harvard MBA, is to this day popularly portrayed as an amiable dimwit. No, Trump represented something entirely new to a great number of Republican voters — a kind of aspirational anti-intellectualism.

Prior to the election it's fair to say that most people, even many who voted for him, would not have mistaken Trump for a man of glittering intellect. But many did see him as a man of decisive action. This, it turns out, was merely an image created for him on his reality TV show, *The Apprentice*. Trump's true management style became evident only after he assumed office, when he revealed himself to be a man of quavering indecisiveness. His opinions would change from moment to moment, depending on which way the political wind was blowing and whoever managed to bend his ear last. In the capricious weathervane of Trump's brain, ideas and opinions could flip in an instant, moved by no more than the passing breeze of the last person to walk by.

He frequently and unconvincingly boasts about his intellect: "I am a very stable genius." "My I.Q. is one of the highest." "I'm a very intelligent person." "I have the best words." But both he and his followers know that this is merely a cover for the deep insecurity Trump feels about his low I.Q., his low intelligence, his lack of "the best" words. For core Trump supporters, however, this is not a badge of shame but of honour. The group euphemistically referred to by political pundits as "low information voters" sees his lack of intellectual polish as a sign that he is like them. It's what distinguishes him from those uppity college-educated types who fill the houses of congress and the state legislatures, and have been in charge of things for too long. Of the many ways in which Trump has changed not just political culture, but American culture in general, his popularization of anti-intellectualism might be the most troubling of all.

There has long been a strain of anti-intellectualism in American politics, but it has mostly stayed on the fringes. What Trump's election has done is to allow those low information voters to come out of the shadows and raucously cheer their leader on.

During the Iowa caucuses in the 2015 Republican nomination battle, Ben Carson had a brief turn at the front of the GOP field. At this time Trump delivered one of his signature barn burners in Fort Dodge, a city in the north-central part of the state. Ridiculing Carson's life story (and his claim of a religious conversion after a knife fight with a friend), Trump delivered a line sure to end any candidate's political ambitions: "How stupid are the people of Iowa?" he yelled at the crowd. "Please don't be stupid!" Despite this, Trump came in a respectable second place behind Ted Cruz during the caucuses, then went on to capture the state by a substantial ten-point margin over Hillary Clinton during the general election. Even being called "stupid" to one's face is not enough to deter his most ardent followers.

As extraordinary as that might seem, it might have been foreshadowed by an equally extraordinary event in January 2016, almost a year before the U.S. election. That was when a whole new kind of hero, never before seen, appeared on American television. He was a self-absorbed, garish loud-mouth who shamelessly celebrated his own ignorance. No, not the leader of the free world. It was the star of a new television commercial for Old Spice, the line of noxious grooming products favoured by over-eager young men.

In this television spot our hero is seen racing across a desert landscape, presumably in an attempt to break the land speed record. But as his jet-powered vehicle streaks across the hot sands, something odd happens. The car begins to disinte-grate. Metal cowlings go flying off in all directions, the con-trols come apart in the driver's hands, and eventually the entire contraption explodes in a fiery ball.

As this disaster unfolds, we hear the driver's thoughts in the voiceover: "Should I stop? Should I have listened to all the crit-ics? Should I have taken even a basic ground-level engineering course of some type?" Yes, yes, perhaps that would have been a good idea, he thinks to himself. But then his true ethos reveals itself: "The most valuable lesson I have ever learned," he says, "is that if you fill your brain with knowledge, then there won't be any room for dreams."

That single line might be the most succinct expression of the Trumpian philosophy ever penned. "My dream is to take the wheel and drive!" shouts the Old Spice pitchman, at precisely the moment his dangerously out-of-control vehicle bursts into flames. In the end, our slightly charred hero survives, but his vehicle is reduced to rubble. No doubt there are many who would see this as a vivid metaphor of America's future with Trump at the wheel. But that was not the advertiser's intention.

This character, who is dubbed "Legendary Man" (because he promises to "Make you smell legendary"), is descended from a long line of rebel heroes in American advertising, from the Marlboro Man to Dos Equis beer's Most Interesting Man in the World. But what makes him different is his open celebration of his own ignorance. That's a first. It's a radical idea for a television commercial, where the hero or anti-hero is always a proxy for the brand and, by extension, for the target consumer. In the long history of advertising anti-heroes, many have been rebels; none have been stupid. However, here was a company proudly saying that the personification of its brand would be the stupidest guy in the room. This was the audacity of hopelessness.

Most people think advertising creates trends. But that is rarely the case. Advertising is, at best, the canary in the coal mine — an early warning signal of emerging social fashions.

What advertising does is sniff out nascent trends and then help to amplify them. And this ad, unwittingly or not, had captured anti-intellectualism's emerging moment at centre stage.

Historically, anti-intellectualism in American culture and politics has been framed as a reaction against the so-called "elites." Perhaps this comes from having escaped the rule of those plummy-voiced English aristocrats over two hundred years ago. In what is perhaps his most famous speech, "A Time for Choosing," delivered in 1964 in support of Republican presidential candidate Barry Goldwater, Ronald Reagan alluded to this idea by saying, "This is the issue of this election: whether we believe in our capacity for self-government or whether we abandon the American Revolution and confess that a little intellectual elite in a far-distant capital can plan our lives for us better than we can plan them ourselves."

The down-home drawl has always worked better on the campaign trail than the upper-class inflection. Reagan, as well as Jimmy Carter, Bill Clinton, and George W. Bush, knew how to turn it on. In the 1950s, following one of his famously eloquent speeches while campaigning for president, Adlai Stevenson was approached by an enthusiastic female supporter who burbled that he would have "the vote of all the thinking people." To which Stevenson quipped, "That's not enough, madam. I need a majority."

While suspicion of the educated classes has long been an undercurrent in American politics, the 2016 election was different. Trump's campaign was an unlikely success, despite careening from one blunder to another like an out-of-control clown car. Nevertheless, he continued to move from strength to strength. His misspelled tweets are, to coin a phrase, legendary. Not to mention his numerous gaffes, from quoting "Two Corinthians" to claiming "I love the uneducated!" to inventing the African nation of "Nambia." None of it impeded his progress.

And once in office, Trump seemed to embrace the Legendary Man ethos with even greater gusto. He became like the macho Slim Pickens yahooing his way to chaos astride an H-bomb in *Dr. Strangelove*, blithely unconcerned about the havoc that he's about to unleash and loving the ride all the way to the bottom. Ground zero for Trump's shameless anti-intellectualism was the Oval Office itself. He carried his particular brand of defiant ignorance from the fringes of American culture into the very centre point of the nation. And in so doing, he brought vividly to life Isaac Asimov's famous summation of that particular brand of defiant and self-confident American anti-intellectualism: "There is a cult of ignorance in the United States, and there always has been," writes Asimov. "The strain of anti-intellectualism has been a constant thread winding its way through our political and cultural life, nurtured by the false notion that democracy means that 'my ignorance is just as good as your knowledge.'"

Asimov, best known as a science fiction writer, was in fact one of the most prolific writers of all time, having written or edited more than five hundred books on a wide range of subjects, in addition to numerous articles and thousands of letters. His article on anti-intellectualism, entitled "A Cult of Ignorance," appeared in *Newsweek* magazine in January 1980. In it he decries the fact that politicians are deliberately dumbing down their language "in order to avoid offending their audiences by appearing to have gone to school." Asimov argues that these politicians are targeting the educated classes, those who are interested in acquiring knowledge and in sharing it with others. "We have a new buzzword...for anyone who admires competence, knowledge, learning and skill, and who wishes to spread it around. People like that are called 'elitists.'" And, he says, "Now we have a new slogan on the part of obscurantists: 'Don't trust the experts!'"

One suspects that Asimov, a futurist, would be unsurprised and a little bemused to find that, decades later, a wave of populist politicians, rising up within Western democracies, have found favour by belittling the so-called elitists and the experts. As Michael Gove, a Conservative politician and a leader of the Brexit movement, asserted during the lead-up to the referendum: "People in this country have had enough of experts!" Instead of trusting the experts who "think they know best," Gove believes voters should simply "trust themselves." Your ignorance, he is saying, is just as good as their knowledge.

TRIBAL LOGIC

Gove, who could pass as a minor character in an episode of *Mr. Bean*, is a graduate of Oxford, a former editor at *The Times*, a former cabinet minister, and a former holder of one of the highest offices in the land: Lord High Chancellor of Great Britain. This did not, however, prevent him from saying, without a glimmer of self-awareness, that those opposing Brexit were "elitist."

In a television interview with Faisal Islam, political editor of Britain's Sky News, in front of a live audience, Gove identified who those elitists were: "The people who are backing the Remain campaign are people who have done very well, thank you, out of the European Union." A line which elicited vigorous applause from the audience. He then defined the opposing side: "And the people who are arguing that we should get out are concerned to ensure that the working people of this country at last get a fair deal."

When Islam challenged Gove to provide details to back up his assertions, he went instead for the ad hominem attack: "You're on the side, Faisal, of the elites. I'm on the side of the people." This time the applause was accompanied by cheers from the audience.

And there you have it: the elites versus the working people. Those experts who think they know best versus the people who should just trust their instincts. The reason anti-intellectualism has suddenly moved into the mainstream is because it offers a way to express the growing tribalism in Western democracies. It provides a convenient shorthand for distinguishing which tribe you belong to.

Jonathan Chait, in a *New York* magazine article entitled "Why Republicans Love Dumb Presidents," has this to say about Sarah Palin, the politician who was perhaps the first standard bearer of conservative anti-intellectualism in the twenty-first century: "The vice-presidential candidacy of Sarah Palin represents an important marker in the evolution of the Republican Party. A candidate who plainly lacked familiarity with national-level public policy was nonetheless not only defended by conservatives, but embraced with a fervor that exceeded the grudging enthusiasm of the candidate who selected her." Tellingly, Chait concludes: "That liberals abhorred her as a rube merely served to confirm her authentic membership in the conservative tribe."

The more the elites point out just how dumb they think Trump is, the more he, like Palin before him, solidifies his tribal position. To his ardent supporters Trump may be a dummy, but he's their dummy.

As Andrew Potter notes in a review of Steven Pinker's book *Enlightenment Now*, "We are not just a social species; we are a tribal one as well, with our group identities giving purpose and meaning to our lives. But being a member of a group involves believing certain things that non-members by definition don't, and if holding that belief boils down to a contest between reality and our sense of self or the esteem of our peers, well, so much the worse for reality."

Our tribal loyalties, Potter notes, outweigh our adherence to logic. "Many tribes insist that their members affirm outright nonsense as a sign of their loyalty. So, just as belief in the resurrection is a baseline requirement for being a proper Christian, denying anthropogenic climate change is the price of entry into contemporary conservatism."

The surprising growth of a kind of celebratory anti-intellectualism in politics and pop culture is a symptom of the widening gulf between hostile social and political tribes. That tribal impulse is the subject of the opening section of this book. It details how politics in a divided age is about energizing small groups of fervent supporters, about being unafraid to antagonize your opponents, and about using tribal loyalties to build support.

Canada, with its articulate and progressive prime minister, Justin Trudeau, thought it had escaped all this divisiveness. Then, within the space of a few weeks in early 2018, the leader of the opposition Conservative Party in Ontario, Canada's largest province, suffered an unceremonious defenestration at the hands of his own party. This followed a sordid scandal involving claims of sexual misbehaviour and the serving of alcohol to minors. At the time this unfolded, the province was less than four months away from a general election, and the Conservatives were well ahead in the polls. The ruling Liberal Party was several years past its best-before date, thanks to numerous scandals of its own and fifteen unbroken years in power.

In the midst of all this, a family name that had for years hovered like a ghostly blimp over Toronto politics suddenly loomed back into view. Doug Ford, brother to the infamous former mayor Rob Ford, sought, and won, the leadership of the provincial Conservatives. His only political experience was as a mostly truant, one-term member of Toronto city council. He entered the race touting his experience as a businessman (by way of inheriting the multi-million-dollar family printing firm); he believed that government should be run like a business. And he was fond of railing against the elusive "elites" — including Margaret Atwood, of whom he declared: "I don't even know her. If she walked by me, I wouldn't have a clue who she is." While he did not share his brother's drug and alcohol problems, an in-depth report in the *Globe and Mail* suggested that, as a young man, Doug had been a small-time drug pusher in his high school neighbourhood.

In a previous political campaign, when asked in front of a Jewish audience about his brother Rob's use of a vulgar anti-Semitic slur, Doug Ford came to his family's defence with what in any other circumstance would be considered the punch line to a decades-old Borscht Belt joke, "You know something: my doctor, my Jewish doctor, my Jewish dentist, my Jewish lawyer." As the crowd laughed and jeered, he kept going, "My Jewish — hold it — accountant." Amid the rising outcry from the audience he finally concluded, "My family has the utmost respect for the Jewish community." His brother and erstwhile comedy sidekick might be gone, but the jokes just keep on coming. At this point it might be worth noting that Ontario accounts for close to 40 percent of Canada's GDP — twice that of the next highest province.

Doug Ford's ascension to the leadership of the Conservative Party in Ontario opened up a fissure in the political landscape of the province that surprised many. Canada had spent the previous couple of years looking condescendingly to the south. Canadians expressed sympathy for their neighbour's political situation with all the sincerity of a contestant on *The Real Housewives*. Now the politics of division have come home. And it is clear that no country is immune.

FIELD GUIDE TO THE FUTURE

This book was intended as a kind of field guide to the future of political and marketing communications in this divided age. But not even the most optimistic prognostications could have predicted how vividly the ideas put forward here have come to life over the past few years. From the surprising Trump presidency, to the chaos of a potential post-Brexit Britain, to the destabilizing forces wrenching governments across eastern and western Europe, the ideas that follow have taken on an even greater sense of urgency.

As you explore the sections of this book, consider the following:

The first chapter, which examines the enormous power small groups of passionate believers can wield, could have been written with America's white evangelical Protestants in mind. This group, which has declined from 23 percent to less than 17 percent of the U.S. population in the past decade, has only seen its political power and influence during the Trump era. They had an outsized impact on bringing him to power and keeping him there. More than a year into his presidency, after numerous sex scandals, a tally of falsehoods in the thousands (as calculated by the *Washington Post*), criminal indictments against some of his closest advisors and friends, and an ongoing investigation into collusion with Russia, evangelical support for Trump reached an all-time high. A survey by the Public Religion Research Institute (PRRI) in April 2018 showed that Trump's favourability rating among this group had reached a staggering 75 percent, compared to just 42 percent among the total population. Considering that Trump's victory came down to roughly 77,000 votes in just three states, it's fair to say that evangelical voters had a hand in taking him over the top. And their steadfast support has also served to keep Republican congressmen and women in line, damping down any criticism of the president. Republicans in congress understand just how much their own fortunes depend on not antagonizing this small but powerful group of voters.

On the other hand, there are some voters the Republicans don't mind antagonizing at all. And that is the subject of the second chapter of this book: how pissing people off can work to one's advantage. No mainstream politician in recent history has tested this theory to such an extreme as Donald Trump. The objects of his ridicule have ranged from a disabled reporter to Pope Francis. Not only does he not mind pissing off large swathes of the population, he actually seems to revel in it. And as he does so, his levels of support barely flicker. In this age of social media–driven belligerence there is a growing tolerance, perhaps even an expectation, that antagonism will be part of public discourse. Trump has embraced this new reality, and set a new gold standard for pissing people off while still prospering in the process.

The social media ecosystem also allows politicians and marketers to shift away from traditional mass communications to individually targeted messages, as explored in the chapter entitled "All Politics Is Individual." Here, too, we have only seen an escalation of this trend since this book was originally published. Highly individualized messaging reached new heights during the Brexit campaign and the 2016 U.S. election. Thanks to Canadian whistleblower Christopher Wylie, we now know that the London-based political consultancy Cambridge Analytica surreptitiously accessed data from tens of millions of Facebook profiles in order to deliver precisely targeted advertising messages to voters in the U.K. and the U.S. One of the ways they did this was to deliver so-called "dark posts" directly to selected individuals. A dark post is an ad that doesn't appear on the campaign's Facebook page but is instead sent directly to an individual's feed. The result is that there is no public record of the ad. It's like a private message, making it virtually impossible to know what was in those ads or who received them. At the same time, Russian bots were also engaged in a similar stealth campaign to deliver individual fake news messages to millions of voters. We may never know exactly how many such ads were disseminated or what effect they had on the final outcome of these votes. What we do know is that, despite promises by Facebook and others that online privacy will be more tightly regulated, the relentless advance of individualized marketing based on consumer profiling is here to stay.

The second section of this book examines the ways in which messages are disseminated in the digital age. It touches on the growing phenomenon of open branding and on the use of political-style "ballot questions" to frame communications. In any campaign, the side with the best ballot question usually wins. And that's precisely what we saw play out during the 2016 Brexit referendum in the U.K. The "Remain" side implicitly posed the following question to voters: "Do you want to abandon all the benefits of remaining in the European Union and thus risk an uncertain future?" The "Leave" side, on the other hand, framed the question this way: "Do you want to take back control of your destiny from the bureaucrats in Brussels?"

Putting these questions side-by-side helps to illuminate the way the Leave side won this debate. Remain was offering a passive alternative, based on a vague set of benefits (unseen by average citizens in their daily lives) and a vague threat of some unknown future. Leave's more active and assertive question touches on the powerful emotions of national identity. It can perhaps be distilled even further into the simple query: "Do you want to be British or European?" During the campaign this argument was bolstered by concrete examples of seemingly excessive regulation coming out of Brussels — defining everything from the decibel levels in vacuum cleaners to how households dispose of their rubbish. This argument echoed the one made by Reagan in his 1964 speech, questioning whether elites in a far-off capital could plan our lives better than we could ourselves. The Leave campaign exploited the feeling of many Britons that punctilious bureaucrats in Brussels were undermining the traditional British way of life. In the words of the editorial writers at *The Telegraph*, "What Britain does not have time for is vexatious regulations.... Traditionally, this has not been the British way. Our historic attitude towards regulation prefers a lighter touch."

Even though the ballot question has been a powerful tool of political communication for decades, it's still possible to witness large and sophisticated campaigns, like that of the Remain side, get it woefully wrong. And as framing the right ballot question becomes more important for politicians and marketers in this divisive age, we can anticipate that many more will get it wrong than get it right.

The other essential aspect of message dissemination in this era of digital and social media is speed. In the chapter entitled "Speed Kills," I argue that, sometimes, the speed with which a message is broadcast can actually trump its content. The first person to get their message to its intended audience wins. And in the age of smartphones, spreading instantaneous messages is only a tap away. No one understands this better than Donald Trump. Roosevelt, with his fireside chats, was the first radio president. Kennedy, who triumphed over Nixon in the first-ever televised presidential debate, became the first television president. Trump, clearly, is the Twitter president. His ability to circumvent traditional broadcast channels, and, in a flash, launch his latest musings directly onto the screens of tens of millions of followers, is unprecedented. And it's a power he wields with gusto. Trump has redefined how politicians communicate. His capacity to instantly communicate to the world without waiting for a print run, or a radio or television broadcast, means that he can control the narrative in such a way that everyone else is responding to his agenda, rather than the other way around.

But for all his skill in communicating with his followers, Trump has flaws that would upend any presidency. Two of these are covered in the final section of this book. One is the ability to build effective teams. When Trump entered the White House he went, overnight, from being a one-man band to being a conductor trying to lead an orchestra. Unlike the CEO of a major corporation, or even the governor of a state, he had no experience managing large, diverse, and complex teams. Nowhere is this inexperience more evident than in the unprecedented turnover among White House and cabinet appointees. In his first fourteen months in office, almost half of the top twenty appointments saw turnover. That compares to two positions experiencing turnover under Obama, and just one under George W. Bush, over the same time frame. And some of these positions have had multiple changes. During little more than a year, Trump burned through five Secretaries of Health and Human Services, four Communications Directors, and, remarkably, four National Security Advisors. This lack of skill in assembling and nurturing strong teams is probably the most significant factor hampering his ability to implement important initiatives, such as an effective replacement for Obamacare.

The other and perhaps more fatal flaw is his inability to plan for failure—the subject of the final chapter of this book. Trump seems only capable of operating in an atmosphere of pure optimism. It is the oxygen that fuels his ambitions, and many of his lies. Self-dictated doctor's reports claiming he would be "the healthiest individual ever elected to the presidency." Claims of having the largest inauguration crowds in history. It seems not to matter that these exaggerations are delusional. They provide the necessary optimism to drive him forward. But such an environment does not admit the prospect of failure. And that might be what ultimately causes Trump's elaborately constructed fantasy, of being the best at everything, to come crashing down to earth. Anticipating failure and imagining the worst that could happen, as shown in the closing chapter, allows one to cope with disaster when it arrives, as invariably it does. Trump may yet discover that the sunny optimism that has sustained him for most of his life has also blinded him to the dangers that lie ahead. His presidency has defied convention in almost every way. But if Trump cannot squarely face the prospect of failure, and cannot contemplate the worst possible outcomes from U.S. Special Counsel Robert Mueller's investigation, he might be wholly unprepared to deal with the consequences. In short, the most unconventional thing about his tenure might be how it ends.

The extraordinary outcome of election night 2016 was, perhaps, an answer to one of the oldest ballot questions of all: "Do you want more of the same or something different?" More than sixty million Americans voted for something different. It's safe to say that many of them had no idea of just how different the Trump presidency would be. And perhaps that is the lesson of this book, with a few years of hindsight. We can predict the trends and techniques of modern communications in this discordant age, but it's a lot harder to predict to what ends they will be used and to what extremes they will be taken.

INTRODUCTION

TILT SHIFT

Change. It was the one-word campaign strategy that propelled one of the most significant presidential contests in recent history. And the hundreds of thousands of supporters who gathered in Chicago's Grant Park, on a clear and unusually warm November night in 2008, had come to see that promise of change made manifest. They would not be disappointed. It appeared in the form of an African-American family stepping out from behind a blue door onto a blue-carpeted runway that stretched like a broad landing strip out into the pulsating crowd. As an announcer intoned, "Ladies and gentlemen, the next first family of the United States of America," the Obamas appeared on stage, smiling unaffectedly, as the cheering throng raised their arms and voices in unison.

In rhythm to the thudding helicopters above, they chanted, "Yes we can! Yes we can!" A fluttering of American flags rippled above their heads. Children were hoisted onto the shoulders of parents to glimpse this moment that would be told and retold for years and generations to come. The lights from countless cellphone screens, held aloft, flickered amid the crowd. Strangers hugged one another. Oprah wept.

The brightly lit runway that extended dozens of feet into the crowd was the end point of a very long road. Some say it was a road that stretched back to Springfield, Illinois, where Obama's election journey began in February 2007; others say it reached back to the march on Washington almost fifty years earlier; and others go back further still, to the dusty trails where the struggle for emancipation began. What everyone can agree on, however, is that this moment represented a significant change in American political life. And the whole world was watching.

"The whole world is watching" was a chant that famously echoed through this same park and the streets of Chicago exactly forty years earlier, during the 1968 Democratic National Convention, when anti-war protesters, who had been corralled into Grant Park, flowed onto the streets following violent attacks from riot police and National Guardsmen, who outnumbered them two to one. It was one of the most raucous and divisive moments in the history of the Democratic Party. But on this balmy night, as Obama strode calmly towards the podium to deliver his victory speech, the party had reached an historic high point and a moment of galvanizing unity. It was evident in the mass of supporters that surged around the stage, undulating as a single body.

As the crowd shifted and swayed, what they did not notice was that another change was taking place, not on the stage above them but right beneath their feet. The socio-political landscape was shifting, almost imperceptibly, but in ways that would affect every voter and every consumer in America and beyond — not just on this day but for years to come.

In the endless back-and-forth between swing states and swing voters that defines U.S. politics, the amplitude of this unseen change could not be measured in ballots cast or electoral votes won; it would be measured by a tectonic shift in the way marketers and political strategists seek to influence what we believe and how we behave.

For decades, there had been a one-way flow of knowledge that travelled from Madison Avenue to Washington. Now the tide was turning. For years political strategists had tapped into the creative brain trust of the advertising world to uncover new ways of reaching and persuading voters. This trend began in the 1960s, at the height of the *Mad Men* era. In fact, it began at approximately 9:50 p.m. on Labour Day, September 7, 1964. It was then, during an airing of the film *David and Bathsheba*, a 1950s toga epic starring Gregory Peck and Susan Hayward, on NBC's *Monday Night at the Movies* that a whole new kind of political ad aired on television, an ad that would change forever the nature of political advertising in America.

The commercial, known as "Daisy Girl," shows a pretty little blond girl standing in a sun-filled field. While birds chirp sweetly in the background, we see her picking the petals off a daisy. As she does so, she counts, "One, two, three, four..." She gets the numbers mixed up a little, adding to the sense of innocence and perhaps bringing a smile to the viewer. "Five, seven, six, six, eight, nine." When she gets to nine, however, the tone of the spot shifts dramatically. Suddenly we hear an echoing and sinister-sounding male voice going through a launch countdown. "Ten, nine, eight..." The girl looks up anxiously towards the sky. "Seven, six, five..." The frame freezes and the camera moves in for an extreme close-up. By the time

3

the countdown has reached zero her pupil fills the screen. The scene then dissolves into a nuclear explosion.

As we see the bright flash and the mushroom cloud forming, we hear the voice of President Lyndon Johnson saying, "These are the stakes — to make a world in which all of God's children can live or to go into the darkness. We must either love each other or we must die." An announcer then says, "Vote for President Johnson on November 3."

The ad caused an uproar. It was never aired again. It didn't have to be. The event was covered in all the major news media, and the spot was played and replayed on television news programs. There had never been a political ad quite like it. Employing a startling juxtaposition of innocence and horror, the spot unleashed a powerful emotional aftershock and tapped into the deepest fears of Cold War America. Without ever naming its opponent, the Johnson campaign had effectively skewered Barry Goldwater and his often-bombastic pro-nuclear outbursts. (Goldwater once quipped that a nuclear bomb should be lobbed into the men's room at the Kremlin.) "Daisy Girl" was saying to Americans, if you care about the safety of your family, don't let Goldwater's itchy finger anywhere near the nuclear trigger.

Goldwater blustered in response that the "weird television advertising" had horrified American voters and insulted their intelligence. But his perplexed outrage came too late. The sweet little girl with the daisy had punctured Goldwater's bloated rhetoric more swiftly and effectively than any amount of reasoning or political argument could have done. And in so doing, she launched a whole new era of political strategizing. Goldwater, it turned out, suffered one of the most humiliating defeats in U.S. presidential politics, eking out a mere 52 electoral votes to Johnson's 486.

The power of that single ad, which made it onto the cover of *Time* magazine later that month for a special "Nuclear Issue," meant that for the next fifty years political strategists would reach out to advertising and market research experts for help and insight into how to communicate their messages to voters. The spot was created by the legendary New York advertising agency Doyle Dane Bernbach. DDB, as it later became known, had made a name for itself with a remarkable ad campaign for Volkswagen starting in the late 1950s. The agency had managed to anticipate the anti-establishment zeitgeist of the sixties and captured it in their ads for the German-made car (less than fifteen years after the end of the Second World War), turning it into the official vehicle of the hippie revolution.

Prior to the 1960s, political strategy was a pretty blunt instrument. In the early part of the twentieth century it amounted to, quite literally, arm twisting and vote buying — not least on the bullying streets of Chicago, American poet Carl Sandburg's "Stormy, husky, brawling, / City of the Big Shoulders." But thanks to the power of the "Daisy Girl" ad, and others like it, political operatives were refining their strategies and adopting the newly emerging techniques of mass persuasion and communication in order to win votes.

The politicos learned well — so well that the pupil has surpassed the teacher. Today, in many ways, political strategists are more sophisticated than traditional advertisers in their mining of Big Data; more insightful in their segmenting of target audiences; more creative in the crafting of messages; and more innovative in their use of digital and social media. The spin doctors have turned the tables and in so doing have upended many long-held assumptions about marketing. Marketers are just now playing catch-up. And in the process they are looking beyond Madison Avenue and towards the data analysts, the media strategists, and the strategic consultants from Washington for help. The flow of knowledge has reversed. This book will trace that transformation, as the lessons of political campaigning move from the political war room to the boardroom, and ultimately to the living room, where the techniques used to sell us on the next president or prime minister are also used to sell us on the next snack food or household cleaner.

This reversal began with the 2008 Obama campaign. And just as the "Daisy Girl" ad marked the turning point at which politicos set their sights on Madison Avenue, so another startling and innovative ad marked the reversal of that trend. It came in the form of a boldly graphic poster entitled "Hope," designed by the artist Shepard Fairey. There are two noteworthy things about this campaign poster. The first is how it was created. There was no advertising agency involved, nor anyone from the Obama campaign. It was created by an ordinary citizen, an artist working by himself in his studio. The second is how it was distributed. On his own initiative, Fairey used social media to broadcast the image and to raise funds so that he could then buy advertising media, such as billboards, to spread the word even further. Fairey's ingenuity underscores the remarkable fact that powerful advertising ideas are no longer the sole domain of advertising agencies.

So iconic did this poster become that in many ways it was the defining brand image of the campaign. It would not be surprising if most people today think that "Hope" was the campaign theme for Obama 2008. In fact, the theme was "Change," or, more specifically, "Change we can believe in." Fairey's striking poster demonstrated just how far political advertising had come, and why it has moved to the vanguard of advertising in general.

In the more than four decades between "Daisy Girl" and "Hope" the American creative landscape has tilted significantly away from the advertising centres of New York and Chicago, and towards the west. The brightest young creative minds today are less likely to be seeking careers as advertising copywriters and art directors and more likely to be heading to California to work for social media companies or to design the latest smartphone app. Forty years hence, when we look back to pinpoint the locus of the golden era of creativity in the early twenty-first century, we will not be looking towards Madison Avenue but towards Silicon Valley. In this altered landscape advertising agencies and their clients are relearning how to manage their communications. And they find themselves in the unfamiliar position of no longer being the most creative guys in the room. Like the Obama campaign, they will have to find ways to leverage the creative output of others while building their brands.

They will also need to survive in a democratized world of communications, where the consumer is no longer just the passive receiver of marketing messages but also the broadcaster of their own messages. It is a world where ordinary consumers can shape and influence brand perceptions just as much as the marketers themselves. Social media is not, as many marketers seem to believe, just another medium for disseminating messages. It marks instead a revolutionary change in the balance of power between marketer and consumer. Consumers have traditionally had the last word, speaking with their wallets, but they have not had the loudest voice. For much of the mass marketing era they have been the mute recipients of marketing messages. That's no longer the case. They have found their voices and they have demonstrated a pent-up eagerness to use them. Going forward, brand communication will be a shared responsibility, and will demand shared vigilance.

This book will not be a rant against the evils of political campaigning — the negative ads and the dirty tricks. Others have dealt with these issues extensively. I have not snuck into the politicians' lair like an investigative journalist to shine a light on their follies and shady practices, which we can agree are plentiful. I've come instead as a kind of anthropologist to dispassionately observe a foreign and exotic tribe, to learn their practices, and to bring those lessons back to my own world, the world of marketing and advertising.

What this will be instead is an agnostic analysis of the techniques of modern persuasion, as seen through the political lens. It's a subject all of us should be interested in as voters and consumers. Because the more we understand how marketers and political strategists work their magic, the more thoughtful and deliberate we can be as shoppers and as citizens.

This book is also not designed to be a prescription but rather a provocation. It's intended to prod consideration of some of the big issues surrounding consumer communication today and how they affect those doing the marketing and those being marketed to. I will touch on three broad areas where consumer marketing is undergoing big change: how consumers are targeted; how messages are delivered to those consumers; and the process marketers use to develop their plans and build their teams.

The first of these, targeting, is arguably undergoing the biggest change of all because of one overwhelming reality: mass marketing as we know it is at an end. For over a hundred years marketers have used the tried and tested techniques of mass marketing to get their messages out to as many people as possible, as efficiently as possible. And they've been tremendously successful at it. For most senior marketers, it's not just the world they grew up in, it's the only world they've known. But as consumers move from a centralized mass-media environment to a distributed digital media environment, the accepted methods will need to be re-examined. Marketers have grown accustomed to travelling along the broad and comfortable highway that was mass media, where all traffic flowed in one direction and got to its destination with remarkable efficiency. That highway has now been joined by millions of arterial roadways with infinite off-ramps and on-ramps and with traffic streaming in all directions at once. Navigating these congested pathways will require a new kind of vehicle and a new set of skills.

In this disorienting climate, marketers will be obliged to reorient their thinking and challenge the received wisdom of the past. They will have to relearn how to speak to their consumers. And the new language is going to be borrowed from the political sphere, where techniques like targeting your most passionate supporters even at the risk of antagonizing the "non-believers" is standard practice. In an atmosphere of open public discourse, where opinions are increasingly polarized, we are going to see brands taking more polarized positions as well. Marketers will be chasing smaller segments of consumers and offering them more personalized messages than was ever imagined in the heyday of mass marketing. And they will do so in ways that will sometimes be unsettling to those micro-targeted audiences.

The second transformative change shaping the industry today is the issue of how marketing messages are disseminated. In a world of perpetual instant communications, the winners will be those who are first out of the gate. Being first to respond to unfolding events will provide significant strategic advantage. Speed can actually trump message content. In other words, how fast you say something will sometimes have greater impact than what you say. Real-time advertising will become not just an optional extra but an essential part of the marketing toolkit. The dissemination of marketing messages will be altered in other ways as well. In the shift to more open branding, marketers will need to welcome the Shepard Faireys of the world into their fold and encourage them to create content and distribute it on their own. These will not be easy changes for marketers to make. They will have to abandon their slow, deliberate, and controlling ways. But the rewards for adopting a more open and responsive stance are potentially immense.

There is a third major transformation facing marketers in the extremely fluid, unpredictable, and competitive environment they find themselves in today: how to build motivated and winning teams. It might seem counterintuitive to look to the often topsy-turvy world of politics for guidance on issues of human resources, but the war room has proven itself time and again to be fertile ground for breeding victorious teams, often made up of the most unlikely assortment of profession-als and amateurs. Ad hoc teams that are nimble, creative, and fiercely driven to succeed will be the ones most likely to pros-per in the new world of marketing. And the blueprint for how to build those teams will come from the world of politics.

What does all of this change signal for marketers and con-sumers? Is it not just another in a long line of challenges the consumer-driven marketplace has experienced over its life-time? After all, throughout the twentieth century mass mar-keting has endured world wars, recessions, and depressions; it has seen the rise of print media, direct mail catalogues, radio, television, and the Internet; and through it all companies and brands have continued to prosper. What insights can political strategists offer marketers who have survived all this upheaval?

What's different this time is that we have entered an era of highly polarizing public debate. The advent of social media, which feeds on the expression of individual passions, has pushed public discourse to the fringes. There is a hollowing out of the middle ground. We are living in a world of red-state versus blue-state dualities. And brands, too, are getting caught up in this bifurcated universe: Android versus iOS, Starbucks versus Tim Hortons, Miley Cyrus versus Taylor Swift. Brands have always had to compete with other brands. Now they have to compete with the fans of those other brands, who might dislike them intensely, and have both the means to speak out and the power to be heard.

But politics has always lived in this world. It is accus-tomed to operating in a hostile environment. In multi-party democracies, like those in Canada and the U.K., it's conceiv-able to win a majority government with less than 40 percent of the vote. That means you have to govern (and work to get re-elected) while an absolute majority of people disagree with you. As one senior Canadian political consultant put it to me, "How do you maintain your confidence if you walk out to the public every day and an absolute majority of people say you're wrong and they disagree with you? That takes a whole lot of confidence." Political parties compete not just with their opponents but also with vocal public opposition, intense journalistic scrutiny, and often-virulent attacks from media commentators. They understand how to communicate amidst the noise of the public square.

Many standing in the enthusiastic crowd in Grant Park on that November night in 2008 may have seen the appearance of an African-American first family on the stage as a healing moment, a reconciliation of the country's racially troubled past. They might also have optimistically hoped that it was, finally, the reconciliation of America's sharp political divide, the great coming-together promised by Obama in speech after speech: "We are not red states or blue states, we are the United States of America."

But only three years into his first term Obama was one of the most polarizing presidents in history. According to a Gallup poll, the partisan gap in approval ratings for the president was massive, with 80 percent of Democrats approving of the job he was doing while only 12 percent of Republicans approved. That gap of 68 points was the highest, by a wide margin, that had ever been seen for a president in his third year in office. It was the highest since Gallup had started measuring approval ratings in the 1950s during the Eisenhower presidency. But we all know the ending to this story. Despite this polarizing view and assaults from many sides, including from well-funded political action committees, Obama went on to a decisive victory against Mitt Romney in 2012. That's because his campaign team had accumulated decades of political learning on how to operate in a highly divisive atmosphere, and they combined it with the latest in technology, data analysis, and social media communication to break through the noise and get their message heard. It's a lesson every marketer is going to have to learn. Brands wishing to communicate their messages will need to discover how to raise their voices above the excited chatter of the virtual public square. For marketers trying to prosper in this raucous environment, one word can serve as both prophecy and rallying cry: Change.

I

THE END OF MASS MARKETING AS WE KNOW IT

The story of the rise of marketing in the twentieth century is really the story of the rise of media. Without media there is no marketing. And without mass media there would be no mass marketing. The capacity for newspapers, magazines, billboards, radio, and television to reach more and more people, more and more cost-effectively, is what made the post-war rise of an advertising-driven consumer society possible. The worlds of marketing and media fed on each other. Media outlets attracted audiences with enticing content, advertisers then paid to get their message in front of those audiences, and the resulting advertising revenue was in turn used to generate more content and even bigger audiences, and so it went. The symbiotic relationship between these two worlds created a cycle of energy that rolled like a perpetual motion machine through the century and into the next.

And then it ran smack into a brick wall called the Internet and shattered into a billion points of light, pulsating at the end of fibre optic Internet cables and smartphone screens.

And with that, the era of mass marketing as we know it ended.

In the old world of mass marketing, most people were exposed to the same mass communication in the same way at the same time. Jay Leno always came on at 11:30 p.m., your copy of the *New York Times* looked the same as your neighbour's, and Ryan Seacrest counted down the American Top 40 in the same order every week. Today, in a universe where almost every form of media can be digitized, content has been untethered from both time and space and is consumable in an infinite variety of ways. Information flow used to be determined by the media outlet; now it's determined by the media consumer. The consumer will decide where, when, and on what screen they want to view video content, what their customized online newspaper will look like, and how they stream their uniquely tailored radio station.

In this exploded universe made up of billions of individuals consuming media in unique ways, the old rules of mass marketing no longer hold.

Most marketers today will talk about micro-targeting and niche marketing, even as they cling to the quaint notion that mass marketing is the answer to all their quarterly earnings pressures. In a war where "make the numbers" is the battle cry, it's tempting to focus all your attention on the biggest number you can find. But we've entered an era of guerrilla warfare where bigger is not necessarily better. Marketers can no longer assume they'll win simply by focusing all their firepower on one big target. Increasingly, consumers expect to be spoken to as individuals, not as part of a giant group. Now, in addition to reaching out to the masses, marketers also need to fight for consumer attention on many smaller fronts at the same time.

They need to engage in conventional warfare and guerrilla warfare simultaneously. Nowhere is this issue better understood than in the political trenches, where techniques for segmenting target audiences and customizing messages have grown more sophisticated, and in some ways more sinister, with each new election cycle.

At the heart of every political campaign and every marketing campaign is you, the target audience. You are the object of all the effort and attention. In your role as both voter and consumer, you are the bull's eye at which billions of dollars are thrown in hopes of changing what you think and what you do. Over time, the dual roles of voter and consumer have gradually been converging. The end of mass marketing as we know it means that the big marketing dogs are having to learn new tricks in terms of how to target consumers. And these lessons are coming from the world of politics.

CHAPTER 1

THE POWER OF THE PASSIONATE FEW

WHERE IDEAS GO TO DIE

In midtown Toronto lies a small industrial park bordered to the east, west, and south by parkland and to the north by a post-war suburban development and a pricey shopping mall. You approach this industrial enclave along a road that gently curves and climbs, passing expansive manicured lawns and low-slung buildings in the modernist style. As the road crests, you can see to the right a long, low, red-brick office building. Beyond this is a large factory where all day long a lumbering ballet takes place as giant semi-trailers manoeuvre back and forth, some bringing in supplies, others hauling off finished product. Inside, workers toil day and night to manufacture chewable latex, inject it with flavour, and then wrap it in colourful packaging.

This is the Canadian headquarters of a multi-billion-dollar American corporation founded over a hundred years ago. It is a global leader in the manufacture and marketing of chewing gum. If you enter the office building and walk up the stairs to the second floor, you will pass by a row of large, glass-fronted offices with tall walnut doors and brass fittings, evoking a 1960s corporate office environment. This is where the senior management is ensconced. Keep going and you will enter a warren of small, windowless offices occupied by the lower echelons. Go farther still and you will come to an equally small, windowless boardroom barely big enough to hold the table and twelve threadbare chairs that crowd the space. It is here, in this room, where many an advertising idea has gone to die.

This is the room where Ipsos, the multinational market research company, routinely comes to present test results for advertising campaigns developed by the ad agencies that work on the gum account. And it is here where one advertising idea died because a small fraction of respondents found it irritating — despite the fact that the vast majority of consumers found the spot interesting and enjoyable and were keen to watch it again. In fact, those who liked the ad were "very enthusiastic" about it, according to Ipsos.

There is nothing unique about this room or about what happens here. There are hundreds, perhaps thousands, of rooms like it spread all over North America. This airless place is symptomatic of a deep and unshakable fear that runs through the corridors of the modern corporation. It is the fear of pissing people off. Companies are unwilling to antagonize any group, no matter how small, with their ideas. Even if there is a much larger group of people who would enthusiastically embrace those same ideas.

The air in all these rooms is permeated by the same odour — the sharp smell of anxiety. If one were to invent collective nouns for the actors in the drama that plays out when the ad agency comes to present ideas, it would have to be a pride of creatives, a cringe of account executives, and a concern of clients. The clients are invariably concerned.

On this day, Ipsos is presenting results from the gum advertising. Glance up at the screen and what you see projected there is a bell curve. This curve displays the reactions, positive and negative, people have towards the ad. Most people give the spot an average rating, so in the middle is where the curve crests. Off to the sides are the most negative and most positive ratings. That is where it tapers off.

Riding that curve is the focus of most marketing efforts. The goal is to make the bulge as high and as wide as possible, with the aim of appealing to the highest common denominator. It is on this coveted mountaintop where mass marketing has traditionally pitched its tent. But this focus on the middle of the curve results in a narrowing of vision. It ignores what's happening at the outer edges. And it's there, on the fringes, where passion lies. And it's passion that can make or break a brand.

The fact is, a small group of ardent believers at the tapering end of the bell curve can influence what the entire rest of the group thinks and does. This is the proverbial tail wagging the dog.

This phenomenon is common in the world of politics. Political pollsters pay particular attention to these small tribes of fervent supporters because they can have an outsized impact on the rest of the electorate. Marketers tend to look past them towards the bigger target, the great middle ground. In so doing, they can miss out on the opportunities these small groups can represent or be blind to the significant dangers they pose.

Of course, there have always been smaller fringe groups orbiting around the great mass market, minor collectives with their own particular interests and agendas. But what's happened in the past decade, thanks to the amplifying effect of social media, is that these groups have become more vocal and more visible than ever before. Get enough of these little groups spinning around and they can throw the mass market off its axis. Sometimes the sheer intensity of one group's passion can overwhelm even a much larger group. The power of the passionate few has long been a persuasive weapon in political fights to control the public agenda and influence voter behaviour.

Politicians have always understood that mass marketing and niche appeals do not constitute an either/or proposition. You need both to survive. That's why politicians spend so much time standing around suburban living rooms, backyard barbecues, and church basements. They know that no audience is too small and that a small group, if it's the right group, can have an enormous impact on your fortunes. Some marketers are still learning to embrace this dichotomy.

As marketers re-evaluate their notions of mass marketing in this new age of hyper-individualism, they're having to shift away from a heliocentric world view where everything revolves around one giant, glowing prize, and instead turn their gaze outwards to the vast constellation of possibilities that lie beyond. That's not to say that mass marketing is going to fade away completely. The sun will come up tomorrow. It's just that there is a universe of other opportunities to be explored, smaller perhaps, but each generating significant heat and energy of its own.

Jake Nickell is a laid-back former art student and college drop-out, now in his thirties, who looks a lot younger thanks to his slight build and mop of boyish blond hair. He speaks in a soft, laconic manner. He likes to wear jeans, T-shirts, and an air of hipster calm. But Jake understands passion.

In 2000, while still a student in Chicago, Jake and a friend decided to start a Web project that matched their artistic interests. As he said later, "I just wanted to make stuff with my friends. That stuff just happened to be art on my computer." Jake knew a little about art but not much about computer programming. So he figured he'd teach himself. As he explained in a TEDX talk in Boulder, Colorado, in 2011, he figured out how to write HTML just by clicking "View Source" on his web browser and patiently working out how to decipher the code.

This instinct for self-reliance and willingness to step fearlessly into the unknown came naturally, and early, to Jake. "I built a tree fort at the age of twelve just by grabbing a hammer and nailing a board in and standing on it and nailing the next board in," he says, as if that's how everyone goes about building things. He taught himself how to use Photoshop simply by clicking every button in the program until he knew what they all did. Mr. and Mrs. Nickell must have raised Jake in a household where the sky was the limit and the floor a giant safety net.

Jake's web project was a simple but radical idea. He created a site called Threadless.com that allows anyone to go online and submit a design for a T-shirt and anyone else to go online and rate those designs. The most popular designs are printed up and made available for sale. This might not seem particularly radical today, but back in 2000 almost no one was using the Internet in this way. Threadless was one of the earliest examples of Web 2.0 — turning the Web experience into something participatory and collaborative, driven by user-centred design. Threadless was using crowdsourcing four years before the term "crowdsourcing" was even coined.

It took a few years for Threadless to become a real money-making business that Jake and his partners could dedicate themselves to full-time. And just a few years after that, in 2008, *Inc.* magazine ran a cover story declaring that Threadless was "The Most Innovative Small Company in America." Today, Threadless supports millions of independent designers around the world by giving them a simple and ubiquitous canvas on which to display their work: the humble T-shirt. And its reach is expanding even further. The company created a line of T-shirts for Gap, to be sold online and at Gap stores around the world.

Threadless has an unheard-of track record for a retailer. Every single product they have sold has been a success. That's because buyers have expressed their passion for the item before it's even produced. It's a retail fashion business that reportedly generates a staggering 30 percent profit margin. Most retailers don't even come close to that. Generally, merchants are lucky to wring out a single-digit net profit margin. The result is that the company, started by a college dropout, is now the subject of business school case studies at Harvard and MIT.

Threadless creates a forum, a meeting place, for designers and buyers to connect. But arguably the same thing takes place every day on the streets of most major cities. Artisans who make jewellery, clothing, accessories, and all sorts of other things set up tables on street corners and at markets and fairs where consumers can see and buy their wares. But at the heart of the Threadless concept lies a critical difference: consumers are allowed to score the designs *before* they're manufactured. This simple mechanism changes everything. When visitors to the site vote on a design, they're delivering a powerful reinforcement to the designer for work that might otherwise never even be seen. And the voters, in turn, are engaged in a way that most ordinary shoppers never are. It's the *American Idol* effect. The more you vote, the more invested you are in the outcome. Research shows that 95 percent of purchasers on Threadless have also voted on designs. Almost no one simply buys; they also engage.

The scoring system is simple. Each design is rated on a five-point scale. In theory, anything that gets an above-average score (2.6 or higher) should be a winning design. And that's precisely how it would work if the folks at Threadless were trained as mass marketers who viewed the world as a giant bell curve. They'd be aiming for the highest common denominator. They'd be focusing all their energy and attention on that bulge in the middle of the curve. But that's not how Jake Nickell and his partners think. They are unencumbered by market research presentations. Their thinking is not funnelled through years of business school training. And they are not interested in aiming for the middle of the road. These guys are used to operating outside the mainstream. So they also pay attention to what is happening at the fringes. And by doing that, Threadless discovered something remarkable: sometimes a below-average score can result in a successful design.

This simple fact runs counter to everything traditional

mass marketers believe. The "concern of clients" sitting in the gum company's dimly lit boardroom could never be persuaded that a lower-than-average score could result in higher sales. But that's precisely what Threadless has found to be the case. Some designs with a score well below average (say 2.0) can still sell very well.

Instead of fixating on the middle of the bell curve, the Threadless team also looks at how many zeroes and fives a design gets. The reason, as they explained in a 2007 interview with the *New York Times*, is "designs that inspire passionate disagreement often get printed because they tend to sell."

Read that sentence again and you'll find the secret to turning below-average performers into winners: passionate disagreement. Polarizing ideas tend to get people more engaged. In these situations, it's not the size of support that's critical but the intensity of that support. A brand seeking to increase its market share by 10 or 15 percent doesn't need to appeal to everyone. It needs to connect in a powerful way with a relatively small group of people. Threadless has succeeded by turning the bell curve upside down.

By expanding its view beyond the broad middle ground, the company has uncovered a powerful idea — that it's better to have a few people who are passionate about your idea than a whole lot of people with only middling enthusiasm for it. And along the way, they've built a whole new level of Web interactivity, a place for people who love design to come together, and an entirely new platform for e-commerce. And they did it simply by nailing one board in, standing on it, and then nailing the next board in.

For years political strategists have been refining the art of engaging a small number of passionate supporters in order to help them win. What Threadless discovered by being observant, political parties have known for some time — ideas that inspire passionate disagreement can lead to success. This runs counter to the impulse of mass marketers, who strive to make the greatest number of people like you, or at least not hate you.

Politicians, however, live in a world of perpetual conflict, where passions can run deep. The most skilled among them learn how to harness that passion in order to keep sailing forward; the less skilled simply get swamped. Everywhere around us are examples of how relatively small tribes of passionate political activists can have a huge impact, an impact out of all proportion to their actual numbers: the Tea Party, pro-lifers, the Occupy Wall Street movement, and so on. The Republican Party is widely considered the party of the pro-life movement, and Republican leaders have been obliged to toe the party line on this issue. Stepping out of bounds can lead to a swift rebuke, as Herman Cain quickly discovered during the Republican presidential nomination contest in 2011. The former CEO of Godfather's Pizza, Cain elbowed his way (briefly) to the front of the crowded Republican race with a simple slogan: "9-9-9." This mantra summed up his plan for a regressive tax policy that would impose a 9 percent income tax, sales tax, and corporate tax on all individuals and corporations. A lot of Republicans liked it. It was zippy, it was simple, and it rolled off the tongue, which is more than could be said of the one-time slogan of Godfather's Pizza: "There's nobody's pizza like Godfather's Pizza."

On October 20, 2011, in the run-up to the Iowa caucuses, Herman Cain appeared on CNN's *Piers Morgan Tonight*. In his awkward, high-school-debate-style of questioning, Morgan asked Cain to consider what he would do if his own daughter were raped and became pregnant. Should she have an abortion? Cain replied that when it came to abortion, "It's not the government's role or anybody else's role to make that decision...It ultimately gets down to the choice that that family or that mother has to make. Not government, not some politician, not a bureaucrat. It gets down to that family. And whatever they decide, they decide. I shouldn't try to tell them what decision to make."

To anyone on the pro-choice side of the abortion debate, this argument would sound familiar. Essentially, Cain was echoing their view that it's a woman's right to choose and the government should keep out of the way. Whether he realized it or not, Cain was about to unleash a torrent of anger from pro-life activists.

The very next day he was obliged to appear on Fox News to quell the unrest. In the introduction to his appearance, former Fox host Megyn Kelly breathlessly announced, "We also have this very big story that is breaking today on the campaign trail." She went on to say, "There's a big backlash that is growing in Iowa today following Herman Cain's recent comments about abortion." A conservative radio talk-show host had blasted Cain for his remarks and had lobbed one of the most explosive insults one can throw at a Republican — accusing him of being pro-choice.

Cain's defence to Megyn Kelly was that Piers Morgan had tried to "pigeonhole" him with his line of questioning. He then made the most astonishing declaration. He completely reversed his position from the night before: "I am pro-life from conception. No exceptions!" And just in case that wasn't clear enough, he went one definitive step further, claiming, "I do not believe abortion should be legal in this country."

To be fair, Herman Cain's nomination bid was unclouded by either reason or consistency. However, to pivot from saying that the government should stay out of decisions about abortion to saying that abortion should be made illegal, in the space of twenty-four hours, was a dizzying *volte-face*, even for Herman Cain. Passions run high on the issue of abortion. And those passions had forced him into pretzel-like contortions so as not to lose the support of the most vocal pro-life campaigners within the party.

But Cain was not the only Republican candidate to make such a dramatic turnaround on the abortion question. Although it didn't happen overnight, Mitt Romney too managed to ride the pendulum from one side of the debate to the other.

As a candidate for the governorship of liberal-minded Massachusetts in 2002, Romney was unequivocally pro-choice. "I will preserve and protect a woman's right to choose," he declared at the time. His views on this subject went back years earlier and were shaped by the death of a close relative who passed away as a result of having an illegal abortion.

As far back as 1994, when he famously and unsuccessfully challenged Ted Kennedy for his senate seat, Romney worked hard to establish his pro-choice *bona fides* in an attempt to match Kennedy's well-established position in favour of abortion rights. In a testy televised debate, Kennedy let loose one of his signature zingers. "I'm pro-choice," he declared. "My opponent is multiple choice." But Romney would not be out-done on the pro-choice question, saying, "I believe that abor-tion should be safe and legal in this country." He went on to add, "I believe that since *Roe v. Wade* has been the law for twenty years, we should sustain and support it." Romney knew that even for a Republican, being pro-life in Massachusetts was simply not an option.

Ten years later, as Romney started looking beyond Mas-sachusetts and towards a role on the national stage, his views began to shift. "My political philosophy is pro-life," he was now claiming. By the time he was running for the Republican nomination in 2011, his conversion was complete. During the campaign, he penned an article for the conservative *National Review* entitled, "My Pro-Life Pledge." In it, he affirmed, "I am pro-life," and then went on to completely repudiate his earlier stand on *Roe v. Wade*. "I support the reversal of *Roe v Wade*," he wrote, "because it is bad law and bad medicine." In the space of a few years Romney had sprinted from one end of the acrimonious abortion debate in America to the complete opposite side of the field.

In that same publication, Romney strategist Mike Murphy tried to justify this about-face by saying Romney had been "a pro-life Mormon faking it as a pro-choice friendly." It was a shameless defence. He might as well have said, "We have our principles. And if you don't like them, we have others."

Despite his call for the repeal of *Roe v. Wade*, the bed-rock upon which all subsequent abortion rights rulings have been built, Romney's stance on abortion was actually the least extreme of all the candidates running for the Republican nom-ination. He was obliged to write his own "Pro-Life Pledge" because he was the only candidate who refused to sign the "Pro-Life Leadership Presidential Pledge" put forward by the Susan B. Anthony List, a hardline pro-life organization that opposes government funding of abortion and has lobbied aggressively for the defunding of Planned Parenthood. The pledge states that, if elected president, the candidate commits to signing into law an act to protect unborn children from abortion.

Politics is a constant balancing act between principle and pragmatism. So one might expect that the rush to the far end of the abortion spectrum by the Republican leadership was supported by the vast majority of Republican voters. But a month prior to Herman Cain's declaration that abortion should be illegal in the United States, CNN/ORC International released a poll showing that only 27 percent of Republicans believed that abortion should be illegal in all circumstances. That number is not far off the figure for the total U.S. adult population, 21 percent of whom believe abortion should be illegal. The vast majority of Republicans (72 percent) believe abortion should be legal in some or all circumstances.

This is the power of passionate disagreement in action. Sometimes balancing principle and pragmatism requires one to step out to the farthest edges of the see-saw. Although only about one in four Republicans believes in making abortion illegal in all circumstances, the candidates for leadership felt obliged to take extreme pro-life positions, even if in some cases this meant renouncing long-held beliefs. They all understood that any other stance would have eliminated them from the race. They knew that the influence of a few passionate believers could shift the prevailing winds and deflate their campaigns entirely.

Political strategists understand almost instinctively what marketers do not: that it's what happens at the edges of the bell curve that can often shape success or failure. Of course appealing to the mass is important, but putting all your focus and energy into the big bulge in the middle can blind you to the dangers that lurk on either side, especially when the issues are deeply personal and highly polarizing, such as abortion — or what design you want to wear on your T-shirt.

THE MAN WHO ATE FIFTY ORANGES A DAY

Right about now I can imagine concerned clients everywhere leaning forward in their chairs and patiently explaining that, sure, aiming for the safe middle ground might not always lead to great success, but at least it will allow you to avoid embarrassing failure. After all, nobody ever got fired for going after the mass market. In response, allow me to offer up the cautionary tale of the man who loved oranges so much he ate fifty of them a day but failed to understand the passion that other people feel for their orange juice. This failure caused two high-flying careers to come crashing down to earth. And it resulted in one of the most embarrassing missteps in the history of marketing.

Peter Arnell grew up in Brooklyn in the 1960s. During his teenage years he would spend summers accompanying his grandfather to his stall in Manhattan's Fulton Fish Market. At his grandfather's knee, he learned such simple homilies as "Fish where the fish are." In the darkness of the pre-dawn drives with his grandfather from Brooklyn to Manhattan, the half-asleep Arnell dreamt about his future. Those trips, he would later say, were all about "yearning to be bigger or better." It's a yearning he was ultimately able to fulfill, in more ways than one.

Arnell founded an eponymous advertising and branding agency that went on to do work for high-profile corporations such as Chrysler, DKNY, Samsung, and Reebok. But success came at a price. Along the way, Arnell acquired a reputation as a boss from hell who frequently humiliated and berated employees, often reducing them to tears. A profile by Daniel Lyons in *Newsweek* magazine reported that one employee saw "Arnell humiliating employees by making them get down and do push-ups in front of clients." It also claimed his language was peppered with profanity and that he was quick to anger, often "screaming at people, even hitting them." Not surprisingly, four former assistants, all women who claimed they'd been abused and degraded, sued Arnell in 1996.

Despite these controversies, Arnell continued his drive to be bigger and better. Unfortunately, as Arnell's business grew, so did he. One day he woke up to find that he'd grown to be over four hundred pounds. He was morbidly obese.

By his own admission, to cover up his bulk he hid behind a brash persona that was extreme, loud, and eccentric, and an unvarying wardrobe of billowy white shirts and elastic-waisted khakis. At photo shoots he'd plop down in a director's chair and use his stomach as a tripod for his camera. His bulk, combined with a carefully tended beard, made him look like a latter-day Orson Welles.

In his book *Shift*, which tells the story of his life and career, Arnell admits, "I've always loved food. I used to devour good food the way I devour life, savouring every new sensation."

Then one day, while watching his kids play in the backyard, Arnell had an epiphany: if he didn't get in shape and lose all that weight, he wouldn't live to see his kids grow up — or his grandkids, for that matter. He embarked on a mission to remake himself. The same obsessive, larger-than-life persona that had driven him to build a successful ad agency, and had led him to be so massively overweight, was now applied to slimming down.

He set an aggressive goal. His doctor said he would significantly improve his health if he could get his weight down to 230 pounds. For Arnell, who stands only five feet eight inches tall, that was not good enough. At 230 pounds he'd still look overweight. He didn't just want to be healthy; he wanted to be thin. So he set his own target. He would bring his weight down to just 150 pounds. That meant he'd have to lose a staggering 250 pounds.

Losing that much weight would require a whole new way of eating. He became obsessively focused on his food intake, even enlisting the help of his favourite restaurant owners and chefs to prepare special meals to suit his new lifestyle. And he discovered oranges.

Oranges became a central part of his new diet. For Arnell, who was frequently on the road to meet clients, oranges were readily available, portable, healthy, and they tasted good. When he arrived at a hotel, he'd order bowls of oranges to be sent up to his room. He began to eat a lot of oranges — twenty, forty, sometimes fifty in one day. He believed that oranges, with all of their fibre, would also clean out the digestive system. He spent so much time peeling oranges that his hands actually became stained a deep orange colour.

Astonishingly, it worked. In the space of just thirty months Arnell had reached his target weight of 150 pounds. His waist size shrank dramatically, from 68 to 28 inches. By any measure it was a remarkable achievement. And much of it was due to those oranges. So it seemed entirely fitting that on a chilly late-January morning in 2009, Peter Arnell was standing in front of the media at a press conference in Manhattan flourishing a carton of Tropicana, America's number one orange juice brand.

Gone were the billowy white shirt and elastic-waisted khakis. The slimmed-down Arnell was dressed in a tailored black woollen jacket with black-and-white checked tie. He also wore a pair of round, vintage-looking tortoise shell glasses. The well-trimmed beard, now greyer, remained. The overall effect was less Orson Welles and more Sigmund Freud.

But Arnell wasn't there to discuss his makeover. He was there to present the redesigned package for Tropicana, which his agency had just completed. The Arnell Group had been hired by PepsiCo, makers of Tropicana, to do a major brand overhaul for all their beverage products, including the iconic Pepsi brand itself. And Tropicana was part of that effort.

The man behind this massive brand initiative at PepsiCo was a suave Italian with the improbably romantic name of Massimo d'Amore. Indra Nooyi, PepsiCo's CEO, had offered d'Amore, a fourteen-year veteran of the company, the job of running its Global Beverages Group two years earlier, as the two of them strolled in the equally romantic gardens of the Hotel Cipriani on the island of Giudecca in Venice. He was a rising star in PepsiCo's international operations and this appointment, some said, would put him on track to one day replace Nooyi as head of the entire company.

D'Amore came to the job determined to make his mark, and with the view that PepsiCo's beverage brands (which in addition to Pepsi and Tropicana included Gatorade, SoBe, Mountain Dew, and others) had become tired and needed to be revived. He hired Peter Arnell to help make that happen. A former senior executive at PepsiCo, who was closely involved with these changes, told me, "Massimo came in and said, 'Peter Arnell is a genius and he is going to tell us how to change all of our businesses.'" In case that wasn't clear enough, Massimo then added, "Everyone get on board or get out." Unfortunately, quite a few marketing executives took the latter option. "We lost a lot of good people because they did not feel empowered to participate in the discussions, to influence the discussions," the PepsiCo insider pointed out.

Nevertheless, d'Amore and Arnell plowed ahead, first redesigning the iconic Pepsi logo, infantilizing it to look like a cross between a beach ball and a smiley face, and then tackling the Tropicana brand. What Arnell was holding in his hand that morning as he spoke to the media in New York was a carton of orange juice that looked nothing like the familiar Tropicana package. Astonishingly, it looked instead like a generic store-brand product. Gone was the instantly recognizable image of a fresh orange with a straw stuck in it, which had been part of the brand's identity for decades and which communicated simply and powerfully Tropicana's promise of purity and freshness. In its place was an ordinary-looking glass of orange juice.

The baffling rationale offered up for this change was that the brand had never shown the juice itself on the packaging before — as if people who'd been buying Tropicana for years needed to know what orange juice looked like. Arnell was particularly proud of the new plastic cap he'd designed for the package. It was in the shape of an orange. Squeezing the cap to unscrew it was like squeezing the real thing, he explained: "The notion of squeezing the orange is implied ergonomically."

Then he took the analogy one arcane step further: "Squeeze also maintains a certain level of power when it comes to this notion, emotionally, of what 'squeeze' means." A squeeze, he explained, is like a hug, a gesture of affection, even love. Sounding increasingly uncomfortable with his own hyperbole, he nevertheless plunged ahead. Squeezing the cap, he suggested, was like "transferring that love…between Mom and the kids."

One may reasonably conclude that only a man mimicking the appearance of Sigmund Freud could say with a straight face that squeezing an orange-shaped plastic bottle cap is like conjuring up feelings of maternal love. But this is often how designers and ad agencies sell their most ludicrous ideas to clients, employing the most esoteric rationale, designed to make you feel like an idiot if you disagree with it. And, not surprisingly, those marketers who feel less self-confident just keep drinking the Kool-Aid.

HE DOESN'T THINK I'M WORTH THE GOOD STUFF?

When the new package hit the store shelves there were howls of outrage from consumers and howls of derision from the marketing community. Consumers were both confused and angry at the change. Some claimed they could no longer find Tropicana on the shelf. Others felt the new package made their favourite orange juice brand, for which they were paying a premium price, look exactly like the cheaper store brands.

Linda Tischler, writing in *Fast Company*, related the story of her adult daughter, Melissa, who was in bed with the flu and sent her boyfriend to pick up some chicken soup and orange juice. She was taken aback when he returned with what looked like a carton of generic supermarket juice. "Gee," thought Melissa, "he doesn't think I'm worth the good stuff?" It was, of course, the newly redesigned Tropicana. It *was* the good stuff. It's just that the packaging was "so bland and undistinguished it looked like the low-rent made-from-concentrate stuff."

PepsiCo had succeeded in taking one of the most venerable brands in the grocery aisle and, through the application of millions of dollars, thousands of hours of work, and the talents of its leading marketers, turned it into a no-name store brand. In less than two months, sales of Tropicana Pure Premium juice plummeted by 20 percent. In 2011, Tropicana had generated revenues of over $6 billion for PepsiCo. If this kept up on an annualized basis, a drop of 20 percent would amount to losses of $1.2 billion.

Driven by social media, the outcry from consumers grew so loud that within weeks PepsiCo capitulated and announced it was scrapping the new design and returning to the familiar orange-and-straw package. It was a humiliating turnaround. Not since Pepsi's arch-rival had introduced a reformulated version of Coca-Cola in 1985, and three months later was forced to bring back the original Coke, had there been such an embarrassing marketing miscue.

How does a $90 billion global marketing juggernaut with a history stretching back over one hundred years and a stable of famous brands — from Pepsi to Doritos to Quaker Oats — get it so wrong? Was this just a matter of d'Amore and Arnell bulldozing their ideas through?

Some within the PepsiCo organization now say there were strong objections to the design from the very beginning: "Nobody liked the designs that Peter Arnell came in with and everyone felt they very much looked private label. In fact, they felt a very strong resemblance to [supermarket chain] Publix's private label orange juice," the former PepsiCo executive told me.

Apparently, those opposing the change included Neil Campbell, who, as CEO of Tropicana, was the most senior person on the brand. The change, the PepsiCo insider says, "was mandated on the Tropicana organization, despite all the naysayers, including Neil Campbell."

But there's more to the story than that. A marketing-driven company like PepsiCo doesn't implement a multi-million-dollar brand makeover just because someone says so — no matter how senior they are. They do consumer research, and lots of it. The Tropicana rebranding was no exception. But to paraphrase Mark Twain, there are lies, damned lies, and consumer research.

Sure enough, Tropicana tested the new package, and sure enough, the results came back saying no problem, make the change. And that's why, when the consumer outcry over the new package had reached its crescendo, Arnell confessed in an interview with the *New York Times* that he was "incredibly surprised by the reaction." He was surprised because apparently the research did not predict that would happen.

When the new design was eventually recalled, it was left to Neil Campbell to explain what had happened. Months earlier Campbell had told the *New York Times* that although the instantly recognizable image of the straw and orange had been around for a long time, consumers were not that attached to it. Now he was forced to admit, "We underestimated the deep emotional bond" with the logo. He was further baffled by the fact that dissent was coming from only "a fraction of a percent of the people who buy the product." But it was the fervour of this small group that was driving the need to change course: "What we didn't get was the passion this very loyal small group of consumers have. That wasn't something that came out in the research."

The truth is not that it didn't come out in the research; the truth is they failed to see it because they were looking in the wrong place. Like so many marketers before them, the folks at PepsiCo were so focused on the bulge in the middle of the bell curve that they failed to see the small but passionate group off to the side, the most loyal and passionate consumers, who could make or break the product's success. It's the kind of mistake that no self-respecting political strategist would make. In that arena, you always gauge the intensity of the opposition to your ideas.

Ironically, PepsiCo had repeated the same mistake the Coca-Cola Company had made almost three decades earlier, a marketing blunder so big that every marketer learns about it in MBA school. Prior to launching New Coke, the company embarked on one of the most extensive consumer research projects ever. By the end of it Coca-Cola had conducted blind taste tests with a staggering number of consumers — over 30,000. Thousands more were interviewed one-on-one and asked if they would buy a reformulated Coke. The response was overwhelmingly positive. The vast majority of people preferred the taste of New Coke and would be willing to switch. The mass market had spoken, and Coke responded by reformulating its decades-old formula.

But lurking in the data was a niggling little fact: about 10 percent of Coke drinkers would be unhappy about this change. The depth of that unhappiness was revealed in focus-group testing, which showed that Coke loyalists believed that trying to improve the product was akin to trying to improve the American flag.

Nevertheless, the executives at Coke kept their eye on the prize: that big, fat bulge in the middle of the bell curve. At the much-hyped press conference to launch New Coke, company chairman Roberto Goizueta proudly announced that when compared side by side with the old formula, New Coke was preferred by a margin of 61 percent to 39 percent. A perceptive reporter interjected to ask what would happen to that 39 per-cent of Coke drinkers who would no longer be able to buy the product they loved. Goizueta dismissed these most intensely loyal consumers with a contemptuous quip. "Well," he said, "39 percent of the people voted for McGovern."

In the pre-Internet age, consumers were left to protest the old-fashioned way, by writing letters and making phone calls. Impassioned and highly personal letters started arriving at Coca-Cola headquarters by the box-load. Tens of thousands of people were actually sitting down to put in writing their feel-ings about the change. The company was forced to hire tem-porary staff to handle an unprecedented deluge of up to 8,000 angry phone calls a day. Protest groups were set up and clubs were organized among Coke loyalists. People started hoarding the original product. The company was stunned and completely unprepared for the consumer backlash.

As the phone calls and letters piled up, other executives picked up on Goizueta's theme and dismissed the complaints as coming from a small group of marginal consumers — the old fogeys. One of them told the *Wall Street Journal* that "Most of the grousing was by older drinkers who aren't big sugar drinkers anyway."

A scant three months after Goizueta's flippant wave of the hand to diehard Coke drinkers, the company was raising the white flag. The original Coke formula was back, now to be called Classic Coke. Donald Keough, the company's avuncular president, was given the uncomfortable job of announcing this dramatic reversal at a press conference before hundreds of reporters. In contrast to Goizueta's dismissive tone, Keough gave a performance that was equal parts Southern charm and Irish humour.

He opened with an astonishing admission: "All of the time and money and skill poured into consumer research on the new Coca-Cola could not measure or reveal the depth and abiding emotional attachment to original Coca-Cola felt by so many people." But, of course, it could be measured. And it was revealed — in both the survey data and in the focus groups. Their own research showed that close to 40 percent of Coke fans objected to the change. The mass marketers at Coke had just chosen to ignore them.

Keough concluded his speech by admitting, "The passion for original Coke — and that's the word for it really, it's passion — that passion was something that had just flat caught us by surprise." A group of people considered to be marginal consumers, the "old grousers" and the "McGovern voters," were able to shift the balance of power away from millions of mainstream consumers and force one of the world's biggest marketing organizations into a humbling turnaround.

New Coke is probably the most famous new product flop in American marketing history. Every marketer knows about it. And yet, decades later, PepsiCo's most senior marketing team was trapped in the same limited view of research, the same mass marketing patterns of thinking, and the same dismissal of the small group of passionate brand advocates that led to New Coke's demise. And so it was that Arnell, the man who loved oranges so much he could eat fifty of them in a single day, failed to understand just how passionate some consumers could be about their orange juice. He was seduced into aiming for the highest common denominator and forgot about the small but fiercely loyal group lurking at the fringes.

PepsiCo's massive marketing machine, which employs thousands of people and spends in excess of $2 billion annually promoting its beverage brands, failed to see what a handful of guys in the funky offices at Threadless had seen: that acknowledging the people who passionately agree (or disagree) with an idea can be highly profitable. And ignoring them can be enormously costly.

Massimo d'Amore retired from PepsiCo in 2012 under a cloud. The romance was over. Beyond the Tropicana fiasco, his main legacy was that during his tenure Pepsi had declined from its long-standing position as the number two soft drink brand in America down to number three, ceding second place to Diet Coke. His appointment, which had started with such high promise in those romantic gardens at the Hotel Cipriani, ended on a sad and sour note. Arnell, who had sold his ad agency years earlier to global advertising giant Omnicom but continued to run the business, was fired in 2011 from the company he had founded and that continued to bear his name until its eventual demise in 2013. He lamented, "I can't believe that for the rest of my life I'm going to be known as Peter 'Tropicana' Arnell." The young boy from Brooklyn who'd been raised on the simple maxim "Fish where the fish are," hadn't realized that where there are giant schools of fish, there might also be sharks lurking nearby. The lure of the mass market is tempting. But sometimes it can distract marketers from seeing the full picture, from noticing that circling the big mass market there are sometimes small but powerful groups that can disrupt even the best-laid plans.

The caution here is not that marketers should ignore the great middle ground (those folks remain critical to mass market success), it's that they *shouldn't* ignore those consumers whose views exist on the extreme fringes. If you always aim to occupy the middle of the road, eventually you'll get run over.

Tropicana did their due diligence; they did their research. They just didn't understand what it was telling them. It was the same insight that Coke had missed: you cannot ignore the power of the passionate few. Antagonizing your most loyal followers is a risk not worth taking. In the post–mass marketing world, that lesson is more urgent than ever.

However, there's a flip side to this coin: there are some folk who are worth antagonizing. And doing so can actually lead to a significant market advantage.

CHAPTER 2

PISSING PEOPLE OFF WORKS

WHEN THE LIGHTS WENT OUT

If you'd been travelling in a low orbit around the earth on the evening of Friday, March 28, 2008, you would have witnessed a peculiar phenomenon, never seen before. Starting in Australia, the myriad twinkling lights of Sydney would have suddenly dimmed at precisely 8:00 p.m. And as the earth spun slowly and silently on its axis, the same phenomenon would repeat itself in Kuala Lumpur, Bangkok, Tel Aviv, Cape Town. At precisely 8:00 p.m. local time, lights began going out. Then in Stockholm, Rome, London. On and on it went. New York, Chicago, Atlanta. Major landmarks — the Sydney Opera House, the Empire State Building, the Golden Gate Bridge — all lost their lights. So too did the CN Tower in Toronto. Had your gaze drifted a little further east, you would have seen the same thing happen in Ottawa, Canada's capital city.

In Ottawa, the Parliament Buildings are dominated by a 300-foot-high Gothic structure known as the Peace Tower. The tower, which sits at the axis of the Parliament Buildings, is the most recognized landmark in the city and is always

45

dramatically lit. But that night it was dark. In the leafy suburbs of the capital, where politicians and ambassadors take up residence, a stillness fell. In house after house, lights were quietly dimmed. The darkness was punctuated only by the occasional glimmer of candlelight glimpsed through a window.

This was the first-ever international Earth Hour. Now an annual event organized by the World Wildlife Fund (WWF), Earth Hour is intended to raise awareness of environmental issues around the world. It has quickly evolved into a global phenomenon with millions of people, in over 7,000 cities and towns in 150 countries, participating.

But back in Ottawa on that cold March evening there was one house, a thirty-four-room mansion sitting proudly on the banks of the Ottawa River, adjacent to the French embassy, where the lights stayed on. This was 24 Sussex Drive, the official residence of the Canadian prime minister. Given its highly visible location, it was easy for anyone to see that two ground-floor rooms remained brightly lit during the entire Earth Hour event.

At the same time, Green Party activists, on Parliament Hill to celebrate the dimming of the lights on the Peace Tower, glanced up and noticed that the windows of the prime minister's third-floor parliamentary office were ablaze with light. An angry jeer rose up from the crowd and then bounced off the cold, silent, and (mostly) dark stone façade.

What happened? Had someone forgotten to turn off the lights? Had the prime minister's advisers neglected to tell him about Earth Hour, an event widely covered in the Canadian media in the preceding days? No, this was Stephen Harper, Canada's twenty-second prime minister, doing what he does best: putting his lips together and blowing a whistle meant to be heard by his loyal supporters.

Two years earlier, Harper led his Conservative Party to a breakthrough election victory, ending twelve years of Liberal Party reign. But he'd managed to win only 124 seats in the 308-seat Parliament, placing the Conservatives in a precarious minority position. He needed all the support he could muster.

And yet, here he was on Earth Hour 2008, only six months away from the next election, defiantly leaving the lights on while all the opposition leaders were tripping over each other to turn theirs off. Earth Hour was a no-brainer, an easy win. It was as uncontroversial as attending a bake sale at the local church. Who could take offence?

But the light in Harper's glowing living-room windows, just visible across the Ottawa River, was really meant to be seen thousands of kilometres away, in the Canadian prairie provinces where the Conservatives held a large and solid base of support. In Alberta, the prime minister's home province, fully two-thirds of the popular vote had gone to the Conservatives. This is where advocating for environmental causes is as popular as talking global warming at a Texas barbecue.

Alberta is ground zero for the country's burgeoning oil industry and its highly controversial oil sands project, which Al Gore has dubbed "the dirtiest source of fuel on the planet." Stephen Harper understood that supporting an initiative by the World Wildlife Fund would not play well in the Conservative heartland. The WWF has made the oil sands a *cause célèbre*, referring to the project as "Canada's devastating oil sands" and claiming it will have a profoundly negative ecological and human impact.

Harper's finely tuned instincts told him that his core supporters, the passionate tribe of Conservative voters, would not be turning off their lights. And he was right. In fact, on that night in 2008, as major cities around the world saw their energy consumption drop noticeably during Earth Hour, in Calgary, Alberta's largest city, energy consumption actually increased. And over the years that attitude has not changed. Earth Hour's own web site reports that "One of the least cooperative areas traditionally has been Alberta." In 2011, during the most successful Earth Hour to date, Alberta's capital city of Edmonton also saw its energy consumption spike.

On that same day, Ezra Levant, a provocative right-wing television host, took to the airwaves on the now-defunct Sun News Network (once known as Fox News North) and delivered a rant about Earth Day, pointing out that it coincided with the birthdate of the Russian socialist leader Vladimir Lenin. Dressed in a lumberjack outfit, Levant declared, "Let me show you how I'm going to celebrate!" and proceeded to fire up a chainsaw and awkwardly hack away at an evergreen tree brought into the studio for the occasion. What Levant was saying was that he was most definitely not part of the tree-hugging tribe of Earth Day supporters.

Given this attitude among hard-core Conservatives, it's not hard to imagine that at precisely 8:00 p.m. on the evening of that very first Earth Hour, Stephen Harper might have settled into his favourite armchair, opened up a book, and with the faintest smile playing across his lips, flipped on a reading light.

Smart marketers, like smart political strategists, understand that avoiding consumer anger and controversy is increasingly difficult. The trick is not to attempt to dodge it but to learn how to manage it and turn it to your advantage. Self-defence instructors counsel that when someone throws a punch your way, the best strategy is not to duck but to redirect the energy of that punch to destabilize your opponent.

Rather than avoiding consumer anger, marketers should be seeking ways to leverage that anger. It takes a fearless marketer to face the hostility of an oncoming crowd. Not just to face it but even to encourage it. There are some who have done it to powerful effect. They are the ones who have taken the lessons of wedge politics and applied them to the world of consumer marketing. They have actively provoked a hostile reaction from one tribe in order to win the support of another. That might seem unnecessarily daring, even foolhardy. But these days, in virtually every consumer arena, people are splintering into tribal groups and demanding to know where the brands they purchase stand on any number of issues — the rights of garment workers, fair trade for farmers, GMO foods, the list goes on.

In recent years there has been much talk in the marketing world about the growing power and presence of consumer "tribes." The term refers to the idea that consumers tend to cluster around common needs and desires, and want to connect with others who are like them. Brands that help them make this connection, and that can lead the tribe, will be more successful. A tribe (or herd, as some call it) is different from the typical way in which marketers define their target audiences.

A target audience, the tribalists point out, is defined from the marketer's point of view (through demographic and psychographic characteristics), whereas a tribe is self-defining. The tribe members' self-image grows organically out of their particular interests and behaviours.

Tribal consumers tend to be more active in shaping the products and services they consume, rather than passively consuming whatever marketers want to feed them. To connect fully with these groups, a brand must become part of the tribe and demonstrate that it shares the same values and interests. By doing so, brands can forge a deeper connection with these consumers. Strong brands can actually help to form and lead tribes, connecting people who might otherwise not have found each other.

This is a compelling idea — the notion that marketers need to go beyond traditional target audience definitions and into a deeper, more tribal understanding of their consumers. But by focusing solely on what makes a tribe unique and what holds it together, this theory misses the bigger and more important idea about tribes. It misses something we all understand intuitively, something that goes back to the very origins of human civilization. That is, the minute you create a tribe, with its internal cohesion, you are by default creating an opposing tribe, with its attendant conflict. A tribe, after all, exists in opposition to others who are not like it. And tribes that are diametrically opposed to one another tend to go to war.

In some parts of the world, ancient tribal wars are still part of everyday life. In modern democracies, however, the tribal conflict tends to play out on, arguably, a slightly more civilized battlefield, the political one. What are Democrats and Republicans, what are Tories and Labourites, what are Conservatives and Liberals, if not tribes in conflict with one another? All the values and beliefs that build cohesion within a given political tribe also put them in opposition to those who don't share their world view. This is where political strategists depart from marketers. While the marketer is focusing all of his or her attention on the internal workings of the tribe, trying to understand its every characteristic and nuance, the political operative recognizes that it's equally important to understand the opposing tribe. It is the tension that exists between tribes that, to the politician, can be a source of tremendous power and leverage. That's why political campaigns put so much effort into researching and analyzing not just their own supporters but those of the opposition as well. Put in marketing terms, who you're *not* marketing to is as important as who you are marketing to.

Thanks to social media, individual brand choices are becoming more public and more vocal. These loud and passionate declarations are causing people to take sides on any number of issues, from the melting of the polar ice caps to the latest monologue by late-night comedians. Individuals are identifying themselves with one tribe or another and making their choices known on Facebook, Twitter, Reddit, and the like. Some get to make their declarations in even more public forums. In 2013, Charles Saatchi, the multi-millionaire London art collector and former ad man, instigated criminal charges against two of his staff, Elisabetta and Francesca Grillo. The Grillo sisters worked as assistants to Saatchi's wife, the TV chef Nigella Lawson, and were accused of fraudulent use of household credit cards to the tune of almost £700,000. But the trial quickly descended into a shadow domestic drama, on the surface dealing with the charges of fraud but below that playing out the hostile disintegration of the Lawson-Saatchi marriage. During the trial, Lawson, a much-loved public figure, was called to the stand for a humiliating interrogation and was accused of drug use by both the Grillo sisters and her estranged husband. In the midst of all this, British prime minister David Cameron declared himself to be a huge fan of Lawson and a member of "Team Nigella." By declaring himself to be on Nigella's team, Cameron was in effect saying he was in opposition to Saatchi and the Grillos. (The women were ultimately found not guilty.) Cameron's comments were highly inappropriate, given that the matter was still before the courts and he was the prime minister. The judge in the case had to instruct the jury to ignore Cameron's "regrettable" statement. But in a time when everyone seems compelled to publicly declare which team they're for and which they're against, even politicians aren't immune to unfortunate outbursts. Add to this true fact that, while marketers are mostly concerned with prompting action by consumers, political operatives are increasingly interested in suppressing action among their opponent's supporters. Arguably, the real damage done by the fake news posts disseminated by Russian trolls in the 2016 U.S. election was to suppress turnout among Clinton voters rather than increase turnout among Trump supporters.

As ordinary individuals increasingly head online to declare their allegiances, they are not just announcing what they stand for but also what they stand against. It's not enough that my brand of choice serves as a connector to others who are like me. I also need it to distinguish me from those who are *not* like me.

What defines me as a Tea Party member is precisely what differentiates me from a liberal Democrat. What defines me as a Coke lover is precisely what sets me apart from a Pepsi lover. And I'd never want to be mistaken for belonging to the wrong group.

The next generation of marketers won't have the option their predecessors had of playing it safe and barricading themselves behind the castle walls. The revolution is here. Every time a marketer does something new, they open themselves up to the potential for backlash and angry words from the crowd beyond the gates. Whether marketers like it or not, they will have to abandon the safety of the high ground and engage with people face to face, some of whom won't like them. Smart marketers will understand that using the anger of some will allow them to win the support of others. The question is, how do you antagonize just enough people in the right way, so that the entire populace doesn't turn on you with pitchforks and flaming torches?

Most marketers aim, at all costs, to avoid the conflict between tribes. The political strategist relishes it and uses it to gain advantage. In fact, pissing off the opposing team is not only a sport in the political world, it's a vital strategic tool. They even have a name for it: wedge politics.

The idea is simple enough: say or do something that appeals to your base of supporters, even though you know it will antagonize others. One senior political strategist describes this dog-whistle approach as "Something which is absolutely the heartland sound your people want to hear. Everybody else won't like it or won't hear it, but it doesn't really matter." In fact, the angrier your opponents get, the more ginned up your supporters become.

This aptitude for knowing how to make a highly polarizing gesture that has the potential to anger many people, but sends a clear signal to his supporters, served Canada's former prime minister Stephen Harper well. In part, it's what propelled him steadily forward to win three successive elections, including a decisive majority in the spring of 2011.

Mere months into his first minority government in 2006, Harper demonstrated his talent for pissing people off by refusing to attend the first-ever International AIDS Conference to be held in Toronto. As former U.S. President Bill Clinton and Microsoft founder Bill Gates were boarding private jets and heading for the conference, Harper was headed in the opposite direction — as far away as he could go while still remaining on Canadian soil. He landed north of the Arctic Circle. The media reported he was there to drum up support for business and tourism in Canada's Far North, a region consisting mostly of permafrost and tundra, where the population density is roughly 0.03 inhabitants per square kilometre. In fact, the number of attendees at the AIDS conference outnumbered the total number of voters in Nunavut, Canada's northern territory, by some 10,000. The symbolism of this act was not lost on anyone.

Media pundits were incredulous at this unapologetic snub. To cheers from conference attendees, Dr. Mark Wainberg lashed out in his opening address, saying, "We are dismayed that the Prime Minister of Canada, Mr. Stephen Harper, is not here this evening." And when Harper's stand-in, the rookie health minister, stood up to speak, he was drowned out by jeers of "Where is Harper? Where is Harper?" In downtown Toronto, at the site of an AIDS memorial sculpture, people scrawled angry messages, including "Stephen Harper you shame us!!" Through it all Harper continued to grin and shake hands with small-town mayors and businessmen in Canada's most remote region.

Major international conferences are usually occasions for governments to make big announcements, especially if those conferences are on home soil. But even as Bill and Melinda Gates were announcing a gift of $500 million to fight AIDS, the Canadian government remained silent. Harper claimed the government would make no announcements about AIDS initiatives during the conference because the event was "too politicized." Of course, this statement simply engendered more anger and dismay.

But what Harper understood is that the louder the voices of protest became, the more his message was getting through to his intended target: those conservative voters who had put him into office. Research indicates that conservative voters are much less supportive of AIDS-related initiatives than the general population. Early on in his new government, Harper wanted to send a signal to those voters, a message that said, "You elected a conservative to office who shares your values."

At the time, online chatter summed up the feelings of those on the right. As one commentator, with the handle "blue-grasscanuck," noted, "I'm glad Harper didn't go...What they wanted was a big gift of money. Should gov'ts be doing things just because they want to be able to be well regarded in the world? Liberals think so, Conservatives don't."

Harper's time in the North was not wasted. For twenty years the Liberals had held the electoral district of Nunavut. Through six elections they had sprinted effortlessly to victory, winning as much as 70 percent of the popular vote. That run ended two years after Harper's much-derided visit. In 2008, Leona Aglukkaq took the riding for the Conservatives, capturing close to 35 percent of the vote. And a few weeks later she was sworn in as the minister of health, the first Inuk in Canadian history to join the federal cabinet.

These seemingly unpopular acts served only to consolidate Harper's personal political power and that of the Conservative Party in Canada. The party steadily increased its popularity over time. In the 2011 election, close to 3 million more Canadians voted Conservative than in the previous election in 2008.

What is more noteworthy is that these controversial stands are not isolated events. They were part of a deliberate pattern of behaviour that began early in Harper's career as prime minister and have continued for years. From scrapping Canada's mandatory long-form census, a move opposed by academics and business people alike, to unqualified and, some say, unbalanced support for Israel; to the dismantling of Canada's long-gun registry, an initiative opposed by every police association in the country; and to a tough-on-crime bill opposed even by judges, Harper has shown himself willing to piss people off at every turn — even those who seem to be his natural constituency. The payoff, however, has been worth it. The Conservatives made dramatic inroads with key voter blocs, from the influential Jewish community in Toronto to rural voters in the Ontario hinterland. The highly targeted appeal of these highly polarizing policies is precisely what helped the Conservatives win a staggering 73 seats in Ontario in the 2011 election and reduced the Liberals to just 11 seats, from 38 in the previous election. Harper repeatedly put his lips together and blew his dog whistle, and all the right ears pricked up.

Of course, western-style democracy is a see-saw affair. In 2015, the balance of power would tilt back in the direction of the Liberal Party, under the leadership of a youthful and charismatic Justin Trudeau. The Liberals would execute a stunning turnaround, going from 34 seats before the election to 184 afterwards. Starting the campaign in third place, behind the NDP and Conservatives, they would win a decisive majority, capturing 40 percent of the popular vote and 54 percent of the seats in the House of Commons.

They did this by understanding that the traditional middle ground in politics is no longer safe territory, and by being willing to piss off large groups of voters. The NDP, the traditional left-of-centre party, began the election campaign ahead of the pack in the polls. Having never won a federal election, they were eager to show they were ready to govern. Their strategy: project gravitas, avoid controversy, and demonstrate fiscal prudence. They would end the race in third place and lose almost seventy seats, swamped by the Liberal tide.

The Liberals, on the other hand, moved aggressively to outflanks the NDP on the left. Trudeau said unapologetically that his government would run a deficit in its first year. He committed to legalizing marijuana. And he promised to bring 25,000 Syrian refugees into the country within a few months of being elected. These policies made the Liberals appear to be the most progressive party on the ballot. And they were certain to antagonize conservative-minded voters. It was a bold gamble in the art of wedge politics, and it resulted in a massive payoff.

Trudeau and Harper were not the first politicians to discover the benefits of exploiting the tension between tribes of supporters and opponents. It's been part of the political arsenal for a long time. In fact, there is another conservative politician who demonstrated the same skill many years earlier and used it to powerful effect — so powerful that it antagonized millions of working people while still bolstering his political support among party loyalists. He was a man many saw as a champion for working people, but who was willing to deprive thousands of them of their jobs to make a political point. He did it without qualms and without hesitation, while the rest of the country nodded in approval.

THEY WILL BE TERMINATED

On the morning of August 8, 1981, Ronald Reagan stepped into the bright summer sunlight in the White House Rose Garden and faced a phalanx of reporters. Looking ruddy-cheeked and with a characteristic sideways bobbing of his head, he delivered a stern ultimatum: "They are in violation of the law and if they do not report for work within 48 hours, they have forfeited their jobs and will be terminated. End of statement." He then marched back into the White House.

True to his word, forty-eight hours later he fired over 11,000 of the 13,000 air traffic controllers who were responsible for keeping safe the tens of thousands of commercial flights that criss-cross America every day, and who had gone on strike two days earlier. This single action delivered a shocking blow to America's once powerful union movement, a blow from which it has never recovered. And it dramatically altered the dynamic of labour relations in America. Prior to the air traffic controllers' strike, American unions averaged around three hundred strikes per year. Since then, that number has gone down to about thirty per year. Reagan's willingness to fire every single striking worker was an unprecedented act and it emboldened private sector businesses to do the same, or threaten to do the same, when workers went on strike. It altered the psychological balance of power between workers and their employers. In effect, it rendered the unions' most potent weapon — strike action — largely ineffective by countering it with a weapon of mass termination. These were Cold War tactics applied to union and management negotiations.

The image of Reagan as the avuncular, optimistic, and patriotic champion of American ideals has been carefully crafted since he stepped down from office, and that effort has only increased since his death. But it overshadows the fact that while in office he was a highly polarizing figure, and one who was not above pissing people off in order to build his base of political power.

Reagan had made it to the White House with the support of many labour organizations. Remarkably, among them was PATCO, the same union that represented those 13,000 striking air traffic controllers. Indeed, only ten months prior to firing most of its members, Reagan had received their endorsement for president. Moreover, he was himself a union man with a record of collective activism. A card-carrying member of the AFL-CIO, Reagan was formerly head of the Screen Actors Guild and had led that organization in its very first strike action, in March 1960, against seven major Hollywood studios.

Reagan was a union man who had actively sought union support. Now, however, he was prepared to antagonize the very people who had publicly supported him for president because he knew it would win him significant support elsewhere. And it worked. A poll taken by Gallup in August 1981, shortly after Reagan's action, showed that 59 percent of Americans approved of his handling of the strike.

One of his earliest and boldest acts as president, the mass firing was intended to send a clear signal not just to the labour movement but, more significantly, to the voters who had put him into office. It was a risky move to turn on an important group of people who had helped get him to the White House, but a risk worth taking if it meant consolidating his support among the millions of others who would help keep him there.

There is an ironic coda to this story. That December, as the 11,000 fired workers faced a holiday season without work or pay, Reagan went on national television to deliver his Christmas address to the nation. He used the occasion to condemn the oppressive Polish government, which was then cracking down forcefully on the Solidarity union movement. The Polish leadership, he said, had broken an agreement "by which the Polish government recognized the basic right of its people to form free trade unions and to strike." He seemed unembarrassed, perhaps even unaware, of the irony of this statement. He looked, as usual, ruddy-cheeked. But he wasn't blushing.

GOVERNING IN POETRY

It might be argued that pissing people off, while effective in the right circumstances, is simply too risky a strategy. The uncomfortable reality is that striving not to piss anyone off is, in fact, much riskier. One only needs to look at the first three years of the Obama administration to see how badly a strategy of compromise, conciliation, and concession can go wrong. Obama brought into the White House the same philosophy he campaigned on: "We are not red states and blue states; we are the United States of America. We can do anything we want to, if we just come together like reasonable men and women and work in unison to find a solution. Yes we can." Well, apparently, no we can't. Obama did not subscribe to the philosophy of campaigning in poetry and governing in prose. He was still waxing poetical four years into office.

When faced with conflict, Barack Obama was inclined to invite his opponents over for a beer or a golf game. What this approach failed to recognize is that while the Republicans might have been interested in playing golf, they were not interested in playing along. Their strategy was simply to block any initiative by the president. By steering a middle course and attempting not to offend voters on the right, Obama was in fact gradually eroding his own base of support.

After eight years of George W. Bush, many voters were hungry for change. Obama was the very embodiment of the change for which they were hankering. But he failed to give his supporters any red meat to satisfy their appetites. He could have made a symbolic gesture to signal that things were going to be different from now on, much the way Reagan had. He could have taken some action, knowing it would piss off his opponents, but knowing also that it would rally his own supporters.

But as time dragged on, the closing of Guantanamo Bay went from being delayed to being cancelled; the healthcare reform bill became so diluted it managed to turn wine into water; the repeal of "Don't Ask, Don't Tell" took so long to implement that when it finally happened it became "Don't Ask, Don't Care." These were all issues Obama had taken a clear stand on during the election campaign. He had the mandate to act, and to act swiftly. Instead he sought compromise with his opponents. And with each passing year, more and more of those eager and impassioned voters who had carried him triumphantly into the White House began to drift away — some in a state of disillusionment, some in anger.

To understand how far those supporters drifted, consider Tom Morello, a passionate and uncompromising political activist and the former guitarist for rap-metal band Rage Against the Machine. In 2008, he said of Obama, "The only time in my adult life that I have ever been impressed by a politician was Barack's speech on race. As someone who has witnessed racism up close his entire life, it's nice to see someone who intelligently, candidly, and honestly talked to the American people as if they were adults for a change."

Three years later, Morello appeared on HBO's *Real Time with Bill Maher*. With Maher and filmmaker Michael Moore nodding along delightedly, Morello unloaded on Obama: "I got a message for him. Dude, it's time to grow a pair! A lot of people who put you in office, put you in office to fight for them, to fight against the Tea Party, to fight against this bullshit in Congress, to fight against those sons of bitches who are attacking the working class and the poor in this country." Raising his voice to be heard above the cheers and applause from the audience, he added, "He hasn't done any of it!"

Obama's election was like Christmas come early for many of his supporters. But his fear of pissing off others made those supporters feel that he didn't care about them and their concerns. As they excitedly scrambled under the Christmas tree, reality gradually set in. There was nothing there for them. Obama, who had carefully built his career by cultivating the image of a black man without anger, was starting to look to some like a president without principle. By striving not to offend anyone, he was inadvertently angering a lot of people who had thought he was going to be their hero. "Justice too long delayed," said Martin Luther King Jr., "is justice denied."

Obama was like the friend who volunteers to do you a big favour. He does so because he's a nice guy with good intentions. But then he delays and delays until eventually you have to start nudging him with gentle reminders. You don't want to be too pushy because he's a friend and, after all, he is doing you a favour. But eventually the delays drag out so long that your entreaties become more urgent. In the end, he finally does what he's promised to do, but by now you resent him for making you beg and you sense that he resents you for forcing his hand.

Obama was playing the role many corporations aspire to in their public personas, that of Mr. Nice Guy. Most companies are afraid to awaken the wrath of a frequently somnolent public. They carefully tiptoe around potentially controversial issues while trying to avoid pressing any hot buttons. This impulse to avoid controversy is felt most urgently in the marketing department, the public face of the corporation. But trying to avoid any sort of negative impression frequently results in marketing that avoids leaving any impression at all. It's no surprise that most advertising has as much impact on the average viewer as a blancmange. Having been absentmindedly consumed, it leaves no trace it was ever there. The unofficial soundtrack for much of what passes for advertising these days is "This bland is your bland, this bland is my bland."

In this changing social geography, as each tribe stakes out its turf, there will be no Switzerland. Neutrality will not be an option. Marketers and the brands they sell will need to stand for something. And in so doing they will need to stand against something. To do this they will need to adopt the lessons of their counterparts in the political world and embrace the idea that pissing off some of the people some of the time can be highly advantageous. Some smart marketers have already figured that out.

THE MOST OFFENSIVE AD OF 2000

In 2000, giant posters began appearing all over London bearing a single striking image. They featured a woman lying on a velvety cloth of dark indigo, her back arched, her head tilted back, her reddish curls sinking into the fabric, and her plum-coloured lips just slightly parted. She wore a pair of gold stilettos, a gold bracelet, a gold necklace. And nothing else. Her hand cupped her left breast. The right breast was fully exposed. The image was shot in such a way as to make her pale and luminous skin stand out from the dark and moody background. In the right-hand corner, in gold letters, were the words "Opium. The fragrance from Yves Saint Laurent."

The ad was hard to miss. It made the reputation of the then twenty-three-year-old model Sophie Dahl. It also made headlines. The Advertising Standards Authority (ASA), the body that deals with public complaints about advertising in the U.K., received over 1,000 complaints about it. That's out of a total of 2,700 complaints about all poster ads that year. It was the single most complained-about ad of the year. And the media quickly dubbed it "The most offensive ad of 2000."

The man behind it all was Tom Ford. Ten years earlier Ford had gone to Milan to work for the then ailing luxury brand Gucci. By 1994 he had been made the company's design director. And he took a staid Italian leather goods company, which had sought its initial inspiration from the horsey English aristocracy, and turned it on its head. Ford single-handedly brought sexy back to the house of Gucci. In the words of his predecessor, Ford changed everything from being "round and brown" to being "square and black."

When Gucci later acquired Yves Saint Laurent, Ford took over design responsibilities there as well. And he chose to make a splash in the YSL perfume business by deliberately appealing to the tribe of fashionistas for whom fashion was all about making daring choices and bold statements. There can be no doubt his message was not intended just for consumers; it was also aimed directly at the fashion influencers — the powerful magazine editors and fashion writers who not only dictated the trends but also decreed who the next fashion stars would be. He was aiming the Sophie Dahl billboards directly at them, knowing that the prim English housewife in her sensible brown and round shoes would likely be outraged.

Two years after the controversial Sophie Dahl ad, he turned up the heat further in a campaign for YSL's men's fragrance M7. One ad featured former martial-arts-champion-turned-model Samuel de Cubber. Shot in black and white and dramatically lit from above to highlight every curve, it shows de Cubber seated on the floor, head turned to one side, leaning back on his hands, legs apart. He is completely naked, in all his swarthy manliness.

In response to this startling image of full-frontal male nudity, *Time* magazine trumpeted, "Break out the champagne, get out the party lights, strike up the band — the last taboo has finally been broken." At last, men were being exploited as sexual objects just the way women had always been. Of course, *Time* never ran the ad, nor did *GQ*. Not even *Out*, a gay magazine with frequently explicit sexual content, could bring itself to display Mr. de Cubber in all his natural glory. The ad ran in the French edition of *Vogue* instead.

The arch and elegant Tom Ford knew exactly what he was doing. Inspired perhaps by Marilyn Monroe's famous line, "What do I wear to bed? Why, Chanel No. 5 of course," he is reported to have justified the ad by saying, "Perfume is worn on the skin, so why hide the body?"

Deliberately creating ads that most magazines wouldn't dare to run, but whose perfectly pitched dog whistle could be heard by just the right audience, seemed to be working as a brand-building strategy for both Gucci and for Ford himself. By 2002 he was once again provoking the scrutiny of the ASA — this time with a brand ad for Gucci that gave a new twist to the old phrase "Opening the kimono." In it, model Louise Pedersen is seen from the midriff down. She is splayed, back against a wall; the kimono she's wearing falls away to reveal her sleek torso and glistening legs. With one hand she is pulling down the front of her panties. In front of her kneels a young man. He is gazing intently at the spot right above the top of her panties, which now reveals her pubic hair, perfectly shaved in form of the Gucci "G." The G-spot, so to speak.

This image was shot by famed fashion photographer Mario Testino and made to look as if the viewer has just stumbled upon the scene. The couple appears to be caught in the harsh light of an amateur's flashbulb, making the intimacy and sexuality of the moment even more arresting.

Predictably, the outcry against this campaign was swift and loud. Mediawatch-UK, an organization whose stated aim is to campaign for family values in the media, led the attack. The director, John Beyer, denounced the ad as deeply offensive and called for an immediate ban by the Advertising Standards Authority. He went on to say, "The companies involved clearly release these kind of pictures to create as much publicity as possible, but it's a thoroughly unpleasant and irresponsible tactic. We can't simply ignore them." Ford might have added, *And that's the whole idea.*

It would be easy to dismiss all of this provocation as just so much fashion industry hoopla, were it not for the results. When Ford began his career at Gucci in 1994, the company was still reeling from a series of financial and management disasters. Two years earlier, its U.S. operations had lost $30 million. That was on top of an accumulated debt of $100 million. Aldo Gucci, one of the sons of the company founder, Guccio Gucci, had spent time in a Florida jail for tax evasion. And the company had been acquired by an investment group from Bahrain, which forced out Maurizio Gucci, the last remaining family member in the business. In 1995 Maurizio was shot dead on the streets of Milan. A subsequent trial would reveal that the murder was arranged by his former wife and that she had used her personal psychic to hire the assassins.

Against this operatic background, Tom Ford sailed into the Gucci offices with an armload of silk and velvet swatches, a few gilt accessories, and a vision for a new and more sensual Gucci brand. By the time he left, revenues had skyrocketed from a couple of hundred million to over $3 billion. And the company's stock value had increased to $10 billion, up from $4 billion only five years earlier.

Any analysis of Tom Ford's tenure at Gucci would have to conclude that it was his artistic vision that remade the faltering brand. From the very beginning his collections were hailed for bringing a new sense of glamour, not just to the house of Gucci but also to the world of fashion as a whole. His velvet hipsters and silk shirts worn open to the waist defined a new long, lean, sexy silhouette. They signalled a shift to a more seductive sense of style, what the *New York Times* admiringly dubbed "a louche sexuality."

Could he have achieved the same results without resorting to controversial ads? Without raising the ire of those outside the cossetted tribe of fashion insiders? Possibly. But there is no doubt that those ads helped tremendously. First of all, they signalled that things were changing at Gucci, and changing dramatically. The once hidebound purveyor of luxury leather goods, known for its iconic horsebit, was striking out in a new direction. And everyone had better pay attention. Secondly, the ads were a logical extension of what Ford was doing on the runway. They were the perfect embodiment of the new, sexy brand image he was creating. From that perspective, the ads made perfect sense.

But, of course, this is fashion. Like the fragrance industry or the beverage alcohol business, it thrives on an intoxicating mix of sex and controversy. Getting people riled up is just part of the job. It's not like selling packaged goods to middle America. It's not like selling apple pie or ice cream. Or is it?

"I CAN'T WAIT TO GET MY MOUTH AROUND THESE BALLS"

Alec Baldwin has hosted *Saturday Night Live* more often than anyone else in history — a total of seventeen times as of 2017. But one of his most memorable appearances was as Pete Schweddy, owner of Seasons Eatings, a bakery specializing in rum balls and other holiday treats. He became so identified with the character that he once said, "For a long time, I thought that 'Here Lies Pete Schweddy' would end up on my tombstone." When Baldwin was interviewed on *Inside the Actors Studio*, host James Lipton referred to the skit as "One of the greatest moments in the history of television." He was being only partly ironic.

In this memorable SNL sketch, Pete is interviewed on a mock NPR radio show entitled *Delicious Dish*. His two straight-laced female interviewers, dressed in ugly Christmas sweaters in keeping with the season, proceed to gush over Pete's "Schweddy balls." The routine leaves no pun untasted. "The thing I most like to bring out this time of year are my balls," says Pete. "I can't wait to get my mouth around these balls," replies one of the hosts. "Mmm, I like the way your balls smell," deadpans the other. And so it goes. The laughter of the studio audience escalates with each fresh quip, reaching its crescendo with Pete's riposte, "No one can resist my Schweddy balls."

It was inevitable, then, that when Ben & Jerry's was creating a new ice cream flavour, consisting of vanilla ice cream laced with rum and loaded with fudge-covered rum balls and chocolate malt balls, that Pete Schweddy would pop into the minds of the marketing team responsible for naming this new concoction. Hence the launch, in September 2011, of Ben & Jerry's Schweddy Balls ice cream.

It was just as inevitable that an outcry would ensue. In this case, it was led by the cleverly branded conservative Christian organization One Million Moms. A project of the American Family Association, One Million Moms appeals to mothers who are "fed up with the filth many segments of our society, especially the entertainment media, are throwing at our children." The organization launched a campaign, for example, to protest the appearance of Chaz Bono on the popular TV show *Dancing with the Stars*. They were outraged not only that a transgendered person would appear on a prime-time television program, but that the show "had the audacity to give a definition of what [transgendered] means for anyone who is not aware."

It's not clear how many moms actually belong to One Million Moms, but their protest over Schweddy Balls ice cream certainly got noticed, generating major media coverage and a good deal of parody. One pundit quipped that the headline for this story should be "Schweddy Balls leaves bad taste in the mouth of One Million Moms."

The marketing folks at Ben & Jerry's must have been high-fiving each other in the hallway. The product sold out in its first two days. After One Million Moms launched its call to action, Ben & Jerry's reported receiving five hundred to six hundred emails in the space of twenty-four hours. And "90 percent were saying 'Keep doing what you're doing,'" according to a spokesperson.

Founded in the late 1970s in a renovated garage by two guys who delivered the product in their VW Squareback wagon, Ben & Jerry's has a long history of social and political activism. And it has a history of in-and-out product launches with catchy names that play on current events: "Yes, Pecan!" in honour of Obama's inauguration, "Hubby Hubby" to celebrate the adoption of same-sex marriage laws in Vermont. The company directs a portion of its profits from these "social mission" flavours to support causes from climate change to fair trade.

In other words, Ben & Jerry's is used to controversy, and it would have known that Schweddy Balls would raise some hackles. And that's precisely why they did it. Not only did the brand benefit from the media exposure this controversy generated, it also managed to get its own user base fired up and motivated to act in support of the brand. The louder One Million Moms shouted, the more Ben & Jerry loyalists were pounding out supportive emails — and emptying the freezer aisle of Schweddy Balls. The product was "flying off the shelves," a spokesperson boasted to Fox News during the height of the controversy. The demand was so great and the product so hard to find, the company set up a Twitter hashtag #helpfindschweddyballs to assist its anxious customers. One Million Moms, which had also protested the launch of Hubby Hubby, saw the provocation for what it was: "It seems that offending customers has become an annual tradition for Ben & Jerry's," they complained. And yet the moms couldn't help but fall right into the company's Schweddy hands. This was wedge politics applied to consumer marketing. It was wedge marketing.

Deploying the tricks of skilled political operatives, Ben & Jerry's was fomenting tribal war in order to gain a market advantage. In the same way that Stephen Harper's absence from the International AIDS Conference was a deliberate provocation designed to antagonize some while at the same time shoring up support with the Conservative Party base, so the marketing of Schweddy Balls was designed to goad social conservatives while at the same time pumping up sales among Ben & Jerry loyalists.

This would all be great fun but not particularly significant if Ben & Jerry's were still run by a couple of hippies from Vermont, operating out of an old garage and a VW wagon. But since 2000, the company has been owned by Unilever, the massive Anglo-Dutch conglomerate that operates in 180 countries and has an annual turnover in excess of 50 billion euros.

Along with Heartbrand (makers of Magnum and Cornetto), Ben & Jerry's has made Unilever the world's largest manufacturer of ice cream. It's a key business for the company. And it's viewed as a major growth area. In short, it's not a business Unilever would want to jeopardize. And yet here was Ben & Jerry's, one of its leading brands in the U.S., willfully taunting an organized group of consumer activists with its controversial naming strategy.

That's because, since its acquisition, Ben & Jerry's has been given free rein by Unilever to be itself, with the understanding that to take the bite out of the brand would be to undermine its true character. Unilever knows what Stephen Harper, Ronald Reagan, and Tom Ford all knew (and what Barack Obama did not) — if you blow the right whistle, you'll attract your most committed tribe of followers. And that can build tremendous loyalty, even while it might anger others. Sometimes pissing people off is not only unavoidable, it's good for business.

Meanwhile, as some anxious researchers and concerned clients sit in their airless, windowless boardrooms wringing their hands over the latest research results, showing that a few people here or there hated their new ad or new product name or new design, the world outside is gathering itself into vocal and sometimes belligerent groups. Eventually, those marketers will have to step outside and face the agitated mobs. They're going to have to take a stand. And the uncomfortable truth is that sometimes they'll have to take a stand that will antagonize even their own loyal supporters.

PISSING OFF THE ONES YOU LOVE

Even the strongest brands, those that have a clear and well-defined identity, sometimes have to resort to pissing off their own customers in order to remain true to their brand values. When Apple launched the original iPhone in America in June 2007, it was a transformational moment in the history of technology — and marketing. The huge pent-up demand for the product served to propel it off the shelves in record numbers. Subsequent generations of the iPhone did the same, as did the iPad. Each new product outstripped the previous one in terms of sales success and marketplace impact. Collectively, these products have transformed many aspects of how we live, work, and communicate. And they have forced entire industries to change the way they do business (*pace* traditional music, video, and bookstores).

What might have been forgotten in the midst of all this excitement is that the original iPhone, and every iOS product since, has been brought to market with a significant design flaw, one that angered and frustrated many loyal Apple users and even led the U.K.'s ubiquitous Advertising Standards Authority to ban one of the original iPhone television spots from British airwaves.

The commercial in question showed the familiar iPhone screen as it finger-swiped, tapped, and pinched its way through a series of web pages. To the tinkling soundtrack of Orba Squara's song "Perfect Timing (This Morning)," the youthful, laidback voice-over intoned, "You never know which part of the Internet you'll need." After taking the viewer on its brief Internet tour, the spot concluded, "Which is why all the parts of the Internet are on the iPhone."

Well, as anyone who owned an iPhone back then knew, and as the Advertising Standards Authority concluded, not all parts of the Internet were available on the iPhone. That's because Steve Jobs, Apple's chief visionary, made a deliberate decision not to support Flash animation on any of its devices. That left a significant portion of Internet content inaccessible on iOS devices. Jobs, whose instincts were more finely tuned to consumer desires than just about anyone on the planet, surely understood that this decision would leave many frustrated and angry.

The day after the first iPhone launched, some wag posted to YouTube a video parodying Apple's television commercial. To the same tinkling soundtrack and a similarly youthful and laidback voice-over, we see a series of iPhone screen shots showing Flash-based web sites. Each screen is blank except for an alert to install the Flash player. The announcer says, "This is not a watered-down version of the Internet. Or a mobile version of the Internet. Or a kinda, sorta looks like the Internet Internet. It's just the Internet, without Flash."

Jobs's decision set off an angry debate among computer geeks (a key Apple constituency). The pro-Flash forces accused Apple of being motivated by greed and a desire to protect its iTunes revenue stream. Others claimed the company was aiming to "strong-arm the industry." One commentator complained, "I can only handle so much of the Apple totalitarianism." The anti-Flash tribe, of course, rose up in defence of their hero.

The debate became loud enough and heated enough that Jobs himself did something he rarely ever did. He stepped into the public fray. He posted a lengthy epistle to the faithful on the Apple web site, entitled "Thoughts on Flash." In it he detailed six reasons why Apple chose not to support Flash on its mobile operating system. But what it really boiled down to was this: Flash is such a power hog, and so unstable on mobile devices, that it would ruin the user experience on iPhones and iPads.

Adobe, the maker of Flash, responded with its own facts, assertions, and counter-arguments. But four years after the launch of the original iPhone, and after Apple had sold a staggering 250 million iOS devices, Adobe quietly capitulated and finally launched an alternative to Flash called Adobe Edge. This new software was powered by HTML5, Apple's preferred platform.

Not only was Apple dominating hardware sales, it was inspiring app developers around the world to make some of the most innovative mobile applications ever seen. By the time

Adobe tapped out of this wrestling match, over half a million apps had been developed for Apple devices, not one of them using Flash.

Through it all, Jobs stuck to his position — and to his vision for the brand. Jobs, whose attention to design detail is legendary, always focused on building the most effortless and enjoyable user experience into each product he developed. Apple's most successful launches did not start with a product idea. The company did not invent the personal computer, the MP3 player, the smartphone, or the tablet. It modernized them. Apple's versions of those products all started with a simple goal: How can we improve the user experience? Anything that got in the way of that experience was ruthlessly cast aside. By creating a family of products that contained a perceived weakness (no Flash animation), he was actually creating a stronger brand by ensuring that the user interface was simple, fluid, and efficient. He was running the risk of pissing people off in order to stay true to his original vision for the brand: to create a better user experience.

Despite this supposed product drawback, Apple went on to establish early dominance of both the smartphone and the tablet markets, significantly outdistancing its competitors — most of whom supported Flash animation and trumpeted the fact that they did.

Jobs knew that as soon as he entered the smartphone market he would have to take a stand on the issue of Flash. There was no middle ground to be occupied. You were either standing with the Flash tribe or against it. He made the tough call that would anger some users in the short term but make many more users happy in the long term. This was an arcane issue, not noticed by most iPhone users. But it serves as a perfect template for the myriad polarizing issues that modern brands must deal with, issues touching on manufacturing practices, social justice, the environment, and human health. On many of these questions there will be no neutral territory, and marketers will need to make the tough call. Which tribe will I stand with? Who will I piss off today? And having made those decisions, they will have to step out from behind the boardroom doors and face the angry mobs and explain themselves.

PUT YOUR LIPS TOGETHER AND BLOW

The point is not that angering people should be the goal for every brand. It's that attempting to avoid controversy at all costs is sometimes the riskier option. It can deprive a brand of its distinctiveness and edge. Too often, marketers strive to please the broadest number of people possible. The result can be communications that no one hates — but that no one loves either.

It would be easy for marketers to dismiss this business of leveraging tribal conflict as just so much sleazy political opportunism. And no doubt a great deal of it is. But they would be ignoring this trend at their own peril. In a social media–driven world where the predictable uniformity of mass marketing has been replaced by polarizing disagreements, marketers can no longer afford the luxury of sprouting bland platitudes about issues that consumers feel passionately about. And they cannot pretend that if they just ignore these conflicts, they can rise above the fray. Whether they like it or not, they will get dragged down into these messy dogfights. Instead of dismissing the political dog whistle as a tactic that's beneath their consideration, a new generation of marketers is going to have to learn how to put their lips together and blow.

But what smart practitioners of the art understand is that pissing people off just for the sake of it is pointless. There are two key questions to consider when taking a stand that might antagonize others. First, is the issue relevant to your most loyal consumers? And second, is it consistent with the brand persona? Stephen Harper needed to establish his conservative bona fides and reassure his base — especially during those years when he was running a minority government and couldn't pass the kind of legislation his supporters had elected him to pass. By making small but highly visible and symbolic gestures designed to appeal to his core voters, he was able to sustain his conservative image even while being hampered in implementing his conservative policies.

Early in his presidency Ronald Reagan was already formulating his cowboy persona, later to be solidified in numerous shots of him with a cowboy hat and horses taken at his vacation home, Rancho del Cielo. But in the waning years of the Cold War, he needed to project a tough-guy image. His uncompromising firing of thousands of air traffic controllers (and pissing off countless union supporters) was as much a message to Mikhail Gorbachev as it was to the country's unions. It simply said, *There's a new gunslinger in town.*

Tom Ford's brand of breathtaking sexiness was integral to his vision for the Gucci brand. And it was like a long, cool drink of water to the tastemakers who attend Paris Fashion Week and who were weary of years of arid high-concept runway shows. They celebrated him for getting back to the most basic impulse in high fashion: clothes are supposed to make you feel sexy.

Schweddy Balls was a perfect fit for the Ben & Jerry's brand, which has a long tradition of using witty and irreverent puns to name its products. Moreover, they knew that, even if the product offended some people, their tribe of core users would get it. In response to the controversy, the company spokesman noted, "It's a great flavor and our fans know it. They get it." The fact that One Million Moms got tied up into knots over it was simply an added bonus. It made the passionate Ben & Jerry's believers even more passionate.

CHAPTER 3

ALL POLITICS IS INDIVIDUAL

NOT TOO BIG TO FAIL

It's a known fact among marketing professionals and researchers that most new product launches fail. Some peg the number as high as 80 percent. In other words, only two out of every ten new products that make it onto supermarket shelves are still there a year or two later. That's a shockingly high failure rate. Imagine if lawyers, doctors, engineers, or airline pilots succeeded only 20 percent of the time. Imagine if your kid's teacher could get only 20 percent of the class to graduate.

This dismal record must be placed in the context of a massive growth in information and technology to help marketers understand consumer behaviour. Today there are highly sophisticated machines to track eye movements as people scan new package designs; virtual electronic store shelves to see how shoppers interact with new products; geo-tagging to monitor the movements of individuals as they wander the aisles. And there's data, vast petabytes of data, that measure virtually every aspect of our lives. It's data so big they actually call it "Big Data."

Mining this consumer data has opened up a whole new career path for Ph.D.s who might otherwise have become economists or stock market analysts. The power of these new tools cannot be underestimated. A 2012 cover article in the *New York Times Magazine* related the story of the retail chain Target, which had used complex data mining to accurately predict when a particular shopper was expecting a baby. They could then send coupons and special offers to that individual, based on her needs as an expectant mother. The project was quietly cancelled after the company received complaints from baffled parents wondering why their teenage daughters were receiving coupons for stuff intended for pregnant females when, clearly, they were not pregnant. It led to some awkward family conversations and, ultimately, to some admissions that Target knew more about their daughters than the parents did.

And yet, even with this explosive growth of consumer data, the failure rate for new products remains stubbornly high. The fact is, data is simply information, and information is meaningless without the capacity to turn it into understanding or insight. It's possible to stare at a bell curve all day long and know what the data *says* but still not understand what it *means*.

FOLLOWING THE DIGITAL BREADCRUMBS

In the post–mass marketing world, the emphasis will be less and less on reaching large numbers of people with the same message and more and more on reaching specific people with highly individualized messages. And just as in the twentieth century mass marketing was made possible by the growth of mass media, in the twenty-first century individualized marketing will be made possible, for better or for worse, by the growth of Big Data. As we travel through our digital lives, wherever we go these days, we leave behind a scattering of electronic breadcrumbs. The result is that much of what we do, say, and even feel can be tracked and recorded. Consider that Facebook's Data Science team has determined that twelve days prior to switching from being single to "in a relationship," the timeline posts between a prospective couple peak at 1.67 posts per day. Theoretically, therefore, tracking such interactions might mean one could predict when two people were about to become a couple. Facebook might know you're about to be in a relationship before you do. Even more extraordinary is the fact that Ray Kurzweil, Google's director of engineering and an acknowledged expert in artificial intelligence, boasted in an interview with the *Observer* that Google will soon know you better than your intimate partner does. By trolling through your emails, computer documents, and Internet searches, Google won't simply answer your questions but will actually know the answer even before you've asked the question.

In the 2016 election it became clear just how dangerous this kind of data capture and psychographic profiling could be. Political consultants at Cambridge Analytica obtained the Facebook profiles and preferences of more than 80 million users, most of them Americans. From these, they were able to create intimate portraits of those people and send them highly targeted messaged — often provocative or completely false. Given that some estimates suggest Clinton lost the election by as few as 70,000 votes, spread across three key states, it's quite possible that this activity had a direct impact on the outcome of the election. In the wake of these revelations,

Facebook promised to increase security and to allow users the ability to more tightly control access to their personal data. But Facebook's business model is built on allowing advertisers to profile their users and deliver them targeted messages. That won't change anytime soon. Not for Facebook, or Instagram, or Snapchat, or Google, or Twitter, or any of the myriad other apps that capture and repurpose our daily online activities.

Each digital trail is as individual as a fingerprint, and it allows detailed and specific profiles to be created for anyone living a digitally connected life. Behind our smartphones and tablets, our web browsers and search engines, our apps and social media sites, are electronic sniffers vacuuming up all those breadcrumbs and then reassembling them to form a picture of each of us. From a distance the data seems to show a general pattern, but up close it can reveal highly specific portraits. It's like one of those photomontages that from a distance looks like an image of a landscape, but when you zoom right in you realize it is made up of thousands of individual faces. The new world of marketing will reverse that zoom, starting with the millions of individual images and then pulling back to reveal the big picture. It will be connecting with millions of individuals and sending out customized messages in order to tell a general story about a product or brand.

This kind of detailed profiling did not begin with Cambridge Analytica in 2016. It was already being used to powerful effect by the Obama campaign in 2012. Assembling massive amounts of digital information and processing it through complex computer algorithms, the campaign was able to deliver highly specific messages, most notably creating individualized web sites for millions of supporters online. When connecting to the campaign's web site through an email link, Jim Smith in Arizona would be logged onto a site customized specifically for him, and different from the one Fred Jones in Nebraska would log onto.

But it wasn't always that way. It's taken decades for political parties to reach this point. At one level, the barriers to getting there were simply technological. Twenty or thirty years ago there were no mechanisms for collecting the vast amounts of data needed to profile millions of individuals. Even if collecting it had been possible, the computing power needed to process all that data was not readily available. And had it been, there was no medium to efficiently communicate customized messages to vast numbers of people all at the same time. In the intervening years, all that has changed.

At another level, it required a significant change of mindset to go from mass communication to micro-targeting. Political strategists actually had to arrive at a different way of thinking about their target audiences. Data and data analysis played a central role in bringing about this change of perception. But it didn't happen overnight. In fact, the evolution of modern political data gathering and analysis has gone through three distinct phases over a period of many years.

FROM INFORMATION TO INSIGHT

In the early 1990s political parties in both the U.S. and the U.K. starting assembling large databases of voters. In this pre-digital age, however, much of this effort was simply cataloguing the basic demographic information such as age, gender, income, employment status, postal code, and perhaps some additional variables such as hobbies or favourite TV shows. This information was used to create a profile of, let's say, what typical U.K. Labour Party voters might look like and pinpoint where they lived, down to a fairly narrow postal area. The data analysis required to arrive at this profile was fairly rudimentary. In the world of data analytics this is what would be called descriptive analytics. As the name implies, descriptive analytics simply tells you what the current state of affairs is: here's what your voters look like, here's where they live, and here's what they like to do on weekends.

As the 1990s progressed, things began to shift. Political researchers were now moving beyond mere descriptive analysis and towards more behavioural analysis of voters. They were using more sophisticated data mining to understand voter behaviour and even attempting to predict future behaviour. In other words, they were able not only to describe the typical Labour voters, but also to explain why they voted the way they did and try to anticipate how they would cast their ballots in the future. This represented a significant step forward for the men and women managing political campaigns. It meant that they could now shape the issues and their messages more effectively. Of course, influencing behaviour is a tricky thing. We humans can be frustratingly unpredictable and irrational. Nevertheless, this type of analysis was creating a shift away from mere description and towards predictive analysis. As we'll see later in this chapter, such predictive analysis was used to great effect by Bill Clinton's pollsters in 1992 to shape the campaign's economic and social message, especially towards disaffected white working-class voters who'd fled to Reagan in the 1980s (the so-called Reagan Democrats), and then to Donald Trump in large numbers in 2016.

It should be noted that, through this entire period, the worlds of marketing and politics were progressing at the same pace. Marketers, too, were creating detailed demographic and psychographic portraits of their customers. They, too, went on to develop greater understanding of the underlying motivations for consumer actions and to create predictive models to anticipate consumer behaviour and find ways to craft their messages to influence that behaviour.

And during this time the magicians behind all the data gathering and analysis were, on the political side, the pollsters and, on the marketing side, the market researchers. (Some firms, like Gallup, straddled these two worlds.) Pollsters and researchers began to occupy positions of substantial influence inside political war rooms and corporate boardrooms.

But since the early 2000s, beginning with the Obama campaign in 2008, accelerating during his 2012 campaign, and reaching warp speed in the 2016 election, we've moved into the third phase of data analysis: using data to drive actionable insights. By actionable insights I mean the ability to find fresh insights in the massive databases that political parties are constantly assembling, and using those insights to drive much higher rates of success in influencing behaviour. It's like the previous behavioural analysis phase, but jacked up on steroids.

These improved results are made possible by two complementary developments: the growth of Big Data (increasingly captured through our online activities) and the capacity for personalized communication. It is here, in the third phase of data-driven insights, where marketers and their researchers are falling behind. As Big Data becomes bigger each year, with more and more information being collected about consumer behaviour, sifting through it all to find new insights is becoming increasingly more difficult. Many marketing-driven organizations are attempting to drink from a firehose of data and finding themselves drowning. The more data that becomes available, the more complicated it is to filter out the signal from the noise. There's an old saw in the marketing world that goes like this: "I know that half my advertising dollars are wasted; I just don't know which half." There's some debate about who said this first, though it was possibly the American department store magnate John Wanamaker. But there's no question it has been repeated by frustrated marketers many times since. The modern-day equivalent of this lament seems to be: "I know that half my data is meaningless; I just don't know which half."

This three-phase evolution of data analysis, from descriptive to predictive to insightful, mirrors the steps that are required to turn data into results. Data in its raw form is just information; to make it useful we must translate that information into understanding; and then to make it actionable we need to transform our understanding into insights. Put another way, information answers the question "What's happening?" It delivers the raw data, just the facts, and it usually describes the current situation. Understanding answers the question "Why is it happening?" This goes a step further by explaining the underlying causes that created the current situation. If we can understand the causes that led to where we are, we can attempt to replicate them. As such, this is a future-oriented stage. It's about predicting behaviour. And last, insight attempts to answer the most difficult question of all: "So what?" What can we do with that knowledge to turn it into profitable action?

Actionable insight is an elusive prize. It does not spring fully formed from our heads once we've filled them with information and understanding. To uncover it requires a combination of skill and instinct. And to be useful, an insight needs to be original. If everyone has the same thought, it doesn't count as much of an insight. At that point it's simply common knowledge. To be actionable, an insight also needs to be exploitable. Some insights aren't. For example, research shows that one of the most common ways in which parents use cookies is to bribe their children. That's an insight. But no cookie manufacturer is about to tell consumers, "We're the best bribing cookie on the market!" Actionable insights also need to be testable and replicable. In other words, the desired outcome has to be achievable and to work on more than a few people; it must be capable of being repeated to deliver results on a sizable scale. That's why data analysts are so critical to the process.

How then have we come to this point where data analysts are supplanting pollsters and market insight specialists are replacing market researchers? And how will this shift from mass marketing to individualized marketing affect us as voters and consumers? To understand this evolution, I thought it would be useful to talk to someone who's witnessed this change up close from the beginning. To do that I travelled to London.

It's a crisp, cool April morning in London and I am standing on the doorstep of a terraced house in trendy Primrose Hill village. It's a neighbourhood that's home to poets and politicians, actors and artists, and media celebrities of all sorts. Glancing down this quiet cul-de-sac you can see two rows of identical houses facing each other across the narrow street. These posh homes date to the mid-nineteenth century, each identically painted white on the ground floor and topped by caramel-coloured brick on the upper floors. This uniformity is punctuated only by the perfect rectangles of brightly coloured front doors in yellows, reds, greens, and blues. The one I'm standing in front of is painted a bright Majorelle blue. It's a curious colour choice because blue is the colour of Britain's Conservative Party, and the man who owns this house has been one of the leading political operatives in the Labour Party for the past twenty years. The Labour colour is red.

The door swings open and I'm greeted by a tall man dressed in a dark blue pinstripe suit, his shirt open at the collar. He is well over six feet tall, with large hands that engulf yours when he reaches out to offer a handshake. And as he does, his face breaks into a ready smile that crinkles his eyes into crescents. His head, perfectly round on top and narrow below, is topped with a fuzzy crown of silver hair and large ears that flop out at the top. The overall effect is of a giant teddy bear.

But this is no teddy bear. This is David Triesman, a political figure who, as the U.K.'s former under-secretary for foreign and Commonwealth affairs, has negotiated tough deals and stared down dictators. Triesman, who also carries the title Lord Triesman of Tottenham, has a résumé that includes positions as General Secretary of the Association of University Teachers, General Secretary of the Labour Party, Member of the House of Lords, Chairman of the Football Association, and chairman of a merchant bank. But ask him to describe his profession and his answer is, "I'm an econometrician by training." Triesman's first love is mathematics, in particular mathematics as it applies to economic theory. He has put that passion to work primarily in the world of politics. In that sense, Triesman is a forerunner of the newest and most in-demand political operatives, the data crunchers, or so-called quants.

Sitting in a cozy, book-lined corner of his living room next to a large window overlooking the back garden, where a collection of terracotta pots warm in the morning sun, Triesman describes the evolution he, and his party, went through on the road to discovering the power of data to transform political strategy. It's a discovery that led to the most stunning political turnaround in modern British history and ushered in the first Labour government, under Tony Blair, after sixteen years of Conservative rule, most of them under the stern gaze and firm grip of that schoolmarm to a nation, Margaret Thatcher.

But as is so often the case when trying to make significant change in an organization, the transformation did not come easily. There were hidebound holdouts who were satisfied to keep doing things the way they'd always been done because, well, that's the way they'd always jolly well done it. Changing the way the Labour Party managed its campaigns had to begin with a change in attitude among its entrenched political class.

When Tony Blair ascended to the Labour Party leadership in the summer of 1994, at the relatively young age of forty-one, he set about making significant policy changes in the party. His first and boldest move was to amend Clause IV of the party's constitution. Adopted in 1918, it was in many ways the party's defining statement. Clause IV made overt the socialist goals of the Labour movement by asserting that workers should share in the equitable distribution of the fruits of their labour on "the basis of the common ownership of the means of production." The party made good on this policy in the years following the Second World War by nationalizing several key sectors of the economy — transportation, energy, telecommunications, and even the Bank of England.

By the 1970s, however, Britain was in a deep economic rut and voters were increasingly disaffected with Labour's policies. By the time Margaret Thatcher took power in 1979, many had lost their faith in these nationalizing programs, which gave Thatcher the impetus to set about determinedly implementing her plan of deregulation and privatization.

Blair knew that if Labour was ever to regain power, the party needed to show that it had ceased looking back nostalgically to its more dogmatically socialist origins and was ready to move forward and modernize. Scrapping Clause IV was critical to this turnaround. In less than a year he had achieved his goal.

But while this struggle over policy was going on in full view of the media and the public, there was another struggle over political strategy going on behind closed doors. Labour had failed to win the 1992 election, despite the fact that the economy was sputtering; the Tories had ousted their now-reviled leader Thatcher; and the country was being led by John Major, a man who brought all the dash and verve of his former profession as an insurance executive to bear on his role as prime minister.

Labour had to do more than just change its policies. It needed to change its politics — the way in which it fought elections. The reformers in the party believed that data — specifically, massive voter databases — would be the key tool to drive this change. For Triesman, who was one of the reformers, it was a frustrating struggle.

"There were people in our own party who thought that the election style of 1983 was still the election style that they ought to adopt because we'd always done that," he says, sounding irritated even to this day.

There were plenty of reformers in the party — Blair himself, of course; his brother-in-arms-cum-rival, Gordon Brown; researcher Philip Gould; key strategists Alastair Campbell and Peter Mandelson; plus many others. They were all long-time party activists who knew change was necessary, no matter how painful. But there was one reformer who was not a member in good standing of the Labour Party. He was a self-described "short, bespectacled Jewish guy with bushy hair who speaks in numbers." He did not come from the clubby inner circles of the British political establishment. He came from Philadelphia.

Stanley Bernard Greenberg is a pollster who was recruited into the Blair campaign after demonstrating remarkable success with another youthful, forward-looking politician: Bill Clinton. Greenberg was a crucial member of the inner circle in the Clinton war room during the successful 1992 presidential campaign — the same year Labour was defeated in Britain, despite polls showing the party was ahead of the Conservatives. Greenberg helped to elevate the role of the researcher as a central figure on the campaign-strategy team. And it was many of the techniques of data gathering and analysis pioneered in the Clinton campaigns of 1992 and 1996 that he exported to the U.K.

What he brought to the Labour Party in the run-up to the 1997 election were the lessons learned from Clinton's success years earlier. He also understood what it meant to deal with a party undergoing the pangs of policy reform. He first gained attention after developing an analysis of why many progressive white working-class voters had abandoned the Democrats in the 1980s. Why, he questioned, had United Auto Workers union members, the party's natural constituency, defected to Reagan in 1984? Greenberg's groundbreaking research and analysis concluded that these "Reagan Democrats," as he called them, felt the Democratic Party had abandoned the average American middle-class white voter in favour of excessive pandering to racial minorities. It was a provocative claim. And it led the old guard of the Democratic National Committee to shun him. But Greenberg found allies among reform-minded groups within the party, who understood that a new type of political analysis — in-depth, unflinching, and grounded in real data — would be needed to return the party to power. And Stan Greenberg was the man to help them do it.

It's a subject Greenberg continues to be concerned with. A few months after Hillary Clinton's surprise loss to Donald Trump, Greenberg penned a lengthy analysis for *American Prospect* magazine — its title: "The Democrats' Working-Class Problem."

When David Triesman encountered Stan Greenberg, he found a comrade with similar attitudes and beliefs, and even a similar background. Both men had a Ph.D. (Triesman's from Cambridge and Greenberg's from Harvard) and both had deployed sophisticated mathematical modelling as part of their postgraduate studies. Both were trying to shake off the old system of political strategizing, which involved a lot of guesswork and gut instinct.

"I believed with the right data you could get a much better understanding than just licking your finger and holding it up," says Triesman. For him, Greenberg's arrival on the campaign team was an invigorating jolt. "When I first ran into people like Stan Greenberg, I found kindred spirits."

BIG DATA, LOCAL POLITICS

Greenberg's arrival in London coincided with two big evolutionary leaps in British political strategizing. The first was a move to develop a clearer description of the voter. This involved assembling more voter data than had ever been gathered in Britain in the almost three hundred years since its invention of parliamentary democracy. These massive databases allowed Labour to gain a much richer image of the voting population. This was the descriptive or information phase of the data evolution. The chief benefit of this more detailed information was that it allowed the party to gain a more finely tuned image of voters, right down to the local level, instead of viewing them simply in large blocs.

Think about the massive amounts of data that Google has gathered to map the earth. The real benefit isn't that it allows us a 30,000-foot view of the world; the real benefit is that it allows us to zoom down to street level. And that's exactly how rich voter data is designed to work. The amount of data gathered is directly proportional to the capacity to see what's happening at the local level. Tip O'Neill, the colourful former U.S. House Majority Leader, coined the phrase "All politics is local," and ever since then political strategists have repeated this not just as a rallying cry but also as an admonishment. Ignore local issues at your peril. What O'Neill meant is that politicians, even at the national level, had better understand the pothole problems in their local constituency if they hope to get elected. Over the years "local" has taken on a new meaning. It's not just about going to the neighbourhood pub and listening to voters' concerns about the condition of their roads; it's about using data in a much more disciplined way to uncover the specific issues that affect specific segments of the population.

Put another way, the more sophisticated the data, the more local the politics. This was an idea the Labour campaign strategists had absorbed while observing both of Bill Clinton's campaigns. There's a long history of shared knowledge between Labour and their American cousins, the Democrats. Party activists frequently travel between countries to observe elections and even to work on campaigns. It allows each side to learn from the other's successes and failures. One of the biggest lessons the Brits brought home with them from the Clinton campaigns was that bigger data makes for better local politics. As Triesman explains it, "The famous Labour Party databases, actually borrowed from Clinton's campaigns and from people like Stan Greenberg...were really granular. It drove us...to becoming more and more and more local. Really local."

But why is what's happening at the local level so important, when most national election campaigns run on broad themes that are meant to appeal to a wide spectrum of the population? "Hope." "Change." "A break for the middle class." These are not local issues. So why is a more local focus important?

In Triesman's view, before political parties can engage with voters on these broader issues, they first need to gain "permission" to talk to them. This idea has not traditionally been part of mass marketing, where brands often blasted out their messages through mass media with all the force and subtlety of a slap in the face. But with the advent of more personal and intrusive online, mobile, and digital media, consumers were finding this kind of assertiveness irritating. The backlash began in the early days of digital marketing, when people started receiving all those unsolicited advertising emails in their inboxes. Remember that? This intrusiveness actually undermined the marketing effort and brought the concept of permission marketing to the fore. Entire books have now been written on the subject. But the idea originated decades ago in the political realm.

Permission marketing, as the name implies, means seeking the permission of the recipients before sending them a marketing message. This begins with an initial "hand-raising" exercise, where the prospect indicates they're willing to be contacted. If you've ever been on a web site and clicked on one of those buttons that says something like "Yes, I'd like to receive more information," you've raised your hand and you can be sure that a marketing message will shortly be headed to your inbox.

In the old days, political campaign workers would pop

brochures in the mailbox (no permission required) and cross their fingers, hoping that people would actually read them and not simply toss them in the bin along with the latest pizza flyer. In the lead-up to the 1997 election, Labour moved towards a different model, based on gaining permission first. They began by organizing mini town hall meetings on issues of local concern — traffic problems, trash collection, or perhaps the local hospital. This was a more subtle form of hand-raising. For the voters, these meetings provided a chance to vent and be heard on issues they cared about, and they also demonstrated that the party was willing to listen. For the party, the meetings provided insight into people's concerns and, perhaps more important, offered valuable information about the language and phrases people were using to discuss these issues.

Armed with this knowledge, the party would "then create something eye-catching so it wouldn't get thrown away," says Triesman, "because we know this [topic] is vital to you." And critically, he notes, the party's communications would "play it back in their language. Let go of political speak and do it in the voter language." Using your audience's own words and phrases is critical to building trust. It makes people feel you understand them and connect with them. It's something we all do instinctively when we're trying to build rapport with someone. We start to mimic their way of talking, not just the words they use but the register of their speech. You might use a more casual and even grammatically imperfect register when speaking to some people and a more formal register when speaking with others. This is not speaking down or speaking up, it's simply an attempt to connect more fully with your audience. It makes everyone feel more at ease.

Connecting in that way is what Triesman means by permission. It is a strategy that says: Before I tell you what I want to say, I'm going to listen to what your concerns are and demonstrate that I've heard them and am willing to do something about them. Only once I've done that will I assume I have permission to talk about my issues. Focusing on voters' own concerns, and even using their own language, means that the chances they'll actually read that item that came popping through the mail slot along with the pizza flyer are much greater. Do enough of this local activity across the country and you will start to see themes emerge that connect the local issues.

That's why what was happening at the local level was critical to developing the national strategy and its major themes and messages. The vast databases that Labour began assembling complemented this local effort by giving the party a much more fine-grained image of their voters. That data allowed the party to divide the population into eighteen distinct segments and then further divide those into sub-segments. All this information, top down from the survey data and bottom up from the local meetings, combined to provide a Google-like street view of the voters. Triesman sums it up: "The process of getting permission drove the knowledge down to a street, sometimes to a block of houses on a street, a block of flats."

This was a major step forward from the old way of doing things, when political campaigns ran on a volatile mix of partisan ideology, received wisdom, and gut instinct. But it remained in the realm of information, a description of what was happening. The data mining had yet to advance to the stage of understanding and insight.

The information the political number crunchers were assembling would be the equivalent of a marketer being able to tell you what kind of people like crunchy peanut butter and what kind like smooth and where each of them lives — down to a specific block of flats. On the one hand, it provides hard statistical data about age, gender, income, location, and so on — the demographics. On the other hand, it offers a more human picture of attitudes, tastes, and perceptions — the psychographics. But this highly detailed profile was simply the precursor to the other significant data evolution that was to come. Knowing who you are and what your issues and concerns are is not enough. Political strategists also need to know your voting patterns. More than your demographic profile and your psychographic attitudes, they also need to understand your past behaviour in order to try to predict your future behaviour. How did you vote last time and how will you likely vote next time? This is the equivalent of knowing not just whether you like smooth or crunchy but also which brand of peanut butter you bought last time and which brand you'll buy next time, or if you're planning to buy any at all. Or maybe you're planning to switch entirely to Nutella, a quirky choice, akin to voting for the LibDems in the U.K. Political data analysis needed to move beyond mere description and into predictive analysis.

Of course, predicting human behaviour is a devilishly difficult thing to do. Much of the field of economics is taken up with this sort of problem — will you buy a car, a house, a refrigerator next month and, if so, how much will you pay, and what impact will it have on your household finances and the economy as a whole? Human beings, however, are stubbornly unpredictable, which is why the dismal science of economics so often gets things wrong. These days, the pop stars of economics are the behavioural economists, who focus less on the numbers and more on the human and psychological factors to try to predict behaviour. These folks like to show videos of cute kids agonizing over whether to eat one marshmallow now or hold off and get two marshmallows later. How kids respond to this delayed-gratification challenge, they tell us, is an accurate predictor of their future success. If only life were that simple. This Willy Wonka branch of economics is no better at predicting the future than traditional economics. And yet this is what marketers and political strategists are called on to do every day.

These days it might seem obvious that political parties need to understand voting behaviour, but it wasn't always so. Just ask Alan Barnard. A longtime Labour Party strategist, Barnard today runs a consultancy called bbm campaigns. His staff works with political clients, but they also take their years of experience with political campaigns and put it to work for businesses and charitable organizations. As they explain it, at his company bbm, "the techniques, skills and knowledge that we've developed and honed over many years of political campaigning are used to achieve success for corporate and not-for-profit goals." Barnard and his colleague Chris Parker have written a book on the subject, entitled *Campaign It! Achieving Success Through Communication.*

Alan Barnard is a shaggy-haired Englishman whose brown locks cascade over his collar. He looks like a slightly aging rock 'n' roller. And he speaks with the intensity of someone who's spent a lifetime in the persuasion business. He's passionate about his ideas and not shy about showing it. He's worked on numerous local campaigns, helping prospective Labour members of Parliament get elected. He also played a central role in the 1997 election that brought Labour back to power. And, like many others, he travelled to the U.S. in 1992 to see first-hand how the Democrats were engineering their White House victory. He spent a month in California working on the campaign and came away with some important lessons, not the least of which was the need to focus on voter behaviour, not just voter demographics.

As Head of Elections for Labour in 1997, Barnard made understanding voting behaviour a critical issue. He points out that, prior to then, the party's approach was pretty crude. "Previously we'd been told to target based on various social demographics and employment criteria, and we were asked to target, for example, nurses with a message about the health service." Intuitively, this makes sense. Nurses are likely to be more concerned about healthcare policy, and butchers, say, might be more concerned about retail taxation. But what Barnard understood is that the nurses are unlikely to define their life primarily around their job. Their main concerns centre on the same things everyone else is concerned about — their families and their personal well-being. This was the simple and radical idea that Labour brought to their 1997 election campaign: nurses are people too. And so are butchers and bakers and candlestick makers.

It wasn't necessary to educate nurses about the party's healthcare policies, because nurses were more aware than the average citizen of where the parties stood on this issue. In fact, they were the people Labour least needed to communicate with about its healthcare policy. "Nurses," Barnard tells me, "know all about the health services. They're going to want to know if they're going to be able to buy their own house with a Labour government." In other words, the issues of financial security and affordable housing were more important to the nurses than how the party planned to overhaul the healthcare system.

Seeing nurses as people first and nurses second marked an important psychological shift for the Labour Party strategists. It signalled the first step in moving beyond mere demographic segmentation and towards a behavioural analysis based on voting patterns. Barnard explains: "The messaging of our targeting wasn't about the demographic group...we were talking to; it was about the broader, wider messaging based on the economy." This shift meant that when it came to analyzing voter segments, "We turned it around, doing it based on the voting intention, voting behaviour, and voting patterns — and likely voting patterns. So that we were going after not women or Asian voters or ethnic voters; we were targeting based on previous Labour voting, potential Labour voting with those who said they were always Tory. So we turned it into voting behaviour much, much more."

These two innovations for the Labour Party — using data to provide a clearer description of the voter and deeper analysis to help predict voter behaviour — were critical to helping the party modernize its campaign strategy. There were other techniques imported from Little Rock: for example, a war room–like layout in the campaign headquarters in the Millbank Tower in London and a swift and aggressive rebuttal team to respond to opposition attacks as soon as they happened. But it's the information gathering and the behavioural analysis that are the precursor to the third and most powerful phase of data analysis — using data to drive actionable insights. This has become one of the most powerful tools in modern campaigning, and it was deployed to powerful effect in Obama's 2012 presidential campaign and to sinister effect in the historic election of 2016. It is now making its way from the campaign trail to the supermarket.

FROM WAR ROOM TO CAVE

From the Labour Party's information gathering that led to a street-level view of voters and their behaviour, the picture has zoomed in even further, not down to a single house but to a single individual. Campaign strategists are now micro-targeting, working at the equivalent of the atomic level of voter analysis. In Tip O'Neill's day all politics was local. Now, thanks to micro-targeting, all politics is individual. And this highly refined focus is allowing political strategists to influence voter behaviour more effectively than ever before, by generating actionable insights.

This new, highly targeted approach was incubated in a cramped, windowless room in the Chicago headquarters of the Obama 2012 campaign — the first truly data-driven election campaign. In Chicago, a group of more than fifty statisticians, engineers, data scientists, and analysts, assembled from around the world, huddled over banks of computers developing algorithms to sift through the immense amount of information that was being fed into the campaign databanks. Campaign chair Jim Messina decided from the very start that this would be a data-driven campaign. What that means is that data was used to inform virtually every major decision they made: which television programs to run ads on; what to say in communications material; how to use digital media; how to craft fundraising appeals and to whom. It would be the first campaign to completely set aside the hunch, the intuition, the gut feel, in favour of the cold, hard facts. David Triesman's long-ago vision of a campaign powered by data rather than a finger held up to the wind began to reach its fullest expression in 2012.

Speaking to an audience at the Milken Institute's Global Conference in Los Angeles just months after Obama's second presidential win, a relaxed-looking Jim Messina explained his goals this way: "In the old days campaigns were smoke-filled rooms with three or four people who...said, 'I've won these campaigns forever and this is how we do it in Montana.'" Then he added, "You don't get a guy named Barack Obama elected if you take the old rules. So we had to run new rules and we reinvented it using data."

The data he refers to was funnelled from all corners of the campaign and from disparate outside sources and was concentrated into the operations in this one room, which served as the nerve centre for the new data-driven approach. If the war room was the heart of the modern campaign structure, this was the brain. It was the job of the analysts working here, like miners heading underground in search of an elusive glistening vein, to delve into the data in search of patterns that would reveal something actionable about the voting population. Aptly, this room was called the Cave.

The scale of the information flow that fed into the Cave was unprecedented. This influx allowed the campaign to accumulate massive datasets, clusters of information that could be analyzed and manipulated. It was through these datasets that they were able to model behaviour to determine how voters would act. The more data, the better the modelling. Consider that the average survey during an election campaign consists of a sample of eight hundred people. The Obama campaign sampled 10,000 people a night. Every night. For fourteen months. This allowed the quants to run a staggering 62,000 computer simulations of the election. Not only had no one ever done this before, no one had even *conceived* of doing it before.

What was the effect of all this data gathering and behaviour modelling? First of all, it gave the campaign a much more precise measure of how the vote would turn out. Many pollsters, especially the Republicans, got the numbers woefully wrong. The venerable Gallup, a name virtually synonymous with American election polling, was showing Obama behind by seven points just days before the election. The Obama campaign, however, was able to predict the final result in *every* state to within 0.5 percentage points. In the notoriously unpredictable swing state of Florida, they came within 0.05 percent.

Big Data also made for a much more efficient campaign, especially when it came to media buying. Presidential campaigns spend massive amounts on advertising. In 2012 the Romney campaign burned through roughly half a billion dollars in television advertising alone. But Obama spent $100 million dollars less on television and still won. That was possible thanks to a much more targeted approach to choosing television programming. And that targeting was informed by the data analytics coming out of the Cave in Chicago.

Specifically, the campaign was able to buy a lot less network television (ABC, CBS, Fox, and NBC) and a lot more cable (the Food Network, HGTV, the Discovery Channel, etc.). Cable buys are more efficient, especially if you know precisely whom you want to reach. If you're targeting women aged 40 to 49 who are passionate about cooking, you could place your ad on Fox's *American Idol* and reach a lot of them. The problem is, you're also reaching millions of other people who don't fit that description. And because advertising rates are based on the total number of people watching, you're paying to reach millions of other people you're not interested in. In ad speak that's called wasted reach. In this case, you'd be much better off buying a spot on the Food Network. The trick, of course, is to know as much about your target group's habits as possible, so that you can target your buy accordingly. How do you know your target is passionate about cooking? Thanks to the massive cache of voter data the team had assembled, the Obama campaign was able to understand these subtle nuances and as a result be much more efficient — $100 million more efficient.

David Axelrod, Obama's chief campaign strategist, explained the process to an audience at Webster University in St. Louis in early 2013: "Generally, the way media buying works is you wanna reach women and you get programming that's... women oriented and you buy that media. But we were able to create a profile of that small sliver of undecideds in these states — 10 or 15 percent — and get a real sense of what their viewing habits were, to the individual programs. And we ended up as a result spending exponentially more money than the Romney campaign did on cable television, going after specific programming that we knew went right to our target voter. We not only saved huge amounts of money — probably 15 to 20 percent — on our buy but we were more efficient in terms of reaching people."

But the real purpose of all of this data gathering wasn't to save money; it was to reach individuals. The goal was to make this the most individualized campaign ever run up until then. Pointing to members of the Global Conference audience in Los Angeles, Messina said, "We had a singular goal: to run a personalized campaign where *you* got a different campaign than *you* did, all based on our ability to move you and persuade you to vote for and support Barack Obama."

He then went on to make a stunning declaration: "We ranked every single voter in America from 1 to 100 ... on whether or not they would support Barack Obama, on whether or not you were going to vote and ... whether or not you were going to be a ticket splitter back and forth." Imagine for a minute such an undertaking — ranking every single voter in America. It's not just a breathtaking act of organization, it's a breathtaking act of vision. To believe you could actually do such a thing requires an extraordinary leap of imagination. It's the equivalent of the founders of Google waking up one day and saying, *Let's create a street-level view of every single street in the world.* The brashness of that vision makes it seem almost foolhardy, so foolhardy that most people wouldn't even attempt it. And yet that's precisely what the campaign's analysts were able to do.

To understand how seriously Messina approached the task of remaking the 2012 campaign into a data-driven machine, it's worth noting that he hired the data analytics director four years ahead of the election, on November 6, 2008. By the time the 2012 election rolled around, the twelve-person data team from 2008 had expanded to 162. When asked what has changed in politics with the advent of Big Data, his reply is simple: "Absolutely everything."

But data is not valuable until you can turn it into insights that drive positive results. Perhaps nothing illustrates the benefit of the highly personalized campaign the Democrats were able to run, thanks to Big Data, than the story of the campaign volunteer canvassing a suburban neighbourhood in Wisconsin. On one street she encountered canvassers for the Romney campaign going from door to door. They went to every single house on that street. She, on the other hand, had been given only two addresses to go to — the homes of potential swing voters. She had on her iPhone six potential scripts to go through with the voters, and before she got to each door, she knew which script she should deliver. When she was done, as the voter headed back indoors, they would have heard a *ping* on their computer indicating an incoming email from the Obama campaign. That email contained a link to a personalized web site, designed specifically for them. The URL was unique — barackobama.com, followed by a backslash and that voter's name. If they clicked on it, they would have found content geared specifically towards them. It was at this point, seeing her Republican rivals going laboriously to every house on the street and talking to many voters who would never vote for Romney, that the Democratic campaigner came to the realization that Obama was going to win this election. They had simply designed a much more efficient vote-generating machine. And it was running on high-octane data.

It's worth noting that delivering this highly personalized campaign was possible only because the social media landscape had completely altered in the four short years between the two Obama elections. Messina notes, "We sent out one tweet on election day 2008 because we thought it was a silly technology that wouldn't go anywhere." David Axelrod echoes this sentiment: "Twitter was nothing four years ago, and look how important it was in this campaign." Facebook had grown tenfold over the same time period and become a highly effective way of getting friends to influence friends. Those voters in Wisconsin who had just received an email from the campaign would, the very next day, be contacted via Facebook to see whether their voting intentions had shifted.

Ironically, technology and social media, which many see as disconnecting us from face-to-face interaction, were essential for the Obama campaign to connect with its voters and lead them to act — volunteer, donate, or vote. Axelrod points out, "What's happened is the marriage of social media and traditional fieldwork so that . . . we're far more efficient at communicating with people. We registered, I think, more voters online in this campaign than we registered altogether in the last campaign." The campaign was able to prompt action because they connected with voters at an individual level. And it's technology, he points out, that made that possible. "So the technology has made it easier to organize, and in a weird way the technology has made it easier to individualize our appeals to voters, and our contact, and our dialogue with voters."

Customized and personalized products and services are blossoming everywhere, from personal shopping lists on Amazon to individualized healthcare based on genetic decoding — all of it made possible by Big Data. People will say they hate having their information tracked. Some would even pay to not have their personal data captured when they're online. A 2013 study by Communispace showed that 30 percent of consumers would pay a 5 percent premium to guarantee none of their information would be tracked. Nevertheless, many more people are willing to give up that information if doing so delivers a direct benefit. The same study showed that more than twice as many people, 70 percent, would voluntarily share their personal data with a company in exchange for a 5 percent discount. Communispace also noted that personalized marketing is much more welcome from a company the consumer knows than from one that is unknown. In short, from the right source and with the right incentives, capturing personal data in order to deliver more personalized marketing is a welcome idea.

Even following the massive data breach suffered by Facebook during the 2016 election, it's hard to believe that billions of users will completely forego the benefits they derive from social media. Regulation will surely come to increase data privacy. But social media and data collection are here to stay.

From as far back as Mary Shelley's *Frankenstein* to Charlie Chaplin's *Modern Times*, to Stanley Kubrick's *2001: A Space Odyssey*, to countless other modern iterations, technology has been portrayed in popular culture as a great dehumanizing force: the creation that consumes the creator, the mythic child intent on patricide. What this view fails to take into account is that much of the endlessly expanding universe of data made possible by modern technology is focused on trying to pinpoint the individual in the multitude. And in the world of politics and marketing the story is no different.

Using data — massive amounts of data — to deliver the most individualized campaign ever was only one of the innovations Messina and his team implemented. The other was to use that data to model behaviour. In other words, to predict how you are likely to behave and then communicate with you in such a way as to influence that behaviour.

WHAT'S DINNER WITH GEORGE CLOONEY WORTH?

One of the most useful tools in this regard was A/B testing, a technique widely used by the Obama campaign. There's not much new in the idea of A/B testing, which simply involves showing people two variations of a piece of communication and seeing which is better at eliciting the desired response — Option A or Option B. However, thanks to the Internet, the Obama campaign was able to scale this type of testing to a whole new level, testing every aspect of the design of each piece of email and every web page they produced. By A/B testing hundreds of variations they were able to determine the optimal design for each item. So when that voter in Wisconsin opened up her email from Obama, everything she saw, from the colour scheme to the size of the text, from the placement of the response button to the headline, had been designed in such a way as to maximize the chances of eliciting a positive response. The impact of this extensive testing was enormous for the campaign. Messina says, "We figured we could maximize our returns by 82 percent by A/B testing all of our emails."

Without the large pool of data crunchers and programmers in the Cave, none of this would have been possible. The other thing that would not have been possible was the myriad serendipitous findings the data threw up. Like the fact that women aged 40 to 49 who lived on the West Coast were inordinately attracted to George Clooney. Armed with this little nugget, the campaign decided to run a variation on a fundraising contest that had been working consistently well. The original idea was simple: donate $3 and you were entered into a contest to win dinner with Barack Obama. This fundraising tactic would reliably generate $3 million in donations. Using the Clooney insight, they offered the chance to win dinner with Obama and George Clooney. The results quadrupled: the contest pulled in $12 million. For the record, then, a date with George Clooney is worth about $9 million. When Messina saw this result, he asked his chief data analyst to find out why this had happened. The reply from the number crunchers was, "You don't need research to figure that out. George Clooney is hot."

One other idea emerged from the Cave that was central to impacting voter behaviour. It was the recognition that, as consumers are increasingly bombarded with information, decision-making is actually becoming more difficult. In theory, the more information we have, the better decisions we can make. But give us too much information and we become paralyzed. If you've ever found yourself staring blankly at a giant wall of books in an airport bookstore, you know the feeling. That's why they create those piles of bestsellers and recommended reads as you walk in. As the flow of digital information has increased, due in large part to mobile technology, many of us are feeling too overwhelmed to make up our minds. And staring at that wall of information, we're reverting back to an old-fashioned way of sorting through the options. We're relying on the advice of our friends. Thanks to Facebook, the same technology that has given us a surfeit of information has also given us a way out.

The Obama data analysts figured that one powerful way to influence voter behaviour amongst those slippery undecideds and switchers was to get their friends to make the pitch for them. There's nothing new in that. Word of mouth from people you know and trust has always been the most powerful tool of persuasion. The challenge has always been how to generate word of mouth quickly and cost-effectively on a very large scale. Facebook became the vehicle for making that happen. In fact, the campaign felt that Facebook would be such an important part of their effort to influence voter behaviour that they spent an entire year and many millions of dollars building a program called Targeted Sharing. This sophisticated data mining tool allowed them to cross-reference the friends of people who liked the Obama Facebook page against a database of undecided voters (remember, they'd already ranked every voter in the country on their likelihood of voting for Obama).

The Targeted Sharing strategy really came to the fore in the closing days of the campaign. In the final six days of the election, roughly six million people logged onto barackobama .com. If you were one of them, you would have been greeted by a twenty-second video featuring Michelle Obama. During those twenty seconds, while you were admiring Michelle Obama's friendly smile, the Targeted Sharing program would have filtered through your list of Facebook friends and found five of those closest to you who were undecided voters. (People who liked the Obama Facebook page or downloaded the app had previously given the campaign permission to access their friends' information. This was precisely the same back door that Cambridge Analytica has accessed in 2016. Only, in that case, the door hadn't been opened by Facebook users but by a third-party who then went on to sell access to Cambridge Analytica.) You were then presented with the option of sending a message or a video in support of Obama to these five friends with just the click of a button. It proved to be a powerfully effective tool for converting undecided voters.

Millions of undecided voters were presented with a direct appeal from one of their closest friends to vote for Obama. The legendary ad man Bill Bernbach, speaking about how best to convey an advertising message, once said, "Word of mouth is the best medium of all." No doubt he could never have imagined word of mouth executed on this scale. The costly year-long Targeted Sharing project paid off in stunning results. According to Jim Messina, of the undecided voters who received the Facebook message from their friends, 78 percent voted for Obama.

After decades of evolution in data collection and analysis, the politics of individualism had reached a new pinnacle. While David Triesman's Labour Party had sought to reach voters by dividing the British electorate into large segments and then narrowing those down to a single street or block of flats, the Obama campaign had come through the front door, walked right up to you, and tapped you on the shoulder. This was the very opposite of mass marketing. It was individual marketing on a mass scale. And it's the direction all marketing will be heading in the future.

What does all of this mean for the world of consumer marketing? Well, as the Cave-dwelling quants who engineered Obama's stunning victory stumble out into the bright light of day, they are opening their eyes to a huge new opportunity. There's a significant gap that needs filling in the corporate sector. Many companies are struggling to sift through the mountains of data that pile up in their computer banks every day. They need people who can find the nuggets of gold amongst the tailings and turn them into improved business results. And that's exactly what the former denizens of the Cave are offering to do.

Alumni of the Obama analytics team are venturing out to start their own companies and to parlay the experience they gained into money-generating businesses that will sell their expertise to corporate clients. Hotshot venture capital firms and high-tech entrepreneurs are eager to get on board to fund these start-ups because they can smell the potential as these data consultants bring their magic arts to the world of consumer marketing.

Among these new companies is Analytics Media Group (AMG), founded by Larry Grisolano, the director of paid media for Obama 2012. AMG advertises itself as "Part tech start-up, part media analytics firm, we are alumni from President Obama's transformative 2008 and 2012 campaigns." It was Larry's team that helped direct the campaign's media buying to deliver greater impact at lower cost. They're now offering to bring the lessons they've learned "to the mainstream." Following the election, David Axelrod noted that the techniques developed by Grisolano's team would ultimately impact the corporate world as much as the political one: "I think that approach is going to revolutionize time buying not just in politics but in the commercial realm."

Another offshoot from the campaign is a firm called Civis Analytics, which offers to "solve the world's biggest problems with Big Data" and is willing to do that not just for politicians but also for corporations. Civis was founded by Dan Wagner, the man who oversaw operations in the Cave. The first thing he did the day after the 2012 election, when he was probably still recuperating from the previous night's celebrations, was take a meeting with Eric Schmidt, the executive chairman of Google. On the day before the election, Schmidt had approached Wagner to ask him about the algorithms he'd used to analyze the campaign data. Too exhausted to explain it all right then and there, Wagner proposed they meet the day after. The two met in a conference room in the Cave. By the end of the meeting, Schmidt was proposing to fund Wagner in a start-up consultancy. Civis Analytics was born.

Dan Siroker, another alumnus of the Cave, also launched a data analytics start-up following the election. His is called Optimizely and it focuses on using the A/B testing methodology developed during the campaign to help companies optimize the performance of their web sites. The main investor in Optimizely is Peter Fenton, general partner at Benchmark, a Silicon Valley venture capital firm with an uncanny ability to bet on the right horse. Fenton was an early investor in Yelp and funded Twitter when it still had only twenty-five employees. Benchmark led a $25 million investment in Siroker's start-up in 2013.

When the Eric Schmidts and Peter Fentons of the world

start pumping big money into a whole new category of business — data analytics firms that can help companies improve their communications and advertising — it's a sign that something is shifting in the marketplace. These investors understand that the future of these companies lies not in working on a presidential election every four years or getting a congressman elected to office. The real opportunity lies in bringing this knowledge and skill to corporate America and helping it to deploy more effectively the billions that are spent every year trying to influence consumer behaviour.

What you'll notice about the names of these new companies is that none of them contain the word "research." They are not offering research but analysis. That's because many companies have come to realize that the answer is not more data but better insight into what that data means. Making this transition has not been easy. Recognizing the need to change, many marketing-driven companies have transformed their former Research Departments into "Insights Departments." Sadly, in most cases this has meant little more than a name change. The new Insights Departments are staffed by the same people doing pretty much the same thing, in the same way, as the old Research Departments. And that's precisely why the data analytics start-ups are likely to find a vast number of ready and willing customers.

The decline of the researcher in the corporate world has been mirrored by the decline of the pollster in the political world. Pollsters used to be the high priests of the election process, poring over the entrails of endless computer printouts and coming forth from their temples to declare what the future would hold. But this religion is now falling out of favour. The most talked-about prognosticator in the 2012 election was not a pollster but a data analyst, Nate Silver. Although he never conducted a single poll himself, the media reported on his election predictions with breathless attention. Silver aggregated the data from existing polls and other sources and put it through his own analysis to derive his predictions. The result was that, unlike the professional pollsters, he accurately predicted which candidate would win in every single state in 2012. Not a single pollster was able to do that. Unfortunately for Silver, he was not able to replicate that feat in 2016. Like virtually everyone else, he failed to see the rapid shift in voting intention in the final days of the campaign that gave Trump his large and surprising victory.

The moment when the credibility of the American pollster came crashing down to earth can be pinpointed precisely. It happened shortly after 11 p.m. Eastern Standard Time on Tuesday, November 4, 2012. And it took place in full public view on national television. It was at that moment that Fox News declared that Barack Obama had won the state of Ohio and effectively had won the presidency. But seated at the election desk was Fox News commentator and long-time Republican strategist Karl Rove, who took issue with the call. Rove, jabbing his finger at sheaves of election result printouts and reaching for his cellphone, could not accept that the election was over. "No, I don't," he declared agitatedly when host Chris Wallace asked if he thought that the results in Ohio had been settled. The conflict of opinion between the Fox election desk, which made the call that the president had been re-elected, and one of its most prominent commentators created some awkward tension on the set. So much so that host Megyn Kelly was dispatched down the hall, cameras in tow, to confront the sequestered election desk number crunchers and have them justify their call. "We're actually quite comfortable with the call in Ohio," they said.

And, of course, they were right. The election was over and it wasn't even close. Earlier that evening several other commentators on Fox had confidently declared that Romney would win the night. In the run-up to the election Rove and fellow Fox pundit Dick Morris had predicted a big win for the Republican candidate. Morris, a former pollster and notoriously inept prognosticator, had called for a Romney landslide and confidently asserted there was absolutely no way Obama could get re-elected. Commentators like Rove and Morris, along with many members of the Romney team, were convinced by the numbers their pollsters had been feeding them for weeks, showing Romney in the lead. Those numbers were wrong, and they remained wrong right up until the end.

Karl Rove was the grand wizard of Republican strategists. He engineered two election victories for George W. Bush, one snatched from the jaws of defeat. He set up the political action committee American Crossroads, which attracted a staggering $300 million from Republican donors to fight Obama in 2012. He was a man both feared and revered. And yet there he sat on election night unable to reconcile what the pollsters had told him with the reality that was unfolding right before his eyes. At that moment, like the Wizard of Oz — who for so long had moved the levers of influence and who had seemed so omnipotent, so omniscient, and even scary — Rove was now revealed to be a desperate and ineffectual character, still yanking away at those levers but producing no result.

The end of mass marketing as we know it is signalling the embarrassing retreat of two of the biggest actors in the world of mass communication: the pollster and the market researcher. These two long-trusted counsellors are being supplanted by data analysts and insights specialists, respectively. In recent years, in election after election, the pollsters' numbers have not added up. Both the 2012 and 2016 U.S. elections were a bust for pollsters. But similarly off-kilter results have happened in Canada in both federal and provincial elections. Meanwhile, in the U.K., the polling predictions for the Brexit vote were spectacularly out of sync with voter intentions. Pollsters are in danger of becoming like the proverbial boy who cried wolf. Keep belting out the wrong information and eventually nobody will take notice. Market researchers are on a similar slippery slope to irrelevance. And both groups are being swept aside by the growth of Big Data.

BLUE IS FOR LABOUR

The path from the Clinton war room to the Labour Party databases, to the Obama Cave, and now into the corporate boardroom, has been one of steady progression. And at each stage the lens has been focused more precisely. In comparison to today, the eighteen voter segments that Labour developed in 1997 seem quaint. And yet the objectives remained constant: to use data to deliver a more individualized campaign and to impact voter behaviour more directly.

The difference is that an election volunteer canvassing a tony neighbourhood like David Triesman's Primrose Hill village, where most of the houses are worth about £2 million, would know, despite the bright blue door, that the person who lives there would never vote anything but Labour. The canvasser's iPhone would tell her so. But the real power of Big Data is that the knock on the door is being replaced by a virtual tap on the shoulder. It's not about targeting a few households on the block; it's about targeting you specifically. It's about your Facebook friend sending you a post suggesting that you donate to a political campaign or vote for a particular candidate. And someday soon, that same friend will be recommending his favourite brand of peanut butter.

And when that happens, it will be the end of a hundred-year-long run of mass marketing — arguably the most powerful communications tool of the twentieth century and one that shaped how we chose everything, from our political leaders to our bathroom cleaners. And just as mass marketing needed mass media in order to grow, so the new age of microtargeting will need personalized media to grow. Social media tools such as Twitter have turned all of us into broadcasters. I don't have to be CNN to broadcast news to the world. An ordinary citizen with a smartphone, standing in the middle of Tahrir Square in Cairo or Times Square in New York, can broadcast to the entire world instantaneously. The mass media have lost their monopoly, and along with it mass marketing has lost a great deal of its traditional leverage. But as the media landscape shifts in unpredictable ways, then surely what you say becomes even more important. Not so. As we'll explore in the next section, in the new age of marketing it's not what you say but how you say it that will take on greater importance.

11

IT'S NOT WHAT
YOU SAY BUT HOW
YOU SAY IT

For most of the last century, the core of every advertising effort was "the message." It was the culmination of all the research, strategizing, and creative rumination, and oftentimes it had to be distilled down to a few seconds of video and audio or a few words and photographs. The message was intended to be the brand's answer to some unmet need amongst consumers. In the Internet age, that is no longer so. Sometimes the answer comes from consumers themselves, not from the brand; sometimes the speed at which the message is conveyed is more important than the message itself; and sometimes the marketer's voice is only one among many and can get drowned out by the chorus of consumers who want to have their own say about the brand and what it stands for. In short, communicating with consumers is no longer a speech: it's a conversation. And that conversation is interactive and taking place in real time.

Crafting the message is a time-consuming exercise in the world of advertising. No nuance is too small not to be fretted over. Words are parsed and deconstructed, then reconstructed, sometimes to absurd extremes. I'm reminded of the time a client declared, "'New' is so overused. Can we use 'introducing' instead?" The transformation of those words into an ad can be even more laborious. A typical television commercial requires weeks of pre-production and at least one full day of shooting to produce just thirty seconds of video. If the production is complicated, that might stretch to two or three days. If the average feature-length movie operated at the same pace, it would require, at minimum, over two hundred days of filming. Even director Michael Cimino's 1980 debacle *Heaven's Gate*, the ultimate example of filmic excess, consumed only 165 days of shooting.

This obsessive fiddling over the details of the message is made possible by the luxury of time. But the altered media landscape, with its emphasis on real-time communication, has compressed time to such an extent that it is squeezing out the opportunity for marketers to ruminate over the subtleties of "new" versus "introducing." This is forcing a different kind of evaluation: not what should we say, but how quickly can we say it. Speed has become its own kind of message. In some instances the impact of a message will be determined by how quickly it gets to its audience rather than by what it actually says.

Even as marketers are occasionally having to favour speed over content, they are also having to relinquish some control of the content to others. A brand's most ardent followers are increasingly having their say in shaping the brand message and brand image. How marketers allow these other voices into the conversation will be a delicate balance. It will demand a new skill: the ability to control the dialogue without appearing to dominate it. This will not be easy for a group accustomed to shaping every minor detail of the brand communication.

Control is an intoxicating drug and can be a tough habit to shake. Nowhere has the allure of complete control been more evident than among movie directors. I'm reminded of the punchline about what God says is still left to do after spending six days creating the world: "I'd like to direct." Michael Cimino's *Heaven's Gate* signalled an end to the era of the dictatorial auteur-director. Cimino squandered the most precious commodity in film production: time. By running a full twelve months over the original schedule and by obsessing over every minor detail of the production, he managed to increase the film's original $7.5 million budget sixfold.

Thanks to social media, many movies are now being crowd-funded. In January 2013, Kickstarter announced it had raised over $100 million in pledges to fund movies. That money came from nearly 900,000 donors, some of whom were given a say in how the movies would be made. When even movie directors start abandoning complete control, you know the world has changed.

In this new world, marketers are finding that the two levers they've traditionally had full control over — time and message content — are no longer theirs to manipulate as they wish. How well they respond to the need for speedier response times, and for more participatory message creation, will be critical to their future success.

CHAPTER 4

THE AGE OF THE OPEN BRAND

THE OPEN BRAND

Just as the Internet and social media have ushered out the age of mass marketing, they have also shown the door to the age of centralized brand control. During the era of mass media and mass marketing, the brand manager was in full control of all aspects of the brand, from how the product was formulated to how it was priced to where it was distributed. In addition, the brand identity (its name and logo), PR efforts, and advertising were tightly managed. Everything flowed from the centre outwards to the masses. But the decentralization of media from the one-to-many to the many-to-many has turned the old brand autocracy into a new brand democracy.

The brand manager must now share control of the brand with the consumer. That's because in the digital age, any piece of communication that the brand puts out into the world can readily be captured, repurposed, and rebroadcast by just about anyone with a computer or a smartphone. In this environment the challenge is how to tap into the creativity of others to help promote the brand while still maintaining sufficient control, because full control is no longer an option.

Giving up control is not easy, and no group has been more possessive and controlling of their message than political strategists. So much so that campaign managers often have to ensure that the candidate's brand image remains intact by muzzling the candidate himself. And yet, in the newly democratized world of communications, it's the politicos, ever the pragmatists, who are leading the way in understanding that by loosening the reins they can actually ride the bucking bronco.

Open branding is not about letting go completely; it's about understanding that others will inevitably have their say. Rather than trying to silence those other voices, marketers must find ways to ensure that those outsiders are singing in harmony with the brand and not creating discord.

HILLARY AND THE BAND

In early 2008, about halfway through the intense battle between Hillary Clinton and Barack Obama for the Democratic presidential nomination, a video was quietly posted on YouTube. In mockumentary fashion it showed a bunch of hipster musicians saying, "For a period of like two, three weeks we were maybe the hottest band around. Suddenly there's this huge audience, everybody's crammed against the wall. Hillary takes the stage."

Cut to Photoshopped picture of Hillary Clinton holding a guitar. "The crowd. Went. Nuts."

Well, actually, the crowd never showed. Three years after landing on YouTube, "Hillary and the Band," as this video was called, had managed to eke out just over 7,000 views, 10 likes, and 74 dislikes.

This ad, created by the Hillary for President campaign team, is painful in its geekiness. It's the equivalent of the awkward guy on the dance floor trying to emulate the guy with all the smooth moves and succeeding only in making himself look even more awkward. To quote one YouTube viewer, the video was "lame beyond words."

Did they launch this video as a pre-emptive strike? Did they know that at the same time they were filming their fake hipster band, dozens of well-known singers and actors were gathering at Ethernet Studios in Los Angeles to record a video entitled "Yes We Can," music by will.i.am of the Black Eyed Peas, lyrics by Barack Obama?

Shot in simple black-and-white on a seamless background, it is a mash-up of Obama's concession speech, delivered on January 8 after losing the New Hampshire primary, and the soulful voice of singer John Legend, plus dozens of famous actors and musicians. With a spare piano and guitar accompaniment, the words take centre stage and they build through a slow but relentless rhythm to the now-famous refrain, "Yes we can. Yes we can. Yes we can." The effect is hypnotic and soul-stirring.

That video was posted to YouTube on February 2, 2008, only three days after the "Hillary and the Band" debut. By the end of the month, it had received over 22 million views. But the most remarkable thing about this clever bit of campaign propaganda isn't that it managed to garner tens of millions of views in just a few weeks. What's most remarkable is that it was not produced by the Obama campaign. In fact, it was produced completely without their knowledge.

Without raising a finger or spending a dime, the Obama

campaign had connected in a deeply emotional way with voters across the country. And it had done so through Obama's own words, albeit put into the mouths of others. The huge success of the video generated millions of dollars in free media coverage for the campaign, the vast majority of it overwhelmingly positive. All the Obama team had done was be open enough to allow others to appropriate his words and use them for their own ends.

And remember, this was Obama's *concession* speech. Hillary Clinton had scored a remarkable and unexpected victory in New Hampshire, against a surging tide of Obama support after his victory in the Iowa caucuses. These were the words of the loser in New Hampshire. But they didn't sound like a concession. They sounded like victory. Watch the two videos side by side and you get a strong sense of which of these two candidates had the momentum to go on to win the Democratic Party nomination and ultimately the White House.

It's been frequently noted that the 2008 Obama presidential run was the first truly social media– and Internet-driven campaign. At the heart of this effort was a simple yet revolutionary philosophy: give ordinary people out in the field the tools to organize and take action themselves, and then stand back and let them do it. The engine for driving this social engagement was the web site My.BarackObama.com (also known by its somewhat more fragrant abbreviation MyBO.com), the brainchild of former Facebook wunderkind Chris Hughes. In the world of politics, where tight control over every aspect of the campaign and every action of the candidate has always been standard operating procedure, the audaciousness of this campaign lay in its willingness to relinquish control when it came to organizing the ground game. The Obama campaign had absorbed the first lesson of social media: control is futile. They understood the odd dichotomy that by loosening the reins they could actually harness more power — the power of millions of individual acts.

REBEL WITH A PAINTBRUSH

Giving volunteers control over local organizing efforts is an idea that makes sense. All that was missing, until then, was the social media tools to make it happen. What makes less sense is to relinquish control over one's brand. But that was the other, less recognized, and even more audacious marketing act of the Obama campaign. The 2008 campaign was the first in history where the strategists, the people charged with carefully managing the candidate's image, allowed others outside the campaign to create marketing images on their own and send them out into the world. As I mentioned in the introduction, the most famous of these was Shepard Fairey's now iconic "Hope" poster.

Fairey is a former skateboarder and punk rocker and someone who'd had several run-ins with the law, thanks to his penchant for tagging public buildings with his street art — work he himself calls subversive. His instinct for combining art with rebellion seems to make him an unlikely "poster boy" for a new kind of openness in political branding. But, in fact, his impulse to reach beyond the traditional channels and take his message directly to the people, in the form of street art and stickers in public places, makes him the ideal revolutionary leader in what is one of the most significant changes in political discourse in our time.

It's not such a far journey from an individual citizen in America creating, on his own, a political poster that came to be seen by millions as the defining image of a presidential campaign, to the Twitter postings from the student leaders of the #NeverAgain movement in Parkland, Florida, to the bloggers covering the Syrian uprising against Bashar al-Assad. The power of individuals to affect what was previously the tightly controlled world of political messaging (and branding) is now an accepted fact. But it wasn't so in 2008, when Fairey was working away in his Los Angeles studio creating what would become known as the "Hope" poster. It's a highly stylized image done in the manner of a woodblock print. It takes the classic American red, white, and blue colour scheme and mutes it, giving the poster a hip yet retro aesthetic. The frame is dominated by a head-and-shoulders illustration of Obama, seen from a low angle, as he stares off into the distance towards some yet-to-be-realized future. On his lapel is the official campaign logo, featuring an "O" that represents the rising sun. Some have likened Fairey's illustration to communist propaganda iconography. Obama looks both calm and determined. This image sits atop a solid plinth of capital letters that spell out the word "HOPE."

Unquestionably it's an heroic image. But its real emotional impact lies in the feeling of solidity, permanence, and strength it projects. To my eye it owes more to the world of classical sculpture than poster art. It has more in common with a Roman bust than a Russian propaganda poster — more imperial than revolutionary. Either way, it works. By Election Day 2008, Fairey had sold hundreds of thousands of posters, stickers, and T-shirts to Obama supporters, plowing the profits into producing billboards and murals across the country. He did all of this without the Obama campaign's involvement or approval — necessarily so, because in some cases he was flouting the law by tagging public spaces with the image. But that did not stop the Obama team from noticing. Campaign staffers started using the image on their email signatures and Facebook pages.

Fairey had gained the attention of the campaign, and it was not long before they came calling to commission him to produce an official image of their candidate. Using photographs supplied by the campaign, he produced two more posters in the same style, using the words "Change" and "Vote." But nothing matched the success of the original "Hope" image and its grassroots impact as it was blogged, tweeted, and posted on Facebook by millions of ordinary voters.

KNIT ONE, PURL 2 MILLION

Imagine a consumer brand allowing a scofflaw to appropriate its imagery and start plastering it all over the place without permission. This would be unheard of in the world of traditional marketing. To understand how closed and controlling most organizations are about their brands, consider the International Olympic Committee. Invariably, every two years during the winter and summer games a news story pops up about some hapless small business owner being sued or threatened by the IOC over copyright infringement. Everyone from small-town butchers to pizza parlour owners has received the unwelcome attention of Olympic organizers over the years. Even the most obtuse reference to the Olympic brand is likely to result in an official reprimand. Perhaps the most absurd of these in recent history was the case of a web site called Ravelry.com. Ravelry advertises itself as a "free site for knitters and crocheters."

In the lead-up to the 2012 London Olympics, the quirky folks at Ravelry decided to host a friendly competition for their online community of fibre fanatics. As in two previous Olympic games, people were encouraged to enter the sweater triathlon, the cowl jump, or perhaps the sock put. So far, this all sounds like fun and games. But then the Ravelers made the mistake of calling their event the Ravelympics. That got the United States Olympic Committee (USOC) on the case. They sent a stern cease-and-desist letter to Ravelry accusing the organization of trying to "denigrate the true nature of the Olympic Games." The USOC's enthusiastic lawyer went on to denounce these heartless knitters of socks and scarves for being "disrespectful to our country's finest athletes."

Once this story got out into the media, headline writers had a field day. Not a single knitting pun was left unexploited. But while the committee did apologize to the knitters of America, it never backed down from its basic stance that the USOC needed to protect its brand. In fact, they feigned surprise at the reaction and pointed out that this was just one of hundreds of such letters they had sent out. To think that something as innocuous as the Ravelympics could somehow undermine one of the world's most famous sports events seems absurd. But it demonstrates the intense level of control marketers try to impose on their brands. As social media changes the dynamics of brand management and control, the International Olympic Committee will need to rethink its approach to copyright protection — or hire thousands more lawyers.

The good news is that at the time of this controversy, Ravelry.com had about 2 million users. A year later they had well over 3 million. And the organization continues to hold its other great competition, the Tour de Fleece, without threat of legal action.

But how will mainstream consumer brands operate in the world of open brands? How can they find the optimal balance that will allow them to cede more control to others while harnessing more power for themselves? To see how this might work in the future we have to travel back in time to one of the earliest experiments in open branding — an experiment that led to one of the most successful marketing campaigns of the twentieth century, and an example of marketing in its purest form.

MAKE MINE COLOURLESS, ODOURLESS, AND TASTELESS

The perfume business is often described as pure marketing because in the end it's really not about the fragrance. It's about the brand name, the packaging, the advertising imagery, and the celebrity endorsements. Just ask Paris Hilton, Britney Spears, and Justin Bieber. But there's an even purer form of marketing. Imagine this as an assignment: take a colourless, odourless, and tasteless liquid and make consumers desire it over other colourless, odourless, and tasteless liquids, so much so that they'll actually pay a premium price for it. That's pure marketing.

And that's precisely the challenge that adman Bill Tragos took on in the early 1980s as head of TBWA advertising (later to be known as TBWA/Chiat Day). I was fortunate enough to meet Tragos in the mid-1990s, when my business partner,

Barry Stringer, and I were negotiating the sale of our agency to advertising giant Omnicom. The plan was for Omnicom to acquire our company and merge it with the TBWA/Chiat Day advertising office in Toronto. During the course of our negotiations we were visited by Tragos, chairman of TBWA/Chiat Day (and the T in TBWA). Tragos was an old-school ad guy. He had actually lived through the *Mad Men* era, working at Young & Rubicam in New York in the 1960s before founding his own agency. He came to meet with us not to negotiate the deal but more as a kind of corporate ambassador, to provide reassurance that the acquisition would be good for everyone involved. He seemed to float on a cloud of self-confidence and bonhomie, untouched by the mundane concerns that weigh down the rest of us. Tragos was then in his early sixties and still a handsome man, tanned and greying. He was casually but expensively dressed in a checked blazer, slacks, and open-necked shirt. His smile reached you a few seconds before he did. Over lunch I couldn't resist asking him about the advertising campaign that had made his company's reputation and helped to define it as a creative powerhouse.

The same high-wattage charm that Bill Tragos displayed over lunch was, I'm sure, on full display some fifteen years earlier when he set out to win a new client, Carillon Importers. Carillon is not a name most people would recognize, but its products are. The small New York–based importer was the U.S. distributor for such well-known European liquor brands as Grand Marnier and Bombay Gin. These were sexy brands with relatively large advertising budgets. Ad agencies love to work on liquor brands because creatives think they allow for more creative freedom than, say, toilet bowl cleaners. Besides, when it comes to cocktail party chatter and someone asks you what you do for a living, it sounds a lot better to say "I make ads for Bombay Gin" than to say "I make ads for Toilet Duck."

Tragos was successful in his courtship of Carillon, but along with the assignment for Bombay and Grand Marnier came the task of advertising a then unknown brand from Sweden. It was a colourless, odourless, tasteless liquor called Absolut. A Swedish company, imaginatively named Vin & Spirit (V&S), was producing the product based on a recipe that dated back to 1879. V&S decided that after a hundred years of satisfying the small but no doubt enthusiastic Swedish market, it was time to look beyond their borders. The burgeoning American spirits market of the late 1970s was the logical place to start. Vodka was still a far cry away from assuming the dominant position it holds today in the hard liquor category. Americans, including the denizens of Madison Avenue, were mostly drinking gin. And whisky. And bourbon. But vodka was gradually moving into a starring role, assisted by the dapper British spy with the palindromic greeting: "Bond, James Bond." Despite being the most British of spies, Bond eschewed the most British of drinks, gin, in favour of a distinctly Eastern Bloc beverage: vodka. Preferably in a martini, "shaken, not stirred."

In the 1962 Bond film *Dr. No* we see a butler preparing our hero's favourite cocktail just as specified. And there, clearly displayed on the tray, is a bottle of Smirnoff vodka. It was the start of one of the most enduring product placement deals in history. Like many vodkas of the day, Smirnoff was cloaked in a faux Russian brand persona, complete with tsarist iconography. But the product was actually made in America (in the 1930s a resourceful American distiller bought the rights to the name from Vladimir Smirnoff, a refugee from the Russian Revolution). The combination of Russian branding and American manufacturing made it the biggest-selling vodka in the country and helped to propel vodka into the leading position among distilled spirits, displacing bourbon. A little wink and a nod from Mr. Bond didn't hurt either. The leading imported Russian vodka at the time was Stolichnaya.

As the Swedes were preparing to launch their product in the U.S., they were facing the challenge of persuading Americans that Russian credentials weren't essential to making great vodka. The austere Swedish sensibility added some further obstacles. They settled on a simple name, Absolut, that conjured up none of the romanticism of the Smirnoffs and Stolichnayas of the world. And they placed their clear liquor in a bottle so plain it would not look out of place in a medical lab.

But they had one thing going for them that none of their competitors had: an ebullient Frenchman by the name of Michel Roux, who was then head of sales for Carillon and would ultimately become its president. It was Roux, along with Bill Tragos and the team at TBWA, who would transform Absolut from an unknown entity into a global brand powerhouse — a transformation that would take the brand from sales of 20,000 cases in 1981 to over 11 million cases annually today. And they did it by being open enough to give others carte blanche to reimagine the brand in their own way.

But first they had to create the brand. The initial print ad the agency developed for Absolut was actually done before they even acquired the account. It was conceived as part of the pitch to win the business. The idea that won the day, and the account, was as simple as the product's name and packaging.

It was a straight-on shot of the bottle, below which was a two-word headline in solid capitals that read "Absolut Perfection." Hovering just above the bottle was a glowing white halo. This ad provided the template for all the ads that would follow in the campaign: a bottle shot, a clever two-word headline playing off the name Absolut, and a little visual reference to reinforce it. Over time the campaign would evolve, but this basic concept was the foundation of everything that came after.

The ad was conceived by copywriter Geoff Hayes, a South African who had worked in London and was now at TBWA in New York. Legend has it that Hayes came up with the idea while in the bathtub. This story was, I guess, invented to give the legendary ad campaign its own eureka moment. The more likely scenario is that he was just sitting at home watching TV and doodling on his notepad. Either way, from this simple premise came an explosion of ideas: Absolut Attraction, Absolut Treasure, Absolut Masterpiece. The options appeared limitless.

One of the ways advertisers evaluate the quality of an advertising idea is to ask, "Does it have legs?" An idea with legs is one that allows for many creative expressions of the same basic idea. The value of this is that over time — often years — the advertiser can build its advertising around a single proposition, thus increasing its stickiness with consumers. It means not having to come up with a brand-new idea every year and start from scratch trying to embed it in the minds of consumers. It makes for more efficient and more effective advertising. When it comes to legs, "Absolut Perfection" was the Marilyn Monroe of advertising ideas. (In fact, there was even an "Absolut Marilyn" ad, showing the bottle with a billowing white dress.) The campaign, which continues to this day, has grown to encompass thousands of different executions of the same basic concept that Geoff Hayes sketched out over thirty years ago.

It's not difficult to see why the client bought this ad. It wasn't because they could anticipate that it would become one of the great liquor campaigns of all time. It was because the ad delivered two things clients always ask for in a print ad: "Make the product shot bigger!" and "Put the brand name in the headline!" Knowingly or not, Hayes was giving the client exactly what they wanted.

Early on, people started to pay attention to these simple but striking ads and sales of the product began to accelerate. Only three years after the first ad appeared, Carillon was shipping well over 400,000 cases of Absolut annually, up from its initial 20,000 cases. By now the unique bottle shape, which at first must have seemed so odd, was starting to become instantly identifiable and familiar. And it was that very uniqueness that allowed the brand to start making ads that replaced the bottle with other objects in the shape of the bottle — a swimming pool, a ski slope, a golf course. Notably, these were all luxury objects designed to reinforce the brand's premium image and premium price. The campaign rolled on in this way for a few more years, with dozens of variations on "Absolut _____."

But things changed dramatically in 1985. That's when Michel Roux, who was by now president of Carillon, commissioned an artist friend of his to do a painting of the Absolut bottle. The friend just happened to be Andy Warhol. Roux had gotten to know Warhol because Absolut was running ads in the artist's *Interview* magazine. It was not Roux's intention to use the painting as an ad, so it didn't matter that when Warhol unveiled the painting, it showed the clear bottle with its colourless liquid painted in black. But Roux was an instinctive marketer with a nose for publicity, so he ran the painting as an ad with the headline "Absolut Warhol."

That decision, which generated huge attention for the brand, triggered an avalanche of creative collaboration between Absolut and scores of artists from almost every creative field. Well-known artists such as Keith Haring, George Rodrigue, and Ed Ruscha, photographer Helmut Newton, and cartoonist Al Hirschfeld all produced ads for Absolut incorporating the now-famous bottle. Then the campaign exploded in a burst of creative energy to include writers (Kurt Vonnegut), fashion designers (Marc Jacobs), shoe designers (Manolo Blahnik), and interior designers (Adam Tihany).

Roux came to see himself as a latter-day Romanoff, a patron of the arts doling out commissions, first to famous artists, and later on realizing that he could also use the power of the brand to introduce unknown artists to the world. It was a level of artistic engagement never seen before, or possibly since, in the world of marketing. Pretty soon, well-known names in the world of the arts were lining up to offer their services to Absolut. Consumers were asking where they could buy the ads. Imagine people wanting to pay money for your advertising, not just your product.

Remarkably, it turned out that the Swedish austerity and simplicity of the name and the plainness of the bottle provided the ideal blank canvas onto which artists could project their creativity. In a stroke of unintended genius, the designers of the product had provided the perfect platform upon which a great advertising idea could grow.

What was even more remarkable was how Michel Roux engaged those creative collaborators. As Richard W. Lewis notes in *Absolut Book: The Absolut Vodka Advertising Story*, Roux placed no restrictions on the artists he commissioned. His only requirement was that they include the product somewhere in the work of art. This was a daring and visionary approach. Even today it would be rare for a brand to give such freedom to others to reinterpret their carefully nurtured image. Of course, Roux always held the trump card. He could simply refuse to run the ad if he thought it wasn't appropriate. But apparently that never happened, even when Kenny Scharf painted some strange cartoon-like figures floating out of the bottle, or when Ed Ruscha depicted the shadow of the bottle as one of his sinister-looking wolf silhouettes. Twenty-five years later you could purchase a lithograph of that Ruscha Absolut ad, along with others, for about $3,300 from a rare bookseller in Chicago.

In his willingness to create an open brand, Roux was unquestionably ahead of his time. But he was operating in the pre-Internet age and he was paying people to create those images for his brand. It's not the same situation as today, when an individual like Shepard Fairey can act independently to produce his own interpretation of the brand without input from the brand "owner." While Roux opened the door to a new way of looking at brand management, it's not clear that he would adapt well to the current environment.

In the 1990s a story circulated in the advertising world that might be apocryphal but which I'm inclined to think rings true. As it goes, Roux was walking through an airport one day and spotted a slobby, overweight man wearing a large T-shirt on which was emblazoned one of the Absolut ads. Roux went up to the man and expressed admiration for the shirt. He loved it so much that he had to have it, and would the man be kind enough to sell it to him right then and there? They reached a deal and Roux walked away with his prize — then he dumped it in the nearest trashcan. Afterwards he explained that having this unappealing walking billboard carrying his ad was damaging to his brand. For all his openness to creating the ads, he wasn't prepared to relinquish complete control.

THE BOXER BRIEF AS CORPORATE UNIFORM

Of course, Roux's stunt would certainly not fly today. Just ask Mike Jeffries, the CEO of Abercrombie & Fitch. Jeffries is a study in what can happen to brands when they try to exert excessive control in an age of open branding. Back in 2006, the online magazine *Salon* published an unflattering profile of Jeffries that left readers squirming in their chairs. He was portrayed as a slightly creepy older guy with an unhealthy obsession with the teenage lifestyle. But the article, penned by Benoit Denizet-Lewis, also highlighted the fact that Jeffries had successfully turned around A&F, taking a fading company that used to sell preppy clothing to old fogies and transforming it into a hip brand with strong appeal among teenagers looking for a California-inspired spring break sexiness.

Jeffries achieved this turnaround through the remarkable trick of selling an audience of teenaged boys and girls an image of all-American masculinity by using Bruce Weber–inspired imagery of soft-core gay male erotica. Its retail environments, advertising, and catalogues are filled with images of bare-chested males displaying their ripped abs and big guns. Half-naked guys with their arms around each other, or play-fully tugging off each other's shorts, form a major part of the brand's aesthetic. The catalogues were eagerly awaited by gays each season.

The article went on to note that Jeffries' vision for A&F was to hire only good-looking people in its stores because they wanted only good-looking people to shop there. He's quoted as saying, "We go after the attractive all-American kid with a great attitude and a lot of friends. A lot of people don't belong [in our clothes], and they can't belong. Are we exclusionary? Absolutely." It's an attitude right out of Michel Roux's school of brand control: don't let unattractive people be seen wear-ing my logo.

There was not much reaction to the article at the time. But that was back in January 2006, the virtual Middle Ages of the social media revolution. The iPhone hadn't been launched yet. Twitter was still two months away from its very first tweet. Fast-forward seven years and that quote gets replayed in *Busi-ness Insider*, an online publication, in an article entitled "Aber-crombie & Fitch Refuses to Make Clothes for Large Women." It's now 2013 and Twitter has nearly 300 million monthly users. And this time the Twittersphere explodes with outrage.

It turns out that A&F won't sell women's clothing in size XL or larger, and their jeans only go up to size 10. That's three sizes below the average woman's jean size in America. Protests erupt online and on air. Ellen DeGeneres delivers a mono-logue on her talk show lambasting Jeffries, concluding with the punchline "Oh, Fitch, please!" — a not-so-subtle echoing of the familiar online rant "Oh, bitch, please!" A social activist posts a YouTube video entitled "Fitch the Homeless," in which he goes to thrift stores and buys up old A&F clothing and gives it to homeless people. By the end of the first quarter, the company's sales are down by 17 percent. By the end of the second quarter, the stock price has dropped by 20 percent of its value from its fifty-two-week high.

Some will argue that Jeffries was simply verbalizing what all companies do but never talk about: targeting a specific type of consumer. But there's a world of difference between targeting a particular consumer and actively rejecting certain consumers. The attempt to control a brand's image to that extent might have worked in 2006, but it won't fly today. It requires a special kind of obsessiveness and blindness to shifting consumer dynamics to try to exert that level of control. And Jeffries certainly brings a special kind of attention to detail to his work. As CEO, he not only fusses over the music, lighting, and decor in his stores but even frets over minor details such as how the jeans should drape on the mannequins.

To get a full sense of his obsessiveness, however, let's forego a visit to the store and instead board the company's Gulfstream G550 corporate jet. Staff on the jet are handed a special manual outlining their duties and expected behaviour. The document, which runs to over forty pages, came to light in a 2010 lawsuit brought by a former jet pilot. It specifies exactly what the male cabin crew should wear, right down to the underwear (boxer briefs). It also tells them how they should smell (a regular spritz of A&F #41 cologne is required while on duty). And it provides helpful hints on how to respond when Mr. Jeffries makes a request ("No problem" is acceptable, "Sure" is not). It's not hard to see how Jeffries might encounter some rough weather trying to navigate through the world of open branding, where enthusiastic consumers, not just brand managers, have a say in how a brand's image is shaped.

There is no harm in aiming for exclusivity. Plenty of companies do. But the key is that the decision about whether the brand is right or wrong for someone should lie in the hands of the consumer. If you've got the means and you're prepared to spend tens of thousands of dollars on a Kelly handbag from Hermès, be my guest. The problem with A&F was that it was denying the consumer the opportunity to choose. Instead, Mike Jeffries was deciding for them, the same way he was deciding what underwear his flight attendants should wear (one wonders if this required inspection). One also wonders what the logical conclusion would be to this neurotic desire for control. Would he prowl the shopping malls of America seeking out unattractive people wearing his clothes and offer to buy them back?

THE STREISAND EFFECT

What Jeffries found out the hard way is that what happens on the Internet stays on the Internet. Trying to assert complete control is a fool's errand. But if you're accustomed to always being the one in charge, giving that up can be difficult. And in the Internet age, the control freaks will find they have about as much command of their environment as a novice on ice skates. The more they try to assert full control, the more it keeps slipping out from under them. Keep it up and chances are pretty good you'll end up on your tuchus. Just like Barbra Streisand.

Back in the prehistoric age of the World Wide Web, in the

early 2000s, Streisand attempted to use her star power (and some high-priced lawyers) to exert control over the Internet. It seems a not unreasonable ambition for someone who is a singer, an actor, a writer, a producer, and a director and who has won an Oscar, a Grammy, an Emmy, a Tony, and a Golden Globe. If anyone could pull that off, it would be Babs. Streisand tried to get an image pulled from the Internet after it had already been posted and reposted countless times. This attempt to turn back the online clock makes about as much sense as that risible scene in the 1978 film *Superman* when our distraught hero flies around the earth so fast that he reverses the planet's rotation, thus turning back time and saving Lois Lane.

The Streisand story begins innocently enough. In 2002 an environmental group called the California Coastal Records Project began the daunting task of photographing the California coastline from the air in order to have a complete visual record that would enable tracking of coastal erosion over time. This was years before Google Earth was launched. These images were posted on the group's web site so that government agencies, researchers, and other environmental groups could easily access them. Of the more than 12,000 aerial images showing the entire coast, one included a shot of Barbra Streisand's home in Malibu. In a superstar display of tetchiness, Streisand declared this an outrageous invasion of privacy and sued the organization for $50 million, demanding that the image be removed. Needless to say, the minute word of the suit got out, people went in search of the image. Streisand's quixotic crusade meant that over a million people who would never have gone to the web site of an obscure environmental group got to see the image she wanted so desperately to hide. Tech blogger

Michael Masnick dubbed this phenomenon of attempting to remove something from the Internet, only to end up giving it more exposure, the Streisand Effect. The Los Angeles Superior Court judge who heard the case realized that both he and Streisand lacked the superhuman power to turn back time, and he sensibly threw it out of court. He then ordered the Funny Girl to pay close to $200,000 in defendant's legal fees.

It was an expensive lesson for the diva but it offers a cautionary tale about the futility of trying to assert control in the Internet age. It's a lesson that brand custodians will have to learn in order to survive. Trying to completely control the brand is pointless. It's an idea that Michel Roux, for all his openness, would have found difficult to adapt to. It's an idea that the Mike Jeffrieses of the world continue to resist.

CROWDSOURCING OUR WAY TO MEDIOCRITY

Fortunately, Jeffries is the exception. Many marketers are embracing a more open approach to branding. Unfortunately, as marketers are tentatively picking their way through this unfamiliar territory, they're sometimes fumbling. The trick is to open the floodgates sufficiently and in just the right places to allow new ideas to flow through and add buoyancy to the brand, but not so much that you're swamped. Take as an example the trend towards crowdsourced advertising. Also known as "co-creation," this involves marketers using social media to invite regular consumers to participate in creating ideas for their ads. Oftentimes this comes in the form of a contest where regular folks can reap cash or prizes for coming up with winning advertising ideas. There are even online companies that facilitate this kind of marketplace of ideas. One of the biggest is eYeka, which boasts a community of "creative talents" that numbers over 250,000 and a client list that includes Coca-Cola, Nestlé, Citroën, and Microsoft.

Clients post creative briefs on the site and eYeka then issues a call for entries from its quarter of a million members. Submissions are made in the form of still images or video. Usually there's a cash incentive for the winners, sometimes totalling tens of thousands of dollars. (The name eYeka is explained thus by the Paris-based company: "Members of our community express themselves in a visual way. This is the 'eYe.' 'Ka' is an ancient Egyptian word meaning the 'spirit' — part of the human soul.")

This sounds like a no-lose proposition. Consumers themselves are telling you what they want to see in your ads. Plus you've got the ancient Egyptian gods on your side. You might wonder why every client doesn't simply outsource its creative assignments this way. The problem with crowdsourcing anything, of course, is quality control. How do you eliminate the irredeemably bad and then sift through the remaining mountain of mediocrity to find the good? Around the same time that Shepard Fairey was sitting quietly by himself at his drafting table sketching out the idea for the "Hope" poster, several companies were sending out open casting calls for advertising ideas from the general public. They were opening the floodgates with abandon.

In the early 2000s big-name marketers like GM, Doritos, Heinz, and Pepsi were all eager to join the crowdsourcing circus, calling for consumers to step right up, folks, and show us your ideas. Until the ideas started rolling in. GM's effort in

2007 was focused on the Chevy Tahoe, a full-sized SUV with a V8 engine and 15 miles per gallon city driving. Conveniently, the company set up a web site with video images of the vehicle that consumers could edit themselves and to which they could add superimposed text and music. It seemed foolproof. Chevy was, no doubt, expecting to receive some clunkers among the submissions. What they were clearly not expecting was the hundreds of hostile ads that ridiculed the very idea of SUVs. One spot showed scenes of a white Tahoe prowling the city streets to the sound of an energetic music track. Overtop of these images appeared a series of supers that read "Forget Iraq's Missing Weapons. Here's the Real Weapon of Mass Destruction." Another ad began with the words "Larger than any mortal needs with four-wheel drive for conditions you'll probably never encounter" and concluded with "So you can continue to drive like a heedless jerk...because you're the only one on the whole damn planet."

GM scrambled to get most of these rogue ads off the site, but some of them spilled over onto other web sites, where they continue to live today. Heinz ketchup encountered similar problems when the company ran a contest offering $57,000 to the winner. The result: videos of people doing unpalatable things with ketchup, including smearing it on their faces and brushing their teeth with it.

The problem is that crowdsourced advertising is not the same as open branding. It is a gimmick intended to generate brand buzz and social media engagement. It's not a sincere attempt to create an open environment for the brand. Crowdsourcing is the digital equivalent of a giant virtual creative brainstorming session. And brainstorming sessions, despite their continued use in virtually every type of organization today, are notoriously bad for developing creative ideas. The underlying assumption of creative brainstorming is that everyone is somehow innately creative. Creativity, we're told, is a birthright. All children are creative; it's the oppressive rules the world imposes on us as we grow up that cause that creativity to shrivel up and die. Adulthood eventually forces all of us to colour inside the lines. This is nonsense. When a child draws a picture of a face and puts the mouth on one side of the head and the nose on the other and the eyes at a jaunty angle and then paints the whole thing blue, that is not creativity. That is lack of knowledge and skill. But when Picasso does the same thing, it *is* creativity, because he knows better and has deliberately chosen to subvert the norms for aesthetic reasons.

This is not to say brainstorming sessions are without their usefulness. Brainstorming has a role to play as a planning tool, but rarely does it work as a tool for creativity. A group of people getting together to strategize how to implement a project that's already planned, for example, could benefit from this kind of open sharing of ideas. But developing a plan of action is not the same as developing original, creative ideas. Yet companies today see no irony in this familiar scenario: We have no one on our team who is creative enough to independently come up with an original idea, so let's put together a critical mass of these uncreative people, and somehow a chemical reaction will take place causing all of them suddenly to be creative. If we can just string together enough dead batteries, we can light this bulb.

Trying to crowdsource advertising ideas is simply this principle writ large. It invites an army of mostly uncreative people (or worse, uncreative people who think they're creative) to submit their thoughts (sometimes funny, sometimes crass, oftentimes boring) and leaves the brand managers to sort through the dross to find the occasional glimmer of gold.

GRUMPY BRANDING

There is a place, however, for crowdsourcing in the new world of open brands. But its role is quite the opposite of what one might expect. Social media and the Internet have made open branding not only possible but also inevitable. They've also created an entirely new branding phenomenon. It's what I call the reverse-engineered brand. Usually, the way open branding works is that a company or organization creates a brand and defines its persona, and then outsiders bring their own variations to that defined brand personality. The Obama brand was well established before Shepard Fairey started sketching on his notepad. But the reverse-engineered brand works in exactly the opposite way. It begins when a disparate group of Internet-connected people starts to define a brand persona and then a company picks it up and markets it.

Perhaps the first and most successful appearance of a reverse-engineered brand can be dated to the fall of 2012. It took the form of a cat named Tardar Sauce, who was born with feline dwarfism. This rare condition gave it shrouded eyes and a downward-pointing mouth that made Tardar Sauce look like she had a permanent scowl. This unlikely brand icon lived in a little town just outside Phoenix, Arizona, with its owner, the aptly named Tabby Bundesen. One day, Tabby's brother Bryan came to visit and thought Tardar Sauce looked kind of weird and cute at the same time, so snapped a picture of the kitty sitting in his lap and posted it on the social news site Reddit. In no time, the picture had garnered thousands of comments and risen to the coveted front page of Reddit.com. And that's when people started reposting the picture all over the Web, but this time with captions added. And thus the Internet meme known as Grumpy Cat was born.

Here's a small sampling of Grumpy Cat captions posted online:

"I had fun once. It was horrible."

"If you're happy and you know it, I don't care."

"There are two kinds of people in this world. And I don't like them."

Within a couple of months, Grumpy Cat was being represented by the leading talent agent for Internet cats. Yes, there's a talent agent for Internet cats. He's a former rocker by the name of Ben Lashes and his clients include Keyboard Cat (a T-shirt-wearing, piano-playing feline) and Nyan Cat, an animated kitty that seems to be using a Pop-Tart as a flying carpet and trailing a lurid rainbow as it goes. These creatures of the Internet have starred in television commercials and smartphone apps. It's a surprisingly lucrative business. And Ben gets 20 percent.

But neither of these wannabes comes close to the success of Grumpy Cat. As you might expect, there's all the usual paraphernalia, from T-shirts to coffee mugs with Grumpy's face staring glumly out at you. There's also a book, *Grumpy Cat: A Grumpy Book. Disgruntled Tips and Activities Designed to Put a Frown on Your Face.* Then there's the line of iced coffee products called Grumpy Cat Grumppuccino (available in three flavours). And then Friskies, the cat food company owned by Swiss food giant Nestlé, hired Grumpy Cat to star in a series of web commercials entitled "Will Kitty Play with It?" These commercials perfectly captured and mimicked the persona that had already been established online, complete with captions superimposed over pictures of the cat.

This reverse-engineered brand started out simply as a photograph posted online. And then, as Ben Lashes pointed out in a radio interview with the Canadian Broadcasting Corporation in 2013, "All the kids out in the meme world start throwing up different quotations and jokes on the pictures and it starts building kind of a storyline and a character around Grumpy that people start to love." In other words, the brand persona itself was spontaneously crowdsourced. And only after it had been clearly defined were marketers able to piggyback onto it and use the brand for their own purposes.

In mid-2013, less than a year after first appearing online, Grumpy achieved the ultimate stamp of brand success. Lashes inked a film option for a one-picture deal based on the Grumpy Cat persona.

Open branding, whether it comes through the front door or the back, whether marketers invite strangers to engage with their brands or vice versa, is here to stay. Marketers and political strategists alike will have to learn the difficult business of trying to harness a crowd that wants to veer in all directions at once. It might prove to be a little like herding cats.

Open branding need not be a change to be feared, so long as marketers understand that it's not about giving free rein to all comers to tamper with your brand. Instead it's about creating an environment where talented people who are passionate about the brand will feel free to engage with it on their own.

Reread that last sentence. It contains the three principles of open branding. First, it's about creating an environment, not about creating stuff. Most crowdsourcing efforts today are about soliciting stuff—send us your ads, your pictures, your videos. The Obama campaign never placed an open call for people to start making their own advertisements and posters. But through MyBO.com and other initiatives, they communicated a strong desire for grassroots involvement. They created an environment that made people feel everyone was welcome to contribute their efforts to the cause. Without that strong sense of openness, Shepard Fairey might never have picked up his paintbrush.

Second, it's about getting the right people to be involved for the right reasons. That is, the ones who are passionate about the brand. An assortment of random individuals who think they might win $57,000 for coming up with a great ad idea for a product they may or may not consume is unlikely to generate the most powerful ideas. Open branding is about getting the people who are most invested in the brand to engage with it. Fairey was a social activist who was deeply committed to getting Obama elected as president. That was his motivation. His personal desire to see Obama in the White House infused his work with passion, drove him to work hard at distributing the image, and made him forego any profit from the venture.

The story of Warhol's commission to paint the Absolut bottle, as told in Richard Lewis's book, is that the idea came not from Michel Roux but from Warhol himself. Over dinner one evening the teetotaller Warhol confessed to Roux that, while he never drank, he was a big fan of Absolut. He used the liquor not as a drink but as a perfume. Before heading out for the evening, one imagines he would dab a little behind his ears or rub it on his wrists. Given that vodka is odourless, it's unclear what the olfactory appeal might have been. But the point is Warhol was passionate about the brand. So passionate he was dousing himself with it. And just as with Shepard Fairey, it was that passion that made him want to paint it and turn it from a familiar image into an iconic one.

In addition to creating the right environment and attracting the right people, the third principle of open branding is summed up in the words "on their own." Warhol and Fairey did not strike a committee or organize a focus group to help them develop their ideas. They were developed through personal contemplation. Even when many people are involved in the execution of a creative project, the initial spark of an idea is most often born in the individual mind. Advertising creatives work in environments where they are surrounded by other creative people. Usually they're in teams. But the creative insight is quite often a solitary thing. When Geoff Hayes came up with the idea for "Absolut Perfection," he wasn't sitting in a boardroom surrounded by a bunch of other creative types. He wasn't even sitting with the art director who was his creative partner. He was at home. Alone.

Michel Roux's ads for Absolut were more about creative collaboration than purely open branding. But they opened the door to a new way of thinking about how ads are made and who controls the brand's image. By expanding the advertising assignment beyond the confines of the agency creative department, Absolut tapped into a vast and diverse array of creative talent, greater than anything that would be available to an ordinary advertiser. They were able to do this only because they gave free licence to those people to do with the brand whatever they wished. The result was not just a gallery of great ads. The openness itself said something about the brand. It told consumers in an indirect way that this was a brand at the leading edge that was willing to take chances — a brand that was embraced by some of the most innovative people in the world. Loosening their grip gave Absolut exponentially more power than they would have got by trying to exert complete control.

There's a middle ground between the obsessive control of Mike Jeffries and the reckless abandon of crowdsourcing. It's a space where brands that have found a committed band of followers will invite those people in to share their ideas and creativity and find new ways of taking the message forward. It's in this open space where successful brands will live in the future.

I say "in the future" because most brands are not there yet. They remain stubbornly clinging to control. This is one area where the boardroom has yet to catch up with the war room. Political operatives have moved significantly ahead of their marketing counterparts in building more open brands. The gimmickry of crowdsourced advertising seems superficial and manipulative compared to the online tools made available to supporters on My.BarackObama.com, which took a proactive approach to managing the inevitable social media outpouring that comes during an election year. For the most part marketers remain in reactive mode, waiting for something to go wrong before engaging with consumers. When companies make big changes to brands that people feel passionately about, they are increasingly obliged to consult first with consumers and allow them the opportunity to provide feedback before the changes take place. Gap Inc. found that out the hard way when it attempted to change the familiar elegant and elongated white typeface inside a blue square that had been the brand's identity for years. Perhaps in an attempt to think outside the box, the company freed the logo from the confines of the blue square and set it adrift, rendering the type in black with a small blue square floating above the "p." Beyond the fact that the new logo showed a remarkable lack of good taste, the elements appeared disjointed and incoherent. They projected an image of a brand that was drifting aimlessly. Like it or not, the old logo said, "We're solid, dependable, and stylish," while the new one mumbled, "We don't know where the hell we're going."

A predictable outcry arose from the social media universe, and within days company executives were backpedalling and promising to keep the original logo. But then, they hastily posted a message to the Gap Facebook page, saying, "We know this logo created a lot of buzz and we're thrilled to see passionate debate unfolding! So much so we're asking you to share your designs. We love our version, but we'd like to see other ideas. Stay tuned for details in the next few days on this crowdsourcing project."

Having developed one execrable design, the company was now planning to compound its error by asking anyone who cared to, to pull out their crayons and start designing. Designs, as it turns out, that would never be used, because ultimately the old logo remained. The entire rebranding effort was a waste of time and money that left Gap management looking as foolish as if they'd been caught with their chinos around their ankles.

This double fumble is what happens when brands try to remain in complete control and then over-correct when things go wrong. What if Gap had run a design competition involving some of the best designers in the world and then had consumers vote on them? It would have meant giving up some control but not all of it. It would have meant inviting consumers in, but on the brand's own terms. It would be acknowledging that the marketers don't always have all the answers. And as we'll see in the next chapter, increasingly marketing is not about having all the answers; sometimes it's about asking the right question.

CHAPTER 5

THE BALLOT QUESTION

START THE CONVERSATION WITH A QUESTION

"Next Tuesday is Election Day. Next Tuesday all of you will go to the polls. You'll stand there in the polling place and make a decision. I think when you make that decision it might be well if you would ask yourself, 'Are you better off than you were four years ago?'"

That's how Ronald Reagan concluded his final televised debate with Jimmy Carter in 1980 and in the process sealed Carter's fate. Millions of people who entered the privacy of the polling booth that November 4 were left alone with two things: a ballot paper and that simple question ringing in their ears.

A generation has passed since then, and in the intervening years political strategists have continued to refine the art of the so-called "ballot question." These days opposing sides in a political campaign frequently make a mad dash to be the first to formulate the overriding question voters will be asking themselves as they step into the voting booth. Political strategists recognize that defining a powerful and effective ballot question can ultimately help you win. The trick is to pose the

160

question but leave it up to the voters to supply the answer. A conclusion reached on one's own is much more powerful than one offered up by someone else. The skill of the truly talented political strategist is to pose a question in such a way that the voter is led to only one unavoidable answer. In the case of Reagan and Carter, for most voters that answer was, "No, I'm not better off. Carter has to go."

It is this talent — the ability to ask the right question rather than always trying to be the final answer — that defines the second big challenge for marketers trying to craft their messages in the digital age. A more vocal and engaged consumer will be increasingly resistant to being told what they want or need and more interested in being asked what they think. The brand is not always the ultimate answer to a consumer's unmet needs. Sometimes it's not the answer at all; sometimes it's just a question that invites the consumer to offer up his or her point of view. Just as the open brand invites outsiders into the process of crafting the message, so too does the ballot question. It's one more step in opening up a two-way conversation with the consumer rather than the top-down approach of the mass marketing era.

There's a certain psychological dynamic to an effective ballot question. It's dependent on three factors in order to succeed. First, a ballot question is fundamentally competitive in nature. It sets up an inherent dichotomy in which there is always a right and a wrong answer. Virtually no one in America in the year 1980 thought they were better off than they had been four years earlier. Even people who weren't going to vote for Reagan knew that the right answer was "No, I'm not better off." Second (and closely aligned with the first), a good ballot question follows the old maxim of trial lawyers: never ask a question to which you don't already know the answer. If you're going to leave it up to your audience to supply the answer, you'd better be sure you know what their response will be. There was no doubt in Reagan's mind how people would respond to his question. And last, the answer should lead the audience back to the brand's basic values, what it stands for. In Reagan's case, the theme of his 1980 election campaign was something that might seem familiar in the post-Trump era: "Let's Make America Great Again!" This was a call to regain America's economic and military strength following a protracted economic downturn, an oil crisis, and a hostage-taking in Iran. The country as a whole felt it had taken a financial and psychological drubbing, and so did many individual households. People wanted to feel great again. The ballot question Reagan posed tapped directly into that longing and into the core message of his campaign.

Oftentimes, the most skillful ballot question is one that is posed so subtly that the audience barely notices it. In the 2012 presidential election the Obama campaign did precisely that, in a powerful television commercial that ran late in the campaign. The spot opens on an oddly downbeat note. We see a black-and-white image of the president's desk in the Oval Office. The office is empty, the president not there. The picture fades out to be replaced by another black-and-white image, this time of the president seen from behind. He is walking away from the camera through a darkened archway; he is silhouetted against the daylight beyond. He is wearing a long black coat. His head is slightly bowed. Two soldiers stand on either side, saluting. Taken together, these images — lasting only six seconds in total — conjure up a stark illustration of loneliness at the top. Walking through the shrouded archway, Obama seems to carry the weight of the nation on his shoulders. He is a man alone with his thoughts. He is the decider.

Over these visuals we hear the unmistakable voice of Morgan Freeman. It is a godlike voice, forbidding and warm at the same time. "Every president inherits challenges," he says sombrely. "Few have faced so many."

Then, as the images shift from black-and-white to colour and an orchestral score swells in the background, we see soldiers returning home, workers at their jobs, eager children in classrooms. Freeman continues, "Four years later, our enemies have been brought to justice. Our heroes are coming home. Assembly lines are humming again."

The narrative is clear. The president has faced unprecedented challenges and he has risen to meet them. At this point the storyline pivots from past to future. "There are still challenges to meet," says Freeman, his voice brightening. "Children to educate, a middle class to rebuild." And then, as Obama's one-word 2012 campaign slogan "Forward" fills the screen, the voice-over concludes, "But the last thing we should do is turn back now."

This powerful thirty seconds of communication does not directly ask for your vote. It makes no grand campaign promises. Instead, while tacitly acknowledging that the state of the nation is far from perfect, it seeds a simple query. Despite his progress, the president still has work to do. The question, never stated but clearly implied, is this: "Should he be given the chance to finish the job he started?"

This question was more deeply human and far more subtle than the one posed by the Romney campaign, which asked implicitly and somewhat drily, "Who do you trust to manage the economy?" Many of us have been in situations where we've been asked to do a job, where we've made progress, and where, if only we had more time, we could get it done properly. It's a circumstance to which many voters could relate. It was an appeal to the audience's sense of fair play. For many of the swing voters at whom this message was aimed, the answer to the Obama ballot question was, "Yes, he should." It was a question that, though subtle, met all the criteria for success. First, there's no doubt the campaign had thoroughly tested this idea and felt confident the targeted voters would answer in the affirmative the question of whether the president should be given a chance to finish the job. Also, the answer contained an implicitly competitive flipside to the same coin: "And Romney should not." Last, the ballot question was linked directly to the campaign theme, "Forward." It also tapped into a core part of the Obama brand persona, a sense of decency and fair play.

Did this ad seal the campaign? Not entirely. There were many other factors at play in the closing days of the election. But it did manage to frame the key question of the election to an important constituency of undecided voters. Like those Reagan voters in 1980, alone with their thoughts in the voting booth, the Obama voters in 2012 had the candidate's ballot question echoing in their heads. And a great many of them answered exactly as the campaign strategists wanted them to.

The ballot question is most powerful when it draws the audience into an internal debate that hinges on an emotional or moral issue. In the case of Reagan it was an emotional appeal to a nation that felt it was slipping backwards, calling on people to move forward and reach for greatness again. For

Obama it was an appeal to fair-mindedness. To answer in the negative would be to deny one's own sense of reasonableness and decency. An effective ballot question is not simply a slogan posed in the interrogative. The 1980s advertising campaign for Wendy's hamburgers, which asked the now famous question "Where's the beef?", was not posing a ballot question. It was simply making the point that Wendy's burgers had more beef in them and doing it in a comical way. A ballot question reaches into much deeper emotional and psychological territory.

The closest thing to a ballot question in the world of marketing is what marketers call a brand positioning statement — a declaration of what the brand stands for in the mind of the consumer. Like a ballot question, a brand positioning statement tries to distill down to its essence the one thing you want people to be thinking about when they consider voting for you, at the ballot box or the cash register. Note that one's a question and the other's a statement. One is open and inquiring, the other direct and declarative. The positioning statement is an essential tool of the mass marketing approach, where the brand always strives to provide the final answer.

Marketers usually develop a brand positioning statement by defining a target consumer and uncovering some unmet need of that consumer — one that relates to their business. Then they align their brand's attributes with this consumer need in order to deliver a benefit. The brand, in short, declares itself to be the solution to your needs.

This approach, which is largely unchanged since it was first developed in the late 1960s, has often been described as "occupying a space in the mind of the consumer." A ballot question does exactly the opposite. By posing a question, it opens up a space in the mind of the voter where individuals themselves supply the answer — albeit one that the questioner has already predetermined. Nevertheless, it creates a sense of participation and control in the target audience.

It's the difference between being at a cocktail party and having your host say, "What would you like to drink?" versus having them say, "I thought you looked like you could use a martini, so I made you one. You're gonna love it!" Marketers have for decades been pressing their oftentimes unwanted products on consumers, all the while telling them how much they're gonna love it. Which is probably what led to the joke about how an advertising executive makes love: he sits on the edge of the bed and tells you how great it's going to be.

But newly empowered consumers have grown impatient and skeptical about this kind of assertive communication. As the Internet and social media have shifted the balance of power between consumer and marketer, consumers are less interested in being told what they want and more interested in being asked what they'd like. Even if the sense of choice is only an illusion.

YOU CAN'T BE THE ANSWER IF YOU DON'T KNOW THE QUESTION

Wendy's hamburgers notwithstanding, the ballot question is no longer the exclusive domain of savvy political operatives. Consumer marketers are discovering the power of daring to pose an implicit open-ended question in anticipation of the consumer's naming their brand as the answer. As with political strategists, the questions are sometimes implied in such subtle ways the viewer may not even be aware of them. In fact, some-times not even the brand's competitors are aware of them. And that can lead to serious missteps in communication, as happened with two of the best-known brands in world in the mid-2000s.

In May 2006 a new advertising campaign started airing on American television. By the time the campaign ended three years later, it had included sixty-six different commercials. Each commercial had roughly the same set-up. There were no special effects, no spectacular locations. In fact, there wasn't even a set. Just two characters against a plain white back-ground, talking to the camera. Nevertheless, *Adweek,* a lead-ing advertising industry publication, pronounced it the best ad campaign of the first decade of the new century. *Advertising Age* magazine gushed that the campaign was a "hit parade of the most memorable ads" of the past ten years. And it went on to win a major marketing industry award, an Effie, handed out to advertising campaigns that had proven themselves to be truly effective and produced exceptional results in the market-place. The Effie jury noted that this campaign had resulted in record sales and had increased the brand's market share by a staggering 42 percent. Moreover, they conferred on it a status most advertising people crave and few achieve. The campaign, they said, was "culturally influential."

From Wendy's "Where's the beef?" to "Got milk?", cultur-ally influential campaigns are those that become so embed-ded in the popular consciousness that they move beyond mere advertising and into the realm of cultural memes — sometimes even entering the vernacular.

Thus it was in May 2006 when millions of television viewers

were introduced to two characters who would ultimately come to seem like part of the family. The very first spot in the series opened, as all the subsequent spots would, with two men standing in front of a white backdrop. They introduce themselves.

"Hello, I'm a Mac."

"And I'm a PC."

The PC, played by comic actor John Hodgman, is dressed in a pair of saggy khakis, a brown tweed blazer, and sensible glasses. He is round and pleasant and exudes a kind of witless charm. His counterpart, played by Justin Long, is in jeans and a T-shirt and hoodie. He sports a scruffy attempt at facial hair. Standing with hands in pockets and legs apart, he conveys an air of laid-back self-assurance.

Through all sixty-six ads the scenarios change but the plot remains the same. PC desperately tries to show that he's just as cool and hip as Mac and each time ends up looking merely clumsy and ineffective. Mac meanwhile talks about his advantages over computers that run the Microsoft operating system: easier to use, fewer crashes and viruses, good for business as well as creative projects, and so forth.

Through all of PC's comic fumbling, Mac looks on calmly, frequently complimenting PC on his strengths ("You should see what this guy can do with a spreadsheet. It's insane."), but always asserting his own superiority ("But he knows I'm better at 'life' stuff, like music, pictures, movies. Stuff like that.").

These ads are part of a long tradition in the marketing world of competitive advertising — where one brand directly challenges another with specific claims of superiority. Think of the Pepsi Challenge, which led Coke to its disastrous reformulation. But two things make these Apple ads, known collectively as the "Get a Mac" campaign, different from almost every other competitive advertising campaign. The first is that they deliver a hard-hitting message in a completely disarming way. Here the iron fist of direct and competitive product claims comes wrapped in the velvet glove of John Hodgman and Justin Long's amusing banter.

The second is that Apple doesn't denigrate its competition in the usual way. The goal of most competitive advertising is to make the other brand seem inferior or untrustworthy. But here both characters are likable. These ads don't attempt to make the viewer dislike or distrust PC; they deliver a much more devastating blow: they make you pity him.

An untrustworthy character can still be powerful. Someone who's worthy of your pity is irredeemably inferior. Hodgman's note-perfect performance as he stumbles from one cringe-worthy act to another gives his character a Mr. Bean–like quality. He's a lovable nerd. We like him. We just don't ever want to *be* like him.

These spots are competitive, but beyond that, what do they have to do with the notion of a ballot question? To understand that we must take a look at the underlying message of these ads and the deeper emotional and psychological territory they mine. At a superficial level they're poking playful fun at the inadequacies of the Microsoft operating system. But at a subconscious level, they're actually taking the viewer back in time to that most fraught of social environments: the high-school cafeteria. As we watch these ads, we are back there holding our plastic tray with the slowly congealing special of the day, and we have a decision to make. Where are we going to sit? Are we with the nerds or the cool dudes?

The ballot question implicit in Apple's enormously success-ful campaign was "Who do you want to be seen sitting with?" Microsoft completely missed that fact. If they'd figured it out, doubtless they would not have responded, as they did, with a campaign starring a cute little girl named Kylie, which ended with her saying, "I'm a PC and I'm four and a half." The com-mercial shows Kylie taking a picture of her fish, Dorothy. She then edits the photo and emails it to her family. You see, a PC is so simple to use that even a four-and-a-half-year-old can do it. Microsoft was battling a perception that it was complicated to use, and at the same time the brand was attempting to counter the challenge that PCs were for spreadsheets and Apple was for "life." The problem was that Microsoft was oblivious to the underlying ballot question in the Apple campaign. The result was that it provided a thoroughly tone-deaf answer. Who would you rather hang with, a wry and fun-loving Justin Long or a precocious yet earnest four-and-a-half-year-old?

THE BURRITO THAT SAVED WALL STREET

The "Get a Mac" campaign preceded the explosion of social media. To see how the ballot question is finding its way into marketing communications in the Internet age, we need to leave behind the cafeteria showdown between Microsoft and Apple and head instead to a small, sophisticated restaurant in New York on a quiet little street in the West Village. By New York standards it is a tiny space, with room for just thir-teen tables. And even though every table is occupied, there is a hushed atmosphere in the softly lit room. The decor is spare; the unadorned walls are the colour of faded parchment.

The attention here is focused entirely on the food. And as if to reinforce the point, the dining area sits on a raised platform. Quite literally, the food has been hoisted onto a pedestal. The menu, which includes frogs' legs with lobster and white speckled grits, and Wagyu beef with escargots and Alba mushrooms, is not for the unadventurous, nor the impecunious.

It is here where I've come to meet Steve Ells, a classically trained chef and one of the most successful restaurateurs in recent American history. But even though he is greeted warmly by the maître d' and the chef comes to the table to shake his hand, this is not Steve's restaurant. Steve has a restaurant a couple of blocks away at the busy junction of Greenwich and 6th Avenue. It's a small storefront location with a grey exterior and large red sign above the door that reads "Chipotle."

The story of Chipotle Mexican Grill began twenty-five years earlier and 1,800 miles due west of New York City, in Denver, Colorado. It is here where a young Steve Ells, freshly graduated from the Culinary Institute of America, decided to open a small burrito shop near the University of Denver campus. His aim? Make enough money so that he could fund a high-end restaurant like the one we're sitting in in the West Village — with lobster and Wagyu beef on the menu. More than two decades later, Steve still hasn't opened his fancy restaurant. That's because he's been busy building Chipotle from a single location in Denver to over 2,500 locations across America, plus an expanding global presence in cities like Toronto, London, and even that bastion of sophisticated gastronomy, Paris.

But what's brought me to my meeting with Ells is not that his is another story of little-guy-has-vision-and-makes-good. I'm here because of *how* Ells achieved his success. He did it by defying every marketing convention of all the successful fast food restaurants that preceded him, restaurants that were mostly created in the mass marketing era and that often continue to cling to their old ways. Most significantly, Ells grew his business by avoiding a simple brand declaration and instead posing an audacious ballot question to his consumers — a question no other fast food restaurant had ever dared to ask before.

When he began his restaurant business, Ells could not have known that the former Dolly Madison ice cream parlour he converted into a "fast casual" burrito bar would, only five years later, attract the eye of the world's largest fast food service retailer, and the company that practically invented the concept of fast food, McDonald's.

In 1998, McDonald's placed a substantial bet on the small but growing Mexican restaurant chain, investing $360 million and committing itself to helping Ells continue to expand his company across the country. On the morning of January 26, 2006, that bet paid off. Chipotle Mexican Grill went public, listing its shares on the New York Stock Exchange. Astonishingly, by the end of trading that day, the shares had doubled in value from $22 to $44. This extraordinary event had a profound psychological impact on the markets. Not since the end of the late-nineties dot-com bubble had a company doubled its value in the first day of trading. Analysts and financial experts were finally ready to breathe a sigh of relief and declare that the dot-com curse had come to an end. After six long years of the high-tech hangover, investors had found something they could believe in again. And it took the form of a warm tortilla filled with rice, beans, and spicy barbacoa.

After the IPO, McDonald's cashed in its chips and hauled off a jackpot worth $1.5 billion, more than quadrupling its initial investment. However, even after the McDonald's departure, investors continued their infatuation with Chipotle. By 2012, the company's shares were trading at $440, ten times the price they were at close of trading on that very first day. This was not simply a display of irrational exuberance on the part of the market. Chipotle was delivering real results. Twelve years after its IPO the company had increased its revenue more than six-fold to $4.5 billion (despite several food safety issues).

What makes Chipotle's success story even more remarkable is that it achieved all this while at the same time eschewing most of the conventional business practices of its fast food competitors. Walk into a Chipotle restaurant and glance up at the menu board. What you'll see are six items: burrito, burrito bowl, soft taco, crispy taco, salad, and chips with guac. That's it. That is all Chipotle sells. Never in the history of humankind have so many restaurants made so much money off so few menu items. The U.S. food menu at McDonald's consists of over a hundred items.

The genius of this abbreviated menu (aside from the fact that it makes for a highly efficient operation) is that almost everything is customizable. Each item is prepared to order in front of the customer. You can choose from braised pork, beef, or chicken; two types of rice or beans; a choice of cheeses and salsas; plus guacamole or sour cream. The result is that the six-item menu expands into a seemingly infinite array of options.

Chipotle is unique in other ways. It has no franchisees. All the stores are company owned. As one financial wag noted, that means "They get to keep all the money they make." The company also spends fully one-third of its revenue on food costs, an unusually high figure for the fast food business. And it makes a serious effort to source local produce and to serve sustainably raised pork, beef, and chicken.

SPENDING LESS TO GET MORE

But of all the things that separate Chipotle from its competition, none is as significant as its approach to marketing. It is this fact that has brought me to the fancy restaurant in New York to meet with Ells, and with Chipotle's chief marketing officer, Mark Crumpacker. Seeing them together, it's not difficult to imagine what these two men must have looked like when they first met, some thirty years earlier as students in Boulder, Colorado. Their younger selves are still quite evident beneath the slightly greying hair. Both men appear to spend a lot of time at the gym. In fact, Ells reports he's just come from there and is famished. The two men share the kind of easy, playful banter that comes from decades of friendship.

Even though they've known each other for years, Crumpacker only joined Chipotle in 2009. Upon his arrival, he did something unheard of in the fast food industry. Even though Chipotle's sales were growing (despite a moribund economy), and even as competition from other "fast casual" restaurants — that is, restaurants that are a step up from fast food places like Subway but below casual dining restaurants like Applebee's — was increasing, Crumpacker took the company's already meagre advertising budget and slashed it. By 2012, Chipotle's advertising spending had been cut by one-quarter.

Media spending plummeted from roughly $8 million to about $6 million.

To put that $6 million in context, during the same period, Panera Bread, whose annual sales are about half a billion dollars less than Chipotle's, was dramatically ramping up its advertising budget to $60 million. Like Chipotle, Panera is a rapidly growing and highly successful "fast casual" restaurant. Panera and its sister brands have over 1,700 locations in the U.S. and Canada, serving wholesome salads and sandwiches made with freshly baked artisan bread in an upscale bakery-café setting. However, even Panera's $60 million advertising budget seems like small beer when compared to the amounts being spent by their fast food competitors. At the low end of the fast food chain, Arby's spends approximately $100 million a year on advertising in the U.S., and at the high end, McDonald's spends about $650 million annually. The average fast food restaurant chain spends between 3 percent and 6 percent of its revenue on advertising. Chipotle was spending a fraction of 1 percent — and it was drastically cutting that spending even further.

This move was even more surprising when you consider that, prior to joining Chipotle, Crumpacker was working on the other side of the client–agency divide as creative director of Sequence, a marketing and design agency he co-founded in 2002. A former ad agency executive is the last person you'd expect to be slashing the company's advertising budget. He made other changes as well, including bringing much of the company's advertising work in-house.

Chipotle has built its business on the promise of "food with integrity," a phrase that may come back to haunt the company after reports of food safety issues, but that was originally intended to capture the fact that the company seeks to use sustainably raised food that respects the animals, the environment, and the farmers. But how to communicate this fact? A conventional advertiser would have created television commercials that talk about where the food comes from and how it's raised. Crumpacker and Ells chose to put aside the old mass marketing handbook and do something completely different. They created a short animated film, just over two minutes long, and posted it on YouTube. The film makes no declarations about Chipotle. In fact, the brand logo appears only very briefly at the end. Instead, it poses an implicit question to the viewer — an unexpected question for a fast food company.

The film is shot in stop-motion animation using handmade figures of humans and friendly-looking farm animals. It unfolds in a single linear tracking shot that follows the journey of one farmer as he progresses from small family farm to massive industrial operation. Eventually he is producing an assembly line of pigs bloated with artificial growth hormones. They are stamped into perfect cubes of unrecognizable pink flesh. All the while, an odd green effluent is being pumped into the surrounding blue waters by the industrial farming operation.

Over this action we hear Willie Nelson. His ancient voice, full of fragility and pain, and accompanied by a single guitar, sings a Coldplay song entitled "The Scientist." Gradually night and a cold winter descend on the scene and the farmer finds himself alone with his thoughts. He reflects on the caged animals, the hormones and antibiotics, the environmental damage, and he has a Damascene conversion. As dawn breaks and spring blossoms on the land, the farmer sets about undoing all he has done. He dismantles his factory farming operation and liberates the animals, allowing them to roam freely and to graze on the land. He goes back to the place where he began. At this moment Willie Nelson, his voice now urgent, sings the final line: "I'm going back to the start."

It's a deeply affecting piece of storytelling. People have reported tearing up while watching it. Crumpacker tells me, "When we showed this in movie theatres, people were applauding." But the movie theatre screenings came later. The film was first posted to YouTube in August 2011. Within just a few months it would log a staggering 5 million views. Eventually that number exceeded 7 million.

Then, in a complete reversal of the advertising norm, Crumpacker decided that, since millions of people were choosing to watch the film online, it might be a good idea to air it on television. The company had never run a television commercial before. It was a good call. That February, the two-minute ad aired just once, on the 2012 Grammy Awards. It was the year Adele's album 21 captured six trophies and the Grammys paid special tribute to the recently deceased Whitney Houston. Viewership of the show jumped 50 percent over the previous year. Forty million Americans tuned in, surpassing the ratings for the Academy Awards.

As soon as the ad ended, the Twittersphere lit up. People reported weeping over it. A Fox News headline declared, "Chipotle Airs New Ad, Steals Grammys Spotlight." The next day Time magazine's TV critic James Poniewozik gushed, "The most enjoyable musical thing I saw last night was not a live performance at all. It was a Chipotle ad." He pronounced the Coldplay-inspired ad to be even better than Coldplay's live performance on the show.

The ad had an impact far greater than the modest advertising budget with which Crumpacker was working. But beyond the fact that the spot was enjoyable to watch and people were moved by it, what was its message? What was it really saying to Chipotle's customers and potential customers? It was posing a question. It was asking, "Do you care where your food comes from and how it's raised?"

Never before had a fast food restaurant dared to ask such a question of its customers. In fact, it's the very last thing most fast food companies want their customers to think about. That's what made the ad so powerful — and risky. Yet it was a question Chipotle, after years of carefully amending its practices and sourcing local, sustainable, humanely raised food, was able to ask with confidence. They knew that for Chipotle's target audience the answer would be "Yes, I do care." By opening up this question in consumers' minds, the company, which had long rejected conventional advertising approaches as being out of character for the brand, was able to engage its customers in a more meaningful and thoughtful way. And it was a question that brought consumers right back to the core value and positioning of the brand: food with integrity.

It was also an implicitly competitive stance. Remember those voters standing in the voting booth staring at the ballot and asking themselves if they were better off now than they were four years ago, or if Obama deserved a chance to finish the job? Chipotle wanted folks standing in line at their favourite fast food joint, staring at the menu, to question where the food was coming from and how it was raised. If that was the ballot question, then Chipotle could win.

The average Chipotle customers are in their late twenties

or early thirties, are better educated, and have a higher income than the average fast food patron. That's part of the reason why the company continued to experience dramatic growth in sales even during a recession — despite having higher prices. The average Chipotle order has twice the dollar value of the average McDonald's order. But the youthful urbanites shelling out for burritos and tacos at Chipotle are also more likely to care about where food comes from and more willing to pay extra for meat that is hormone-free and humanely raised.

They are the Millennial generation (born after 1980), and they dine out a lot. Given their numbers, spending power, and frequent restaurant-going, they've been labelled the generational group that has the highest impact on restaurants, especially fast casual restaurants like Chipotle. They are the generation raised on a diet of Anthony Bourdain, Gordon Ramsay, and Michael Pollan. They see food as part adventure, part competition, and part social cause. They grew up in an era when television cooking shows came into such prominence that entire cable networks were devoted to 24/7 food programs and their celebrity chefs. And they've been cataloguing their food experiences, from the mundane to the sublime, by uploading a torrent of food pics to social media. The food you eat and where you eat it have become critical markers of one's personal identity and values. For this generation, where you eat might be a more important signifier of social status than where you went to college.

Chiptole's promise of "food with integrity" prepared the way you want it, right before your eyes, was pitched perfectly to this cohort.

Aside from hitting its target audience so precisely, how did Chipotle drive such extraordinary growth with a premium-priced product in a recessionary time, without the power of a massive advertising campaign? A significant part of the brand's success was the question it dared to pose to consumers through the "Back to the Start" video. But figuring out how to ask the right question is no easy matter. As noted earlier, a successful ballot question has a three-part dynamic: it must set up an inherently competitive choice; the answer to the question must already be known before you ask it; and the answer must bring the audience back to the brand's core values and positioning. In addition, there are three important attributes a great ballot question must have in order to succeed. The Chipotle video had all of them.

A powerful ballot question, one that connects deeply with its audience and moves them to think or do something different, resides within the magic triangle bordered by believability, credibility, and humanity.

Believability is about engendering a head-nod from the audience. It's about tapping into a pre-existing belief — one that is widely held and accepted by the target audience. On this front Reagan's question delivered in spades. By the end of the 1970s, America was suffering through an oil crisis that had resulted in a dramatic drop in world oil supplies and a corresponding rise in prices. This in turn led to rationing of gas for American drivers, some of whom had to wait in long lines to fill up their tanks and could do so only on certain days, depending on whether they had an odd- or even-numbered licence plate. The 1979 oil crisis was not only felt at the pumps;

it sent shockwaves rippling through the economy. Inflation shot up as employment and economic growth declined. Consumer confidence took a beating. It wasn't a stretch for Reagan to suggest that Americans were not feeling better off than they had been four years earlier. It was the truest thing he could have said.

Identifying an issue that consumers care about is only the beginning. The second gauge of a successful ballot question is credibility. The audience has to accept that the questioner can opine on the subject with a high degree of authority and trustworthiness. In theory, McDonald's could have talked to consumers about the fact that sustainably raised, hormone-free meat is an important issue. But they could never have done so with any degree of credibility. People would simply not have believed them — not without massive and sustained changes to the way in which the company sources its food. A discussion about sustainability from McDonald's would have been dismissed as crass opportunism in an age when people are increasingly concerned about this issue. But fast food diners were open to hearing Chipotle on this subject because the company had spent years building up its credentials. A good ballot question is not just about the question; it's also about the questioner.

Finding a subject that consumers believe in and that is credible coming from the questioner is not easy, but it's a lot easier than the third part of this triangle — humanity. There is some art involved in finding a question that connects with people at a visceral, emotional, and human level. This is the most abstract and elusive part of the puzzle. And oftentimes that deeply human connection is simply serendipitous.

To understand the full force of Reagan's simple query, "Are you better off than you were four years ago?", one needs to understand what was happening to the American psyche at the time. It was undergoing a crisis of confidence unprecedented in the history of the republic.

On Election Day, November 4, 1980, Iranian revolutionaries had been holding U.S. embassy personnel hostage in Tehran for precisely 365 days. Every day since the hostage-taking, Walter Cronkite, the voice and conscience of the nation, had signed off his nightly newscast with a grim accounting: "The 324th day of captivity for the American hostages in Iran...The 325th day...The 326th day..." A supposedly rag-tag band of Iranian students was holding the most powerful nation on earth hostage. And for months on end it seemed that America could do nothing about it. The country that had invented the countdown as the soundtrack for its ingenuity and strength had been forced to turn the clock around and was now collectively counting up. And as the numbers clicked by relentlessly, day after day, they were adding up to failure. Defeat is sometimes experienced simply as an emotion, but this was quantifiable defeat. It was tangible. You could track it. And each day was a fresh reminder of the failure. By Election Day, a full year into the crisis, many Americans were feeling frustrated, angry, and diminished.

It was against this background that Reagan posed his question, a question that tapped into all those powerful underlying emotions. The hostage crisis had opened up a deep vein in the American spirit that had never been exposed before. The country that was the very embodiment of unquestioning self-confidence was now experiencing an unprecedented *crise de confiance.* "Are you better off than you were four years ago?" wasn't just a question about middle-class income levels and job security; it was an existential question about America's vision of itself and its place in the world.

The subliminal power of this question raised it above the level of mere political rhetoric and made it click in the collective subconscious of the nation. On November 4, 1980, the 365th day of captivity for the American hostages in Iran, more than 79 million people went into the polling booths. Close to 44 million voted for Reagan. It turned the electoral map into a sea of red with only a handful of blue islands scattered here and there. It was the beginning of the Reagan revolution. And more than a few of those Reagan voters must have had that ballot question echoing in their ears as they cast their votes. "Are you better off than you were four years ago?"

Had Reagan's team figured all this out? Had they carefully crafted their ballot question, knowing it would tap into a much deeper and more profound emotion? Probably not. No doubt luck played a role. But as anyone who's worked in communications will tell you, that's often how it works. Hard work, planning, and strategizing make serendipity possible.

Luck had a similar role to play in helping Chipotle create a corporate video that resonated so powerfully with people that many of them were brought to tears. What is noteworthy about the "Back to the Start" video is that it doesn't take the expected route. It avoids the typical us-versus-them approach — the approach that Apple took in their Mac-versus-PC ads. The obvious choice would have been to show a small independent farmer pitted against a powerful industrial farming operation that slowly squeezes him out of existence. Instead it follows one man's journey of enlightenment. This single journey is echoed in the single linear tracking shot that comprises the film and that shows our farmer travelling through a cycle of all four seasons. The farmer is both villain and hero of the spot.

This simple device of showing an individual rite of passage, from heedless progress to enlightenment to change, gives the film added force because it echoes the journey many of us have gone on — from naive enjoyment of the convenience of fast food to a growing awareness and concern for how our food is raised or grown, and towards a desire to change how we eat and what we eat. It is the same journey that Steve Ells himself went on. Unhappy with the way his pork tasted, Ells went to visit the farms where the meat was being raised and was shocked at the conditions he found: cruelly confined animals, hormone-laced feed. Around the same time, he also read an article entitled "The Lost Taste of Pork" by Ed Behr, publisher of a quarterly foodie bible called *The Art of Eating*, which completely changed his view of farming and food production. Ells decided that more humane farming practices would not only result in better-tasting pork but would also be better for business.

He met with Paul Willis, founder of the Niman Ranch co-operative, which raises pork the old-fashioned way — free range and free of antibiotics — and started buying his pork from Niman Ranch farmers. Not surprisingly, pork raised this way is more expensive, so Chipotle had to raise the price of its *carnitas* burrito, not by a few cents but by almost 25 percent. The price jumped from $4.50 to $5.50. And then something extraordinary happened. In defiance of every principle of the fast food business handbook, sales increased. Soon Chipotle was selling twice as many *carnitas* as it had before the switch to Niman-raised pork. Perhaps consumers could actually taste the difference, as Ells did. Or perhaps they just believed that humanely raised pork was worth paying more for. Either way, they were lining up by the thousands behind Steve Ells on his journey of discovery.

The Chipotle farmer's personal journey of conversion allows us to put ourselves in his shoes, to experience his journey with him, because in a way we've all been there. His awakening echoes our own. And for that reason we feel connected to this narrative more intensely than we might have been otherwise.

Remarkably, all of this was purely accidental. When I ask Mark Crumpacker about the decision to depict one man's journey, he confides that it was all happenstance. The original script followed the story of an individual farmer facing down an industrial farming giant. But the British director of the video called midway through production to say that he was having difficulty telling the story that way. He couldn't fit everything into the linear tracking shot. Crumpacker goes on to explain: "So he asked if he could just show one farmer and depict his change from family farm to industrial farm and back. I said, 'Sure.'"

Would the video have had the same emotional pull for viewers if it had followed the us-versus-them formula? Almost certainly not. The happy accident of needing to simplify the storyline allowed Chipotle to complete the triangle and create a piece of communication that was not only believable and credible but also deeply human. It tells one of the oldest human stories of them all — paradise lost and paradise regained.

In the opening chapter of this book I talked about a change in targeting strategy that pushes beyond the middle ground in the bell curve and strives to appeal to a passionate few, even if it means pissing off a lot of other folks who don't share your views. During the 2014 Sochi Olympic Winter Games a commercial started airing on American television that managed to combine that new kind of consumer targeting with the new kind of messaging represented by the ballot question. In the spot, entitled "Poolside," the camera follows a character played by actor Neal McDonough. Looking ruddy-faced and sounding just shy of angry, he wanders through his lavish California-style home from pool to living room (populated by two silent kids) to kitchen (populated by one silent wife) and out to the garage, where his new Cadillac ELR awaits. He unplugs the electric extended-range car before hopping in and getting ready to drive off. So far the only controversial thing about this commercial is that it features a plug-in hybrid from that most American of luxury vehicles, Cadillac.

But turn up the sound and what you hear is McDonough delivering part rant, part call to arms. "Why do we work so hard? For what? For this? For stuff? Other countries, they work, they stroll home, they stop by the café. They take August off. Off. Why aren't you like that? Why aren't we like that?" He then goes on to name a few icons of American ingenuity and tenacity: the Wright brothers, Bill Gates, Muhammad Ali. He talks about landing on the moon. "We went up there, and you know what we got? Bored. So we left. Got a car up there, left the keys in it. Do you know why? Because we're the only ones going back up there. That's why." Hard work, he tells us, makes anything possible. Then, with one final knock at those endlessly vacationing, *café au lait*-sipping Europeans, he concludes, "As for all the stuff, that's the upside of only taking two weeks off in August. *N'est-ce pas?*"

This was wedge marketing delivered with a punch. It was followed by a predictably polarized response, with some cheering its celebration of American exceptionalism and others denouncing it as a crass appeal to the worst kind of consumerism. The debate split along political lines, with commentators like Rush Limbaugh enthusiastically defending the spot while others like Carolyn Gregoire, a features editor at the *Huffington Post*, penned critiques. Gregoire's was entitled "Cadillac Made a Commercial about the American Dream, and It's a Nightmare."

The marketing team at Cadillac anticipated all of this. They were well aware that the aggressive tone of the spot would engender controversy. In fact, at the very last minute, as the commercial went into production, they decided to switch cars and feature Cadillac's new plug-in hybrid as a way to soften the harsh tone of the spot. Uwe Ellinghaus, the German-born former BMW executive who is chief marketing officer for Cadillac, told *Advertising Age* that consumer research had shown the ad "Would break through the clutter and generate a hell of a lot of buzz. Mission accomplished."

Ellinghaus and his ad agency, Rogue, knew the spot wouldn't appeal to everyone. And they were okay with that. They were pitching the ad directly at a particular segment of the American car-buying public, those who believed that hard work and personal sacrifice ultimately entitle one to material rewards. Callers to Rush Limbaugh's radio program were giddy with delight. "Kudos to the advertising agency that would actually make an ad like this and make a pro-American, pro-work ad," said one. "Oh, my gosh. I want to go out and buy a Cadillac now," gushed another. Comments on YouTube alternated between calling the spot delusional and praising it as one of the greatest commercials in a long time. But the likes far outweighed the dislikes, by a margin of more than two to one. Cadillac had taken the risk of pitching their message to the margins of the bell curve, and it seemed to be working. The company had concluded that conservative-minded Americans in the post–Tea Party political atmosphere would find the message of industriousness and personal reward highly appealing. And taking a page from the political playbook, they decided that angering some people on the opposite end of the political spectrum would not be a bad thing. In fact, it might actually be good for business.

At the same time as it was taking a daring approach to targeting, the spot was also using the political trick of the ballot question to communicate its message. It opens with a question "Why do we work so hard?" and then follows that up with about half a dozen more. But all of these rhetorical queries really add up to just one question that is never overtly stated but clearly implied: "What makes America great?" The answer, also implied, is that American grit, hard work, and determination make anything possible. That's what makes the country great.

This query about American greatness should come as no surprise from a brand that was seeking to appeal to more conservative consumers. It has been a long-running theme in Republican politics from Reagan's "Let's Make America Great Again!" to Trump's punchier version, "Make America Great Again."

At this point you might be wondering what all this has to do with Cadillac. After all, we see the car only briefly at the end. And the only mention of it is made silently, in the last four seconds of the sixty-second ad, when the words "The First Ever ELR" zoom onto the screen, followed by the Cadillac logo. Unlike most car commercials, and most commercials in general, this spot makes no mention of the product, its features, or its benefits. This commercial is not about selling a specific car (which is why they could so easily switch the featured vehicle at the last minute); it's about selling the brand's values. This is an attempt to reset the brand's image, which had come to be seen as older and perhaps a little tired (despite the success of the compact and sporty Cadillac ATS, which had succeeded in attracting younger buyers). The brand was trying to assert a muscular and energetic American voice amidst the elegant hum of all the foreign luxury imports.

It's not unusual for brands that are trying to reposition themselves to create ads that talk to the brand values rather than product attributes. In fact, the Cadillac commercial has an antecedent in one of the most famous television commercials of all time. The 1997 Apple "Think Different" spot, which showed archival footage of famous innovators from Albert Einstein to Muhammad Ali to Pablo Picasso, all hailed as "the crazy ones" who thought they could change the world, and did. That campaign was part of an effort to remake the Apple brand following the return of Steve Jobs after several years of exile from the company. As Jobs told a group of Apple employees when he introduced the campaign, Apple was a great brand that had suffered from neglect and this ad was an effort to get back to the core values of the brand, as summed up in its closing line: "Because the people who are crazy enough to think they can change the world are the ones who do."

Like the Apple "Think Different" campaign (which ran on television, in print, and on billboards), the Cadillac ad references great American pioneers. Both mention Muhammad Ali, for example. Like the Apple campaign, Cadillac celebrates the crazy ones. "Why do we work so hard?" asks an intense Neal McDonough. "Because we're crazy, driven, hardworking believers."

"Were the Wright Brothers insane?"

"Were we nuts when we pointed to the moon?"

Yes and yes is the answer. And look how much better off we are for being the crazy ones. But while the Apple spot was celebrating thinkers who had worked to "push the human race forward," the Cadillac ad was celebrating those who had worked hard to push themselves forward. "You work hard, you make your own luck." It was as if Gordon Gekko had been asked to redraft the "Think Different" ad for a new age of conservatism where the philosophizing of Ayn Rand had taken on the aura of holy scripture. Instead of a Jobsian anthem to the ingenuity and creativity of the human race, Cadillac delivered a paean to personal advancement, American-style. But love it or hate it, the highly polarizing ballot question ad is here to stay. And Neal McDonough's red-faced tirade is its perfect embodiment.

CHAPTER 6

SPEED KILLS

THE FIRST TO SPEAK WINS

The nexus between technology, news reporting, and conflict is a long-standing one. During the American Civil War the relatively new technology of telegraphy, using Samuel Morse's code of dots and dashes, made possible the more rapid dissemination of news. It also fed a tremendous growth in the newspaper business. At the start of the war there were roughly 3,000 newspapers in America. Twenty years later that number had more than doubled to 7,000. Prior to the widespread adoption of the telegraph, newspapers had to rely on steamships, the pony express, and even pigeons to transmit the news. Samuel Morse's invention changed all that.

More than a hundred years later another American visionary, Ted Turner, conceived of using the latest satellite technology to change television news reporting, away from its fixed position at a certain time of day to a constant stream twenty-four hours a day. CNN launched in 1980, but it really earned its place as a major force in news reporting in 1991, during the first Gulf War. Its live twenty-four-hour-a-day coverage of that conflict transformed television news forever and generated a multitude of imitators around the world. But the network's coverage consisted largely of newscasters on rooftops and hotel balconies reporting on explosions happening in the distance.

Today, social media (most notably Twitter) is transforming news coverage of military battles in ways never imagined by Samuel Morse. The capacity to instantaneously broadcast from the middle of the action is changing our concept of what is news and how it's delivered. At 1:22 p.m. on November 14, 2012, the Israel Defense Forces' official Twitter feed, @IDF-Spokesperson, issued a message that read, "We recommend that no Hamas operatives, whether low level or senior leaders, show their faces above ground in the days ahead." Fifty-nine minutes later, it issued a follow-up tweet that showed a blood-red picture of Ahmed Jabari, head of Hamas's military wing, with the word "Eliminated" stamped overtop. And in a message entitled "In case you missed it" the IDF tweeted an aerial video of the instant when the Israeli missile strike hit Jabari's car, which exploded in a giant white flash — all of this within moments of the actual events.

At each step of its evolution, from the carrier pigeon to the telegraph to the live satellite to the instantaneous Twitter feed, the pace at which news is transmitted has grown faster and faster. Speed has itself become part of the story. CNN made its reputation thanks to live coverage of events. It was the immediacy of that coverage that separated the cable news broadcaster from its rivals in the world of conventional network news, which was still focusing on prepping stories for the six o'clock report. Increasingly, the speed at which information is disseminated is becoming the measure of its value.

In the interconnected world of marketing and mass media, the issue of speed is becoming a central concern for marketers as well. Not only is everyone with an Internet connection or a smartphone a potential broadcaster or publisher these days, they're also capable of communicating to the world instantaneously. Real-time communication is changing the way some marketers send their messages out to their customers. And sometimes the speed at which those messages are sent is the most important factor of all. In an atmosphere of instantaneous communication, being the first to say something can mean the difference between success and failure.

The famed Democratic political strategist James Carville figured this out decades ago. He understood that speed was critical to controlling the political narrative. It was Carville who determined that when it comes to shutting down your opponent, rapid response is the key. One of the greatest innovations of the Bill Clinton campaign was the speed at which it responded to attacks and statements from the Republicans. During the 1992 Republican convention that nominated George H. W. Bush, the Democrats did something that was completely unheard of until then. They were rebutting statements made by the speakers at the convention while they were actually speaking. Bear in mind that this was at a time when the most technologically advanced communications device was the fax machine. Carville coined several important maxims during the 1992 Clinton presidential campaign, but the one that formed the campaign's core operating principle was "Speed kills!"

Since Carville's days on the Clinton campaign, that adage has only become more important as the pace of communications has increased. But marketers, for all their vaunted creativity, are slow to change. Embracing speed might prove to be one of the more difficult changes marketers have to make in this time of rapid response. In part, that's because most marketing organizations have complex decision-making hierarchies that create a drag on rapid action. The capacity to react quickly is dependent on having all the decision makers in the same room at once. That's rarely the case in a large marketing-driven organization. That's the other innovation Carville and the Clinton campaign team developed. They understood that if you're going to speed up reaction time, you need to get rid of the decision-making hierarchy, and to do that you need to get rid of the physical hierarchy that separates decision makers from each other. But more on that later. To see how real-time communication has altered the way politicos and marketers attempt to control the narrative, we need to go back in time and look at how slow things used to be.

HURRY UP AND DON'T WAIT

In the fall of 1996 I was sitting in my office at Stringer Veroni Ketchum, the Toronto-based advertising agency my partners and I had founded six years earlier, when my assistant put through a call from the president of a large market research company. He was a man I had worked with years earlier and he had a client that needed help. Urgently. In a tone that seemed unnecessarily conspiratorial he said, "I can't tell you the name of the client or what the project is. It's extremely sensitive and very urgent. At this point I just need to know if you are interested in taking this on."

When you work in advertising, you become accustomed to calls from clients who need help "urgently." You also know that what this really means is that the client wants you to do something very quickly (produce a proposal, an idea, or even a campaign) that they'll then spend weeks or even months mulling over. Then you'll engage in a lengthy game of hurry-up-and-wait — urgent calls for quick turnaround of each new step in the process, followed by long periods of silence while the client ruminates, until the next urgent call.

The research company president was a colleague I'd known for years and someone I liked and respected. Even though he was being oddly secretive, I trusted him enough to know I'd help him out. When I offered up a reassuring "Sure, we'd be happy to help," I also knew that this assignment, whatever it was, would probably drag on for months on end. I couldn't have been more wrong.

I had no idea that, once I'd hung up the phone, every resource in our small agency would be focused on developing a new television commercial that would air in just three days — a process that, even under ideal circumstances, would normally take months. If you'd asked me prior to that call if we could pull off such a feat, my answer would have been a derisive snort. To take on board a brand-new client, get briefed on the assignment, develop an advertising idea, get it approved, find a director and production team, shoot and edit the spot, record a voice-over, complete post-production, and ship the finished product to television stations across the country in just a few days is a task no agency could accomplish — especially not a small agency like ours.

But this was no ordinary ad campaign. This was crisis

management. And everyone working on it — the client, the research company, and our agency — approached it like a political campaign, not a marketing campaign. And that attitude made all the difference.

HOGS IN THE WAR ROOM

For students of politics, *The War Room*, the 1993 documentary by Chris Hegedus and D. A. Pennebaker, is a master class in political strategizing. The film chronicles Bill Clinton's extraordinary 1992 presidential campaign through the eyes of the odd couple of Democratic politics, with communications director George Stephanopoulos playing punctilious Felix to campaign strategist James Carville's anarchic Oscar. In it we see Carville wandering around the campaign war room on Election Day, November 4, 1992, proudly sporting a T-shirt with the words "War Room Staff" printed in a military-style font on the front. On the back, in bold capital letters, it reads, "SPEED KILLED…BUSH."

Carville, who bears a striking resemblance to Gollum from the Hobbit movies (if Gollum had less hair and a penchant for salty language delivered in a Southern drawl), is a man never at a loss for an amusing anecdote or a colourful turn of phrase. And he's a master of the political aphorism. His succinct summaries of political strategy are legendary. Most famous among them is the oft-quoted "It's the economy, stupid."

"Speed kills" was less famous but no less important to the success of the 1992 campaign. Carville believed that speed of communication was critical to success and to killing the opposition. Metaphorically speaking, of course. In his view, getting your message out rapidly was essential to shaping public opinion, especially when faced with negative news, whether self-inflicted or coming from the opposing side. And Clinton had plenty of self-inflicted negative news to contend with. Does the name Gennifer Flowers ring a bell? How about Monica Lewinsky?

Speed is critical not just for deflecting negative information but also for disseminating positive news. We have moved beyond the clichéd twenty-four-hour news cycle, the constant flow of information that we could dip in and out of as we pleased. Now, thanks to our connected lives, we are swimming in a sea of it. The tide is both unrelenting and ubiquitous. In this environment, opinions, especially if they're negative, can spread rapidly. The trick is to be fast enough to shape the wave and not just ride it or, worse, be overcome by it. In this environment, the first-mover advantage takes on much greater significance. In prepping for a televised debate between Clinton and Bush, one of the Democratic War Room staffers points out, "As we always say . . . 'Speed Kills,' and we will die in this debate if we're not there first with our answers."

Many marketers would say they work to extremely tight deadlines. Walk through most marketing departments or ad agencies and there is frequently a low but insistent hum of urgency. But compared to the political campaign environment the pace seems positively glacial. Planning cycles for marketing campaigns often begin twelve months in advance. That's several lifetimes in the world of political campaigning. These days during presidential elections, campaigns can release as many as 100 items per day, from ads to press releases to online content. By comparison, in the world of consumer marketing, a single television script can take weeks or months to meander from the ad agency, through the marketing department, and up to the executive suite, with a detour to the legal department, before it gets approved — just to go into testing. A fully fledged campaign, with multiple ads and other communications materials, can take even longer.

Contrast this with a moment captured in *The War Room*, a scene that would be incomprehensible to most marketers. Carville, Stephanopoulos, and other senior campaign staff are on a conference call with media consultant Mandy Grunwald, trying to finalize the script for a television ad they want to put into testing that night. After a bit of toing and froing about the exact wording of the copy, Carville hangs up, angry and frustrated. He complains that it took too long to get agreement to the changes he was suggesting — getting Bush Senior's lamentable phrase "Read my lips" into the script three times. "Every time you suggest changes to a media person, their first reaction is 'We can't do that,'" he complains. Just one time, he says, he'd like to get agreement to his suggestions right off the top.

The rest of the team look at him, bemused, and one of them chides, "James, this idea was suggested, what, a half-hour ago? The script has been made in twenty minutes!" Then he adds, "We've gone in a half-hour from a concept to a spot. What the fuck do you want?" Carville finally concedes, chuckling. "I take it back. Okay, I'm a hog, I'm a hog."

But it's precisely that hog-like insistence on wanting everything *right now* that helped to drive the campaign's success. As Carville points out, it would take most campaigns two days to get out a new television spot. They were scripting one in a matter of minutes. The final spot would be ready for testing in a few hours. Deploying cutting-edge 1990s technology, including satellite dishes, faxes, beepers, and brick-sized cellphones, the Clinton campaign team moved with unprecedented speed to respond to every shift in the political winds, sometimes even intercepting Bush's television commercials with satellite dishes before they made it to air.

All this took place in a pre-Internet age. And the one thing that's changed since then is that things have gotten exponentially faster.

CHEATING BABIES

Back in 1996, when the world was a lot slower and I felt pretty cool because I had a cellphone hard-wired into my car, our idea of speed was a little different. But that all changed the day I received the call from my friend at the research firm. Once I'd agreed to take on the assignment, he sent me a copy of a press release. This was not one of those dreary statements that get churned through the PR machine and manages to be both puffy and bland at the same time, like some good-for-you cereal. This was an incendiary device. In public relations terms it was explosive. The headline read: "Heinz Is Cheating Canada's Babies."

No corporation, especially one that sells ketchup and baby food, ever wants to see its name in a sentence alongside the words "cheating" and "babies." What made this statement even more volatile was that the press release was not put out by some aggressive baby food–selling competitor; it came from one of the largest and most respected consumer-interest groups in North America, the Center for Science in the Public Interest

(CSPI). CSPI had been created in the early 1970s by a group of concerned scientists to advocate for greater awareness of nutritional and environmental issues. It was a major player in the movement to get nutrition labelling on all food products in the U.S., and it had exposed the nutritional deficiencies of everything from movie theatre popcorn to fettuccine Alfredo. Now it was claiming that Heinz was cheating Canada's babies.

Needless to say, that headline caught the attention of the media. News organizations across the country were starting to run with the story. As I quickly scanned the document, it became apparent to me why there was such urgency and secrecy behind the phone call I'd received. CSPI's contention was that Heinz was using cheap fillers, including starch, to plump up its baby food, thus delivering less real food and, it claimed, less nutrition. CSPI had prepared a detailed report on the formulations of Heinz baby food in Canada and had concluded that the products Heinz was selling were nutritionally inferior.

To understand the impact of this news on Heinz, it helps to know that the company had been steadily building its reputation as a trusted and well-loved food brand for over 140 years, ever since Henry John Heinz started bottling and selling his mother's horseradish recipe to the good people of Sharpsburg, Pennsylvania, in 1869. Heinz ketchup would follow seven years later, in 1876, serving as the sweet and tangy fuel that propelled the company into the $12 billion multinational corporation it is today.

It also helps to know that in Canada Heinz had been selling baby food for well over sixty years and in that time had come to dominate the market, with a 90 percent share of the jarred baby food business. But baby food wasn't just big business; it was central to the brand's image as a trusted food company. One of the most sacred duties parents have is to provide their children with healthy, nutritious food. Millions of Canadian moms and dads, too busy to cook from scratch every day, were fulfilling that duty with the help of Heinz. The hard-earned bond between the brand and its users was about to be broken, perhaps irreversibly.

Corporate reputations that have taken decades to build can shatter in an instant with news of serious wrongdoing. And cheating babies is right up there on the serious-wrongdoing scale. After all, if Heinz could cheat babies, what else were they capable of? If they couldn't be trusted to make something as serious as baby food, what about something as frivolous as ketchup? And what is in ketchup, anyway? This crisis had the potential to spread beyond Canada and beyond just baby food. The panic at Heinz was palpable. This one-page press release from CSPI had the power to undo almost a century and a half's worth of corporate goodwill.

What made all of this worse was that the CSPI report was true. Well, it was true with one important caveat. It applied to only a small proportion of Heinz products. The vast majority of Heinz baby food had no additives. That fact was being lost in the media coverage, however. And even if the media did make it clear, it wouldn't matter — the only thing people would remember was that Heinz added filler to its baby food.

Where the company had fallen down was in failing to clearly identify those products that had additives and those that didn't. This was the 1990s, and product labelling was not what it is today. Heinz decided to put in place a two-part plan.

One: fix the labelling issue and clearly identify which products had additives and which didn't. Two: communicate the full story to consumers. That's where we came in.

Heinz knew it had only a small window in which to act. Once opinions hardened or the story started to leak beyond the Canadian border, it would be difficult to get the baby food back into the jar. The company needed to get its side of the story out, fast.

In moments of crisis the most powerful tool a company (or a politician) can have is not communications, it's information. That's why the first phone call that went out from the Heinz marketing department was not to us, an ad agency, but to their research firm. Heinz engaged its research company to do something that marketers rarely do but that is a standard tool in the political arsenal. They decided to conduct ongoing daily tracking of public opinion. That meant every day hundreds of consumers across the country would be polled on their views of the Heinz brand and its baby food. In those pre-Internet-survey days, that required a virtual army of pollsters making thousands of telephone calls each day just to reach the few hundred who qualified and were willing to answer the questionnaire. Overnight, the results would be collated and in the morning pored over by the clients, the researchers, and the ad execs.

Within days, the impact of the CSPI report was evident in the polling data; key metrics slowly started slipping downhill. On every critical measure, from likability to trustworthiness to quality of food, the brand was in decline. On any given day the declines were small — just a little bit, then a little bit more. But the cumulative effect was devastating. If things continued on that trajectory, the fears of the Heinz executives would be realized. The brand would sustain significant damage that might take many years and many millions of dollars to repair.

We understood that the heart of the matter was that Heinz was being portrayed as providing inferior nutrition for babies. So, early on we made an important strategic decision. We needed to shift the focus and responsibility for the child's nutrition away from Heinz and towards the parent — where it rightfully belonged. This insight came from the creative team and my business partners, Barry Stringer and Kathy Doherty. They had worked together for years, Barry as art director, Kathy as copywriter, on countless television, print, and outdoor campaigns. Their long history together made them act like an old married couple. They frequently bickered with one another — occasionally good-naturedly. Clients who didn't know them well would ask, "Are you two married?"

"Yes," they would reply in unison, "but not to each other."

Both of them had an instinctive understanding of how to sell. Kathy's laser-sharp ability to cut to the psychological heart of an issue, combined with Barry's natural salesmanship, made them the rarest of breeds among creative people — they knew how to close the sale with the consumer, not just win advertising awards. Advertising creative people frequently see themselves as frustrated entertainers, or even artists. Barry and Kathy had no such pretensions. They were proud to see their job as selling things. Barry picked up many of his selling skills as a young man growing up in the north of England. On Saturdays, to make a few extra pounds, he'd go and sell chickens at a market stall near his home. Surrounded by all the barkers and pitchmen, he absorbed the kind of lessons you'd never pick up at a sales seminar. There was, for instance, the time the man selling factory-reject clothing in the next stall over was confronted by a customer who complained that the jeans she was trying on had one leg longer than the other. "See," cried the salesman with glee, "I am saving you money! You only have to shorten one leg!"

The instinct for how to turn a negative into a positive was coming in handy right about then, as Barry and Kathy pondered the issue of Heinz. They knew parents were probably feeling that their responsibility for feeding healthy food to their children had been undermined. They needed to take back control. That's why the television commercial we developed began with the words "Heinz has always believed that every mom and dad deserves the best choices for their baby." The word "choices" was the hook from which the entire ad was suspended. It established a simple truth, designed to elicit a head-nod from the viewer: *Heinz is not feeding your baby, you are. And the choice of what to feed them is yours.* It's a point that's hard to argue. The first job of selling an idea is to get people to listen. Barry's favourite quote was "You can't sell to a man [or mom] who isn't listening." This opening line was designed to get them to listen. To reinforce the idea of choice, the video slowly dissolved through still images of smiling babies as the word "choices" appeared not once but three times on the screen. In the art of persuasion, repetition is one of the oldest and most effective tools.

Having established its central idea, the commercial then went on to explain what those choices were: "Today we offer over sixty varieties of baby food with no added starch or sugar... And we make varieties that do contain added starch or sugar." Think about it. Over sixty varieties with no additives. That's an impressive number, a number that didn't appear anywhere in the "Cheating Babies" press release. To reinforce this point, the number sixty appeared onscreen superimposed over more faces of happy babies. The "see/say" technique of showing what you're saying is as old as television advertising itself. It seems a bit old-fashioned these days, and fresh-faced young creatives might reject it for a more subtle approach. But the fact is it works, as countless artless yet deadly effective political ads will attest.

But sixty varieties without additives raises the question "Why make baby food with added starch and sugar at all?" To close the loop on that logic, the female announcer went on to say, "To enhance their texture and taste." And then she delivered another simple but powerful truth that would have every parent's head nodding once more: "Because the greatest baby food in the world is no good if your baby won't eat it."

In a few short seconds, the commercial had tackled the "Cheating Babies" claim head-on by expanding consumer perception of the situation. It acknowledged that Heinz made baby food with additives, but it gave a reasonable explanation why. And it pointed out that a huge number of these products, in fact the vast majority, had no additives at all. Then it left the choice up to you.

The spot also noted that a new label would be launched in a few weeks, making that choice even easier. Then it closed with a nod to the decades of goodwill the brand had built up. "Heinz. Feeding Canadian babies for over sixty years."

Heinz had actually been feeding Canadian babies for a lot more than sixty years, but there was that repetition again.

Repeating the number — sixty varieties, sixty years — allowed us to bring the figure back up on the screen, thus reinforcing it in the mind of the viewer. Hopefully, that would make it easier to remember those two key facts.

There's an old adage in the advertising world that says communicating a message is like tossing a ball. If you throw one ball at a person, chances are they'll catch it. If you throw three at the same time, chances are they won't catch any of them.

As soon as this commercial went to air, people started catching the ball. Rarely in advertising do you get to see the impact of your work on consumers' attitudes in real time. But thanks to the overnight polling Heinz was doing, we could watch day by day as the numbers shifted. Within a few days the attitudinal scores for the brand, which had been drifting steadily downward, began to slow their descent and then level off. Despite significant media coverage of the CSPI press release, the brand message appeared to be getting through.

Then something remarkable happened. The numbers started to climb. Not only had we halted the growth of negative attitudes towards Heinz amongst moms and dads, we were now actually winning back their trust and confidence. Within weeks the conversion was complete. We had made back virtually all the lost ground. This could never have happened if Heinz had not acted swiftly. If they'd moved at the usual deliberate pace that marketers do, the slide would have continued unabated for weeks or months, and winning back that lost support would have required a massive investment of time and money. In the meantime, the impact in terms of lost sales could have been in the millions. By taking a political-style crisis management approach, all that was avoided.

Was the Center for Science in the Public Interest right to issue their provocative press release accusing Heinz of cheating babies? Absolutely. In fact, their actions helped to bring about a significant change in the way Heinz labelled its baby food. But Heinz was equally justified in responding with its own message that clarified what the company was doing and why. In the end, a venerable brand with a long history of making products that many people loved was able to protect its reputation and regain consumers' trust.

But despite Barry and Kathy's heroic efforts, the single most important factor in the success of this campaign was not the careful analysis of what consumers were thinking or the skillful crafting of a script idea. It was the speed at which it was executed. Had Heinz taken months to rebut those accusations, had they hemmed and hawed over the creative idea, had they implemented a complex, multi-layered approval process, it wouldn't have mattered how good the ad was. The brand would have sustained enormous and possibly irreparable damage. In political terms, it would have been the equivalent of being accused of some scandalous impropriety by your political opponent and then taking weeks to respond. Silence would have equalled guilt. And with each passing hour the burden of guilt would have grown heavier. The only way to halt that momentum is through rapid response. When it comes to dispensing with a negative perception, speed kills.

The three-day turnaround for the Heinz ad seemed like a miracle at the time. And it still does, especially considering we also created an accompanying print ad that ran at the same time, with a headline borrowed from the TV spot: "The greatest baby food in the world is no good if your baby won't eat it."

This ad was one of the first ever in Canada to be distributed electronically to newspapers across the country, rather than sending out film and print proofs by courier. It meant we got the ad distributed nationally at least twenty-four hours faster than we could have done previously. Rarely can clients and agencies respond as quickly as we did, even to a crisis situation. It was possible only because we adopted the proven techniques of overnight political ad-making — editing together a series of stock images of babies rather than shooting original film; foregoing an original music track and using existing stock music instead; recording the voice-over and editing at lightning speed — and not getting a lot of sleep. But those three days pale in comparison to the few hours James Carville and his team took to develop an ad for the Clinton campaign. Yet none of this compares to the speed at which advertisers must react today — making ads in real time.

THE TEN-MINUTE AD

At 8:38 p.m. on February 3, 2013, about two minutes into the second half of the forty-seventh Super Bowl — or to use its more familiar and gladiatorial title, Super Bowl XLVII — the blazing corona of white light that ringed the inside of the New Orleans Superdome suddenly dimmed. Stadium officials, standing in the control room with their headsets and microphones strapped on, looked dumbfounded and perplexed. Meanwhile, down on the field the gladiators would have to wait for more than half an hour in the twilight glow while engineers worked to restore electricity and bring the arena back to its full brilliance. Without full lighting, there could be no television image, and without television there could be no Super Bowl.

The last time the Superdome had experienced such a public disaster was during the devastation of Hurricane Katrina, when it became a shelter for thousands of displaced people. For five hot and humid days in August 2005, without electricity or air conditioning, with garbage and human waste spilling everywhere, people filled the dome because they had nowhere else to go. The chaos and stench were overwhelming. One observer described it as a scene from Dante's *Inferno*.

Now, on the pristine AstroTurf in the half-lit stadium as players and officials wandered listlessly on the field like attendees at a humdrum picnic, one wag noted that at last rich people could find out what it was like to be in the Superdome without electricity. With the minutes ticking by, the NFL's vice-president of special events, Frank Supovitz, struggled to get a handle on the situation. In the operations nerve centre, a kind of mission control, people were calling out NASA-like commands: "We're going to manual override... Do we have access to PA?"

One of the team said, "Frank, we lost the A feed."

To which Frank replied, "What does that mean?"

"It means we have to do the bus tie."

"What does that mean?"

As this fumbling scene played out in a perch high above the field, another group of executives was gathered in a command centre more than a thousand miles away, in New York City. They were equally fixated on the blackout that had just interrupted the most-watched sports event in America. But here there were no headsets with microphones, no NASA jargon.

Instead there were about fifteen hip-looking, mostly young people hanging out in the loft-like offices of 360i, a leading digital marketing agency. They were copywriters and art directors, marketing strategists and digital media experts, PR executives and brand managers. It was not their job to figure out how to fix the blackout; it was their job to figure out how to take advantage of it.

They were assembled at the behest of their client, Mondelēz, a $35 billion global food company headquartered in Deerfield, Illinois. More specifically, they were there to work on one of Mondelēz's leading brands: Oreo cookies. The 100-year-old cookie brand had made a major investment in the Super Bowl. They had paid close to $4 million to run one thirty-second television commercial during the game — a staggering amount for a single airing. And they'd spent an additional seven figures producing a spot entitled "Whisper Fight." In addition to the millions of dollars, months of planning, creative development, and production had gone into crafting that one thirty-second spot.

But the folks at 360i had nothing to do with all that. The television spot had been created by renowned advertising agency Wieden + Kennedy. As Oreo's digital marketing agency, 360i was responsible only for the social media aspect of the brand's communications. That's why 360i had set up this command centre in its offices in lower Manhattan. Social media feed on speed. The team that was gathered together in New York knew that if they were going to use social media to reach out to the more than 100 million viewers tuned in to the Super Bowl, they needed to be able to react instantaneously to any surprising developments in the game. They needed a war room.

What no one could have predicted was that the biggest surprise of the night would play out not on the field but somewhere deep in the bowels of the Superdome, where an electrical relay device would suddenly malfunction, causing the lights to go out. But when it happened, the 360i team spun into action. They were able to do so because their command centre was modelled on the same principles that Carville and his team had developed during the Clinton campaign.

The very structure of the Clinton war room was a significant innovation in presidential politics, and arguably the campaign's stealth weapon. It completely flattened the traditional hierarchical structure of campaign headquarters and put every relevant function in the same room rather than stacking them one floor above another above another, with the most important people at the top. They collapsed this tower to enable rapid decision-making and speed to action. In the old vertical model, ideas had to swim upstream through many levels before they made it to the decision makers. Many ideas, even good ones, would die along the way, killed off by active resistance or simply starved to death by indifference.

As any advertising executive will tell you, the biggest frustration in getting ideas through to an organization is to sit in meeting after meeting filled with lots of people who have the power to say no and no one with the power to say yes. In the Clinton war room the people who generated ideas, the people who could execute ideas, and the people who could approve them were all in the same place and attended the same meetings. And that's what the Oreo digital ad team had done as well. The command centre in New York was their version of the non-hierarchical war room: the strategists, the creatives, the production people, and the client, all in the same place at the same time.

So when the lights went out in the Superdome, they were able to respond in real time. Within a few short minutes the team had developed an ad they were ready to tweet to the world. It was a simple and elegantly designed image, consisting of a black square with a spot of light illuminating the bottom left-hand corner, where an Oreo cookie was peeking into the frame. A few tiny crumbs lay scattered around the cookie, somehow making it look more mouth-watering. Along the bottom ran a single line of copy, punctuated at the end by a stylized illustration of an Oreo. It read, "You can still dunk in the dark."

This was a shorthand reference to years of marketing that highlighted the most popular way to eat Oreos — by dunking them in milk. There was no question that any American seeing this ad would get the reference instantly. It was certainly not the most brilliant advertising idea ever conceived, but it was clever enough to bring a smile to the face of anyone who saw it, assuming that they saw it while the lights were still out. And that was the key. The team gathered at the 360i offices conceived and produced this ad not in days or hours but in minutes. Because they had to. Its impact was entirely dependent on getting it out to the public while the stadium was still in the dark. The same ad run a day later or even an hour later would have been completely meaningless. The timing of the ad is what gave it meaning.

More than a thousand miles from the stadium in New Orleans, from behind the glow of its computer screens, 360i was about to launch an advertising drone attack in real time.

This tweet would land with greater impact than most of the multi-million-dollar television ads that aired during the game. At 8:48 p.m., precisely ten minutes after the lights went out, a simple keystroke sent out a message from the Oreo Twitter account. It read, "Power out? No problem." Attached to that tweet was the "You can still dunk in the dark" ad they'd just created. At that same moment, Frank Supovitz and his team at the Superdome control centre still had a full twenty-five more minutes to go before they'd get the lights back on.

Meanwhile, thousands of people with no game to watch were checking their Twitter feeds and saw the Oreo ad. Within an hour, 10,000 of them had retweeted it and a further 18,000 people had liked the ad on Facebook. By the next day it was clear that the Oreo tweet had photobombed the advertising event of the year. While all the high-priced, high-production-value TV ads were lining up in front of the television cameras for their shot in the spotlight, Oreo popped up from behind and stole the limelight. Over 24 million tweets were sent out during the game. None of them generated as much buzz as Oreo did. Imagine being given the task of getting your voice heard when 24 million other people are speaking at the same time. The Oreo ad managed to break through a massive amount of web noise.

Major media outlets from the *Wall Street Journal* to National Public Radio picked up the story of the little tweet that could. The trade media declared the Oreo tweet a creative coup. *Wired* magazine gushed that Oreo had won the marketing Super Bowl. The story spread around the globe, with news items appearing in over 100 countries from Argentina to Romania. By the time it was all done, the tweet had generated over 500 million media impressions. A media impression is a measure of how many times an item is seen. One set of eyes looking at an ad or news story once represents one media impression. So if all 100 million people who were tuned in to the Super Bowl had their eyes on the screen at the exact moment when Oreo's television commercial was airing, it would have generated 100 million impressions. In other words, the half a billion media impressions generated by that single tweet delivered five times the impact of the multi-million-dollar television ads that were airing during the game.

While tens of thousands of people were liking and re-tweeting the Oreo message, the pricey "Whisper Fight" television ad the company had run only minutes earlier garnered an anemic 373 Facebook likes. The media cost for that TV ad: almost $4 million. The media cost for the "Dunk in the Dark" tweet: zero dollars.

"Whisper Fight" was not a minor effort. In addition to the stratospheric media cost there was also the seven-figure production cost. The ad is built around the belief that people feel passionately about this simple cookie with its vanilla cream sandwiched between two chocolate biscuits. That passion might explain why the brand has over 43 million followers on Facebook. The folks at Oreo also noticed that on social media people frequently debated the merits of the cookie part versus the cream part. Some loved the cookie more, others the cream. The agency decided it would be a good idea to make a commercial about that.

The spot opens on two men in a library engaged in the cookie versus cream debate. Even though they're having a heated argument, they're whispering. They're whispering because, well, it's a library. Pretty soon books and tables are flying. Then everyone else in the library joins in the argument. People are crashing through banisters, bookcases are tumbling like dominoes, and fire breaks out. But through it all, everyone is whispering. When the firemen and police eventually arrive, they hold up their megaphones and break out in...a whisper.

This is an extravagantly produced commercial. To shoot it, ad agency Wieden + Kennedy built an elaborate two-storey library in an unused airport terminal in California, and then destroyed it. But the lavish production values don't make up for the lack of creative engagement in the spot. It's essentially a one-note tune. It tells the same joke over and over again. It's surprising how long thirty seconds can seem when you keep getting hit by the same punchline. Five seconds in, you get the idea. Fifteen seconds in, you're tired of the idea. Twenty seconds in, you're rolling your eyes and waiting for it to be over.

Compared to Oreo's ten-minute tweeted ad, the television spot received comparatively few media mentions. It's safe to say no Romanian news organization was covering it. This mammoth undertaking, which demanded thousands of person-hours, months of effort, and millions of dollars, produced comparatively little impact on game day. The advertising elephant had laboured mightily and produced a whispering mouse.

But as a creative idea, is "You can still dunk in the dark" better than a whisper fight over cookies versus cream? No. The reality is that neither idea is creatively outstanding. Both feel like obvious answers to the creative challenge they were asked to address. What made the tweeted "Dunk in the dark" ad so successful was not its creative brilliance but the sheer speed with which it was executed in response to an unanticipated turn of events. In an age of real-time advertising, if you need to ask yourself whether it's better to be clever or better to be fast, all one needs to do is remember James Carville's maxim, "Speed kills." And in that sense, "Dunk in the dark" killed it.

The Super Bowl experience was so successful that setting up a war room for special events is now an integral part of the Oreo marketing effort. During the 2014 Sochi Olympic Winter Games, Mondelēz Canada set up a war room at its advertising agency in Toronto so they could fire off real-time ads on behalf of Oreo.

To understand the value of Oreo's decision to set up a war room at the Super Bowl, staffed with a full complement of highly trained and highly paid individuals, just in case something dramatic might happen, consider the case of Allstate Insurance, another big advertiser on that same Super Bowl Sunday. Allstate had been airing a television campaign entitled "Mayhem" for more than a year prior to the big game. The campaign dramatized all the disastrous things that can go wrong in one's life and against which the only insurance is, literally, Allstate. The creative trick in the ads is that "Mayhem" is actually personified. The character of Mayhem is played by well-known television actor Dean Winters, a man who is to sinister what Cary Grant was to charm.

In a succession of ads, Winters plays everything from a terrible downpour gushing water into the open sunroof of a car, to a malfunctioning GPS that directs a driver right into oncoming traffic, to a faulty hot water heater that explodes through the roof of a house. Following each disaster, "Mayhem," looking considerably the worse for wear, smugly lets the viewer know that without Allstate Insurance these disasters could have a terrible financial impact. In the ad that ran during Super Bowl XLVII, Winters plays "your lucky team flag," flying from a post on a pick-up truck as it speeds along the highway. Eventually, all that flapping in the wind causes Winters to break loose from the flagpole and fly into the windshield of an oncoming car, resulting in the inevitable highway disaster.

The "Mayhem" campaign was tailor-made for the unforeseen power failure in the Superdome. Quite literally, mayhem had struck. The problem was, there was no Allstate war room. There were just the Allstate marketing folk, all in their own homes watching the game, and the agency creative and account people, doing the same. When the lights went out, all those people must have had the same sinking feeling: *We're about to miss out on the biggest social media opportunity of the night.*

Emails and texts started flying back and forth between agency personnel and clients. "In the end," one senior executive at Allstate's ad agency, Leo Burnett Chicago, told me, "the client decided it was going to be too difficult to co-ordinate the whole thing." The agency had suggested prior to the game that the client set up a mechanism for dealing with just such an eventuality, but they had declined. "So a couple of creatives sitting in their living rooms just posted something on the Allstate Facebook page." That posting passed by unnoticed.

The lesson for Allstate, and for many other advertisers that day, is that in the highly digital, highly connected social media environment in which we're living there is no off switch. In the good old days of mass media it would have been sufficient to expend a huge amount of effort, time, and money to produce a television ad and then broadcast it to the world and sit back and relax, waiting for the accolades and sales to start rolling in. Today a speedy response to unfolding events can mean the difference between achieving a major marketing bounce and simply falling flat. But the capacity to react quickly to any change in the environment requires a lot of planning and putting into place the right organizational structures.

The Clinton war room ran twenty-four hours a day. They had a team called the Overnight Crew, which tells you pretty much everything you need to know about them. Once everyone else had gone home, those folks stoked the coffee machines and fired up the microwave popcorn, passing it around in large pleated coffee filters. Their job was to scan media from key regions across the country, pull out the most pertinent information, and summarize it. All this had to be ready for the daily 7:30 a.m. team briefing. Without this kind of unblinking attentiveness, it would have been impossible for the campaign leadership to react rapidly to developing issues and events. Speed became not just a motto for the Clinton team, it was one of the chief organizing principles of the campaign.

DELIVERY MAKES THE MESSAGE

Speed is about how the message is delivered. But what about the message itself? Does how you say it actually trump what you say? Political television commercials are often of surprisingly low quality. They sometimes look they've been shot and edited by amateurs. They frequently use fuzzy pictures and grainy news footage. They deploy onscreen titles and voice-overs that would not be out of place on late-night 1-800 TV spots. But sometimes speed has to trump quality in the political arena. Had we been given months or even weeks to produce the Heinz commercial, I have no doubt the end product would have looked a lot slicker. We would have shot live images of cooing babies instead of cobbling together some stock photographs. We would have filmed perfectly lit slow-motion images of the luscious fresh fruits and vegetables that go into every jar of baby food. They would have spiralled slowly through the air, spraying water droplets as they fell. And we would have scored an original music track to punctuate each edit point and heighten the drama of the whole piece. But that would have all come too late. Getting it done was more important than making it pretty.

Producing the Heinz commercial (and the accompanying print ad) was a three-day high-speed rollercoaster ride. But it is noteworthy only because that kind of rapid response happens so rarely in the marketing world. Despite that, it doesn't come close to matching the turnaround times for modern political campaigns, where television commercials can go from concept to finished product in a few hours. In our digital, social media–driven era the race to get your message out is now down to minutes. And victory will go to the swift. Today more than ever, speed is critical to controlling the narrative.

The Oreo tweet depended on timing to give the ad its relevance. Seen outside the short window in which the stadium lights were out, the ad would have been nonsensical. Both its impact and its meaning were dependent on its temporal context. In a world of instantaneous real-time communications, speed will be the new lingua franca. To rework Marshall McLuhan's famous dictum for the digital age, the timing is the message.

III

MINDSET
OVER
MATTER

So far we've looked at how technological change, in the form of more instantaneous global communication, and social change, in the form of a more engaged and activist consumer, are shifting the way in which marketers are targeting and talking to their customers. The cues for how to manage these changes are coming from the political arena. In the areas of targeting and messaging, some marketers have become gifted students, learning the tricks of their political counterparts and applying them to the business world. But there's a third area where big change needs to happen in the communications business, and that's with the marketers themselves.

Most marketers have yet to figure out how to bring about change inside their own organizations, because the hardest change to make is the internal one. To deal with the creative challenges of a dramatically shifting social and media landscape, marketing-driven companies will need to rethink two things: the types of people they hire and how those people approach the work that they do. This will require not just a change of process but also a change of mindset. And once again the inspiration for these boardroom changes is coming from the most unlikely of places, the war room. Fans of the Netflix drama *House of Cards* might think the political backrooms are the very last place to look for human resources advice. After all, the underlings and colleagues who work with the show's sociopathic duo Frank and Claire Underwood are likely to find the only career path assistance they receive leads straight over a cliff. Our popular conception of political strategists does not generally put them under the heading of "good with people."

But we have to square this prevailing view with the reality that political campaigns do a remarkably good job of building loyalty and teamwork among their staff. And they do it with none of the lavish inducements that companies deploy these days to attract the brightest and the best. While the hippest companies around are trying to entice talented employees not only with juicy pay packages but also with promises of play-pen-like offices and round-the-clock gourmet dining on the premises, political campaigns are still managing to attract creative and talented people who are willing to work extraordinarily hard and for long hours in cramped, windowless, airless boxes, fuelled by little more than caffeine and takeout pizza.

The people attracted to these political jobs are not just the freshman class of future Nerd Prom attendees. Not all the bright young things of our day are heading to Silicon Valley; some are heading for the political hills. And the sharpest minds, when it comes to analyzing consumer behaviour and influencing it, are not coming out of consumer research firms or the marketing companies that employ them; they're emerging from the political war rooms. The work that they do requires a particular blend of logical analysis and creative risk-taking. And they combine those skills better than most of their counterparts in the marketing world.

Add to this brew the fact that campaign teams are often made up of an oddball mixture of professionals and amateurs, highly paid experts and volunteer labour. And yet they seem to coalesce quickly into a functioning and often effective workforce. How do they do it? The way campaign teams are assembled and how they operate offer some important lessons for marketers, who are increasingly struggling to assemble their own teams that demonstrate passion and drive and that are peopled by nimble movers and creative thinkers.

I've been lucky enough to work with some remarkably talented and successful teams over the years. But what made those teams click was rarely the superficial trappings of the job. There were four critical factors to success: a strong and almost obsessive focus on winning; a diverse group of people with different backgrounds and experiences and even from different cultures; an environment that dissolved hierarchies and forced collaboration; and, most important, a truly inspiring mission that everyone believed in. All of these factors are present in successful political campaign teams, but rarely have I seen all of them present in a team of marketers and their agency partners. If marketers are going to attract young creative minds to work on their businesses, they're going to have to learn how to create this new kind of team dynamic.

CHAPTER 7

THE IMPROBABLE TEAM

WHEN YOU REACH FOR THE STARS

Inside an unremarkable office building in downtown Toronto, facing Lake Ontario, are three floors of office space whose sole claim to fame is that they were designed by the renowned architect Frank Gehry. As you wander the open-plan space with its cubicles made out of varnished particleboard, you might conclude that this is not his best work. There is, how-ever, one wonderful and whimsical touch. As you step off the elevator into the main lobby you're confronted by a bathtub, out of which rises a large metal fish. Gehry has long found inspiration underwater. The undulating and iridescent surface of fish is reflected in his buildings from Los Angeles to Bilbao. But this bathtub sculpture is a simple homage to his childhood in Toronto, when his grandmother used to keep carp in the tub to make gefilte fish for the traditional Friday night Shab-bat dinner.

I was greeted by that fish every day for two years when I went to TBWA/Chiat Day Advertising as head of client servi-ces after selling my agency to its parent company, Omnicom.

For me it was a kind of talisman, a good luck charm. Its arcing grace delivered a little spark of positive energy to start the day. I was particularly in need of its powers one bright and brisk morning in the summer of 1998, when I headed into the office to face one of the biggest new business pitches of my career. Ours was one of six ad agencies that had been shortlisted to pitch the highly coveted Bell Ontario account. Bell is Canada's leading communications company, and back then its annual advertising expenditure in Ontario alone was in excess of $60 million. It was a sizeable account, making the competition for its ad business both high-profile and intense.

My role was to kick off the pitch and lay out for the assembled Bell executives our analysis of their business issues from a consumer perspective, and then offer up an insightful and original solution to those issues. I'd spent weeks developing my opening pitch, working with an ad hoc team of planners, account execs, media strategists, and the creative team. Some of us had not worked together before. But it is the nature of new business pitches, especially large ones, that a disparate group of people within the agency gets thrown together to work intensively for a few weeks.

We decided to forego the traditional PowerPoint presentation for something more immediate and tactile. I had several large foam-core boards printed up by the art department, laying out my argument in words and diagrams. As I revealed them one by one, I could feel the tense atmosphere in the room start to relax and then shift. The audience was coming with me. As I laid out the last few boards, reaching the heart of our case and our vision for the future of the company, the positive energy in the room seemed palpable. I felt like a poker player slowing unveiling a royal flush, card by card. When I was done, I sensed that, even though we had yet to present our creative ideas and media plan, somehow we'd already played a winning hand.

The week following the pitch, rumours and phone calls began filtering into the office. The first of these came from headhunters, those predators who are always quickest to smell blood in the water. They placed calls to Steve Hancock, the president of TBWA/Chiat Day, saying that we were going to get the business and they'd like to help us hire all the new people we were going to need to staff a $60 million account. Word also started to leak out from some of the other agencies on the short list, saying we'd won. Then came the news that John Sheridan, the most senior executive at Bell Ontario, was coming for a tour of our agency prior to announcing the final decision.

"Yours is the only agency he's going to visit," it was whispered.

Several days after Sheridan's visit, the official announcement came from Bell. The advertising assignment had been awarded to Cossette Advertising, one of the other contenders.

We were stunned. Of course, agencies are often stunned when they lose a hard-fought new business pitch. But this was entirely different. Others were surprised as well. Rumours started to spread in the tight-knit Canadian advertising industry that the selection committee's decision had been over-ruled at the last minute by Bell's CEO, Jean Monty. The media picked up on these rumours. The trade press speculated that the close personal friendship between Monty and Cossette's CEO, Claude Lessard, had led to the last-minute change. (Many years later, in an interview with a Canadian newspaper,

Lessard would bemoan the fact that the era had passed when relationships cultivated over the three-martini lunch would help agencies to win business.)

Then industry representatives picked up the issue of Bell's decision. In an extraordinary and unprecedented move, Rupert Brendon, the CEO of the Institute of Communications Agencies (ICA), a leading industry association, issued a stinging public rebuke. "ICA has been told by various different sources that Bell's search and selection team's choice was overturned by a higher authority not involved in the process," he announced. Incredibly, he then went on to say, "The ICA challenges Bell to publish the selection team's scorecards to demonstrate the objectivity of the decision. If it was not objective, the only equitable recourse for a reputable and principled advertiser such as Bell is to fully reimburse all the participants for their total costs." It was a shocking accusation, levelled at one of the largest corporations and biggest advertisers in the country.

Of course, all this furor was for naught. The decision would stand. But the story didn't end there. A few weeks later, my phone rang. On the other end of the line was the head of Cossette's Toronto office. He'd like to chat. Could we meet for lunch?

We met in a small, tony restaurant in midtown Toronto, favoured by ladies who lunch. There wasn't a lot of small talk as we settled into our corner table, surrounded by well-dressed women delicately nibbling their butter lettuce salads and *omelettes aux fines herbes*. The president of Cossette got straight to the point: his agency had just acquired the massive new Bell account and they needed someone to run the business. Would I be interested? As I stared, dumbfounded, at the slightly disgruntled-looking man sitting across the table from me, it dawned on me that he really didn't want to be there and he didn't want to be doing this. Clearly the client had told him to take the meeting. They had decided that if they couldn't hire TBWA/Chiat Day, at least they could hire me. I politely declined.

I relate this story because it touches on the first important attribute that drives successful political campaign teams: the notion that winning is everything. Indeed, it's the only thing. Coming in second place is as good as being in third or fifth. Nobody remembers and nobody cares. In politics the only position worth occupying is first. As one senior political consultant put it to me, "In a first-past-the-post system winners are geniuses and losers are idiots." Complaining that the Bell selection committee's decision had been overruled was like saying that in 2000 George Bush was elected by the nine members of the United States Supreme Court rather than the millions of people who had cast their votes in the election. The Supreme Court's decision in the controversial Florida recount opened the way for certification of the vote in favour of Bush, giving him the one extra electoral college vote he needed to take the election from Al Gore. In the end the only thing that really mattered, for better or worse, was that Bush won. Whining over Bell's scorecards was as useful as wrangling over hanging chads.

In the world of marketing things are a little different. Being in fifth place can still feel like winning if you're lifting your market share from 10 percent to 12 percent. In fact, some marketers have tried to make a virtue out of their losing positions. For decades Avis rental cars sold consumers on the idea that they were actually the better choice because they weren't in first place, with their memorable slogan "We're only No. 2. We try harder." The underlying philosophy of that line, penned in the 1960s by copywriter Paula Green at the storied ad agency Doyle Dane Bernbach, is that it's the striving that matters, not where you end up. It's the how-you-play-the-game philosophy. Interestingly, fifty years after that slogan was introduced, Avis remains stuck in second gear, still holding the number two position in the global car rental business. They've been trying hard, it seems, to remain number two. Leo Burnett, another great adman of the 1960s, crafted a similarly defeatist line that has since become his eponymous agency's central philosophy. Burnett, a truly gifted copywriter, was obviously having an off-day when he dreamt up this leaden dictum: "When you reach for the stars you may not quite get one, but you won't come up with a handful of mud either." We're not sure if old Leo was just having a lark, but his successors at the agency took him quite seriously, and the hand reaching for the stars has now become an integral part of Leo Burnett Advertising's brand image. But what Burnett was saying is, it's okay if you don't reach the celestial prize, because, well, you'll end up with something (anything?) somewhere between there and the sludge beneath your feet. This idea of settling for less than the ultimate trophy has never been part of the political culture, probably because it breeds complacency and compromise. A win-or-lose ethos has tremendous power to focus the mind and motivate teams. Marketers and their agencies might consider that "We're number two!" might not be the most inspiring battle cry for their teams.

The other distinctive characteristic of political campaigns is the diversity of people they throw together — some professional, some volunteer; some experts, some amateurs; some who've worked together before, some complete strangers — and how they manage to transform them into a cohesive team in short order. These improbable teams are able to operate with remarkable effectiveness. Not even in ad-agency new-business pitches would such a diverse group of people be expected to coalesce so quickly as a team. It's a scenario that is virtually unheard of in the business world. How do political campaigns do it, and what does it mean for the future of how businesses, and marketers in particular, organize their workforces?

FINDING THE PATTERNS IN THE DATA

When Dan Wagner was recruiting his team for the Cave during the 2012 Obama election, he did not limit himself to data jockeys who had political experience or even just to those from the U.S. He reached out to the best people he could find anywhere in the world. Here's Andrew Claster, the campaign's deputy chief analytics officer, in an interview with the *Yale Daily News*, describing what they were looking for: "It was important for us to have a number of people who had worked on political campaigns before." But then he added a surprising twist: "It was at least as important to us to bring in people who had never worked in politics before." A mix of people with and without political experience was seen as an asset in building the analytics team. Frankly, I can't think of many businesses that would say, "We need to hire more people who've never worked in our industry before." Usually it's exactly the opposite. What the Obama data analytics team was trying to create was an environment where the differing backgrounds of the people involved would lead to some fertile cross-pollination.

People with different backgrounds can offer different perspectives, but how is that helpful in the business of data analytics? To answer that question, we have to consider what is the fundamental underlying skill of data analysis. It turns out it's the same skill most professionals use to find innovative answers to a problem where there are large amounts of data. It's the same skill lawyers use when poring over boxes full of files while analyzing a case, or scientists use when sifting through reams of data while exploring a thesis. It's also the same skill I use every day in developing brand strategies, sorting through reams of market research and sales data. It's pattern recognition.

Pattern recognition, in its simplest terms, is about finding useful patterns of meaning in a collection of data. And it requires two things. The first is lots and lots of good data. It would be difficult for a lawyer to develop an effective case without having all the available facts and without ensuring those facts are accurate. The second is a talent for making unexpected and surprising connections, like connecting the appeal of George Clooney with campaign donor lists. It's about joining the dots between seemingly unconnected things to develop a new insight or idea. But unlike data gathering, pattern recognition is a highly individualized skill. It can't be taught. It can only be given the right environment in which to flourish.

While it's difficult to develop this talent in an individual, it is possible to improve a team's capacity for pattern recognition. The key is to ensure that there is as much diversity of experience among the team members as possible. For a pattern to be useful, it first of all needs to be original. There's no value in seeing the same pattern as everyone else. Value comes from looking at the same information as everyone else but seeing something different. The greater the diversity of the team members, the greater the chance of seeing something different.

In a 1982 speech to the Academy of Achievement, a non-profit foundation that brings together world leaders and accomplished students, Steve Jobs offered up his definition of human intelligence. He noted that part of it has to do with memory. But the other part, he said, is the capacity to rise above the landscape, to see the lay of the land, "Like you're in a city and you can look at the whole thing from about the eightieth floor, and while other people are trying to figure out how to get from point A to point B reading these stupid little maps, you can just see it all out in front of you... You can make connections that just seem obvious because you can just see the whole thing."

What Jobs is describing here is pattern recognition, the ability to lift oneself above the data and connect the dots that reveal a unique pattern, while others are still stumbling around in the forest, lurching from tree to tree. But then he gets to his main point: "The key thing is that if you're going to make connections which are innovative — to connect two experiences together — you have to not have the same bag of experiences as everyone else does, or else you're going to make the same connections and then you won't be innovative." The trick to seeing something different in the data, he's saying, is to bring a different set of experiences to the task.

Jobs then encourages his student audience to seek out different life experiences: "You might want to think about going to Paris and being a poet for a few years. Or you might want to go to a Third World country — I'd highly advise that... Fall in love with two people at once." Then, in a perfectly Jobsian aside, he says to his young listeners, "Walt Disney took LSD, do you know that? He did, once. And that's where the idea for *Fantasia* came from."

Smart people, Jobs argues, make the connections and see the patterns that others don't. And the key to doing that is "that they had a variety of experiences which they could draw upon in order to solve a problem, or attack a dilemma, in a kind of unique way." Some went to Paris, others took a trip to a place called Fantasia, on LSD.

When Dan Wagner was setting about staffing the Cave, he was trying to improve the chances of generating innovative patterns and connections by having a diversity of experience in the team. If everyone in your marketing department has a marketing MBA, chances are they're all going to think like business-school graduates with a marketing MBA. Every business problem will look like a case study. And sadly, real-life problems don't progress in a linear fashion like a business-school case study. One of my clients is a large Fortune 500 packaged goods company. One day, in a lengthy conversation with the chief marketing officer in his glass-enclosed, sun-dappled office, he confided that his toughest challenge was finding creative thinkers to staff his marketing departments around the globe. Building marketing teams that can think innovatively is a constant challenge. The issue, I suggested, was not the limitations of any one individual, but rather the fact that those teams as a whole consisted of people with remarkably uniform business backgrounds and education. Too many MBAs and not enough arts grads, perhaps.

My own higher education consists of a B.A. and M.A. in English literature. (I also started working on a Ph.D., which I never finished, thanks to a crisis I had in class one day: I looked around the room at my fellow Ph.D. students and thought, "I've got to get out of here.") The basic skills I acquired as a student of English are the same skills I use today in my work consulting with corporations large and small. My literary education helped me develop three important mental processes.

The first of these was pattern recognition. For a student of literature, university assignments usually involve reading several poems or plays or novels and then finding the patterns of meaning in the "data" — seeking out the themes or ideas that run through the works. I use that same process today to sift through consumer data and seek out patterns and connections that others might have missed. The next step is to develop a thesis about the pattern. What does it mean? Why is it significant? A pattern that isn't actionable or that can't be turned into an advantage isn't of much use. And last, one has to play back that thesis to someone in a coherent and compelling way. In university that was usually in the form of an essay. Today it's more likely to be a PowerPoint presentation.

Corresponding to these three processes are three useful skills, also learned by analyzing poetry, plays, and novels. The first is non-linear thinking. Despite what the purveyors of public-speaking courses might tell you, the most compelling stories don't boil down to simply a beginning, middle, and end. The complex structures of great literature often require us to move back and forth in time and space. This is the very opposite of the linear unfolding of case-study analysis.

The linear approach of MBA school says, here's the problem. Find the best possible solution. The analysis of literature says, here's some data in the form of a text. Tell me what it means and why that's important. The mental processes are different, as are the outcomes.

The second skill is empathy, the capacity to understand the world from someone else's perspective. This is one of the fundamental elements of literature: taking the reader into the mind of a character who might be nothing like him or her and allowing that reader to peer out at the world through the character's eyes. This is not an insignificant skill for business people to acquire. But for marketers in particular, it is vital. When I was still in the business of hiring people to work in advertising, I would often be asked what was the single most important thing I looked for in a creative person. My answer was always empathy. You might be a young copywriting hipster living in an urban loft and DJing on the weekends, but if you're selling laundry detergent to a suburban housewife with two kids you'd better be able to see the world the way she does. Empathy is not on the curriculum at B-schools. Which might explain why many of them, like Boston University's School of Management, are now requiring students to take an ethics course. There is no required ethics course in English lit. It's all ethics.

The third thing one acquires through regular reading is narrative skill. I'll leave it to others to decide if I absorbed this lesson well enough. But what I do know, from years of developing marketing and branding strategies, is that a good strategy needs a good narrative. A strategy is not just an articulation of the way forward; to be effective it must also be a call to arms. To get people to understand the strategy, to believe in it, and then to want to act on it requires narrative flair. It is like the oft-repeated legend that when Cicero spoke people praised, "How well he spoke." But when Demosthenes spoke, people said, "Let us march!" One of the most celebrated rhetoricians of his day (his day being three hundred years before Christ), Demosthenes clearly knew how to spin a narrative.

"Innovate or die!" is a popular rallying cry among the new generation of tech start-ups. The humiliating downward slide of Microsoft's Zune, the Blackberry smartphone, and the ill-fated Google Glass demonstrates that without innovation it doesn't matter how big you are; you're never too big to fail. The same is true for non-tech consumer products companies. The need for a constant flow of innovation has never been greater. Companies looking for more creative thinking and more original insights should start by bringing greater diversity to their marketing departments. It begins with hiring more people who can demonstrate non-linear thinking, who have genuine empathy, and who possess narrative skill. If corporations want to develop more creative solutions to business problems, if they want people who see things in a new light and who find patterns in the data that no one has spotted before, they might want to look beyond business schools. The English department would be a good place to start.

THE DAILY DISCO

Once he had hired the suitably diverse team that would occupy the Cave, Dan Wagner put them into an environment that was the antithesis of modern ergonomic office planning. They were squirrelled away in a small windowless space and forced to sit mere inches away from each other. There was little room to move and even less privacy. Why? "We wanted to create a hub of innovation," he explained. This is the third element of successful team building for winning campaigns: a work environment that forces creative collaboration. It seems to defy logic that this cramped, uncomfortable space could help to create a hub of innovation. With its disco ball and strands of fairy lights, random posters stuck on the wall, and the general clutter of a small space shared by several people, it looked more like a college dorm than the nerve centre of a massive high-tech data-analysis operation, much less a hub of innovation.

But, remarkably, out of this cramped chaos arose a spontaneous culture. Every day at 4:30 p.m. work would stop, the overhead lights would be switched off, and the disco ball would light up the room. The soundtrack invariably consisted of one of Andrew Claster's robocalls remixed with anything from Psy's "Gangnam Style" to vintage Milli Vanilli. Even though, and perhaps because, they were working intensely hard and for many long hours in a claustrophobic environment, the team was able to coalesce and develop their own bonding rituals — an important sign of a well-functioning team.

The Cave also borrowed a key idea from the political war room: the flattened hierarchy. Placing everyone in the same room in close proximity to one another ensured that information and ideas could flow freely and rapidly from one person to the next. Ideas could emerge from casual interactions. Recommendations didn't have to climb some imaginary ladder to get approved, because all the decision makers were within hollering distance of one another.

Consider the environment of the Cave compared to its counterparts out in the modern world of high tech. The norm these days is to build elaborate playpens to house the cosseted employees of companies like Apple, Google, and Facebook. All three of these companies have engaged in massive building projects to expand their office complexes — invariably called campuses, in keeping with their general collegiate culture. Apple's new 2.8-million-square-foot headquarters in Cupertino looks like the spaceship from *Close Encounters of the Third Kind* set down in the middle of a 150-acre California field. Twelve thousand people occupy this single ring-shaped sanctuary, which opened in 2017. The exterior of the building is sheathed in 40-foot-high sheets of curved glass imported from Germany. It cost $5 billion to build. By way of comparison, the world's tallest building, the Burj Khalifa in Dubai, cost $1.5 billion to build in 2010.

Google's Mountain View headquarters, dubbed the Googleplex, offers a lavish array of onsite perks: free meals in a variety of cuisines three times daily; the obligatory employee lounges with pool tables and retro video games; hundreds of bikes and scooters for zipping around campus; subsidized massages and haircuts; car washes; free dry cleaning services; seven fitness centres, some with swimming pools; a bowling alley and climbing wall; the list goes on. The 3,000 employees in the company's New York City office, which occupies an entire city block, have their own set of whimsical perks, from a Lego play station to private reading rooms hidden behind concealed doors to free weekly eyebrow shaping, if that's your thing. One suspects it will be no different in London when Google completes its £1 billion office complex near King's Cross Station.

Not to be outdone, Facebook's new digs in Menlo Park, California, and in New York are designed by none other than starchitect Frank Gehry. The concept for Menlo Park is to create essentially a ten-acre room. Staff can go from one end of the building to the other without passing through a single door. There are no private offices or cubicles, but there are war rooms for planning sessions, and at the centre of it all is a glass-enclosed space housing the captain of this ship, Mark Zuckerberg. Beyond the walls is an outdoor restaurant serving California's favourite cuisine, sushi. Up on the roof, a massive landscaped garden, spanning the length of the building. There are skateboard-friendly ramps to get you from one place to the next.

What all these companies are creating is a kind of dude's dreamland. Google's own description of the Googleplex captures the essence of all this: "It's easy to feel like we're back in college." Except this is a college where you never have to cook, there's always a refrigerator full of snacks, Mom does your laundry, you can play awesome retro video games between brainstorming sessions, and you can skateboard your way to the john. Sweet.

It's easy to see how these temples to high tech can function as bait in the highly competitive hunt to recruit smart young programmers and engineers. Hey, over here, we've got scooters! No, over here, we've got Segways! We'll give you a massage! We'll give you a massage while we do your laundry!

But it's less easy to see how these work environments and perks function as a means to create more effective and efficient teams or how they increase innovation. The one thing they do manage to get right is the flattened hierarchy. There's a reason why leaders like Zuckerberg like to make a show of sitting right in the midst of all the other employees and not on some hushed executive floor. It indicates accessibility, openness, and an egalitarianism that suggests everyone is part of the team.

A HIGHER CALLING

Let's head back to the Cave at Obama headquarters for a minute. Arguably, the fifty-odd people working there for months on end coalesced into a formidably powerful team. They achieved remarkable results and did it by sparking innovative connections and developing proprietary algorithms that gave the candidate a massive advantage over the airwaves and on the ground. And they did it all on the fly, taking time out only for the afternoon disco break. When Dan Wagner was approached by Eric Schmidt, who offered to fund his vision of a new company to the tune of many millions of dollars, Wagner didn't say he wanted to build the next great data-mining business. He said, "My main motivation was to keep together this brilliant group of people we had built in the analytics team over several months." This wasn't mere feel-good rhetoric.

There was something about that team. And it had nothing to do with the environment they were in. There were no free massages, unless your desk-mate was friendlier than most. There were no snack pods stocked with gourmet chocolate, no organic meals freshly prepared three times daily. And the closest thing to a fitness centre was the Ping-Pong table located somewhere in the building, where Obama actually played a match with one of the Cave dwellers. What the team had was a bold mission. The thing that brought them together and moved them forward was a common purpose. And it wasn't just any purpose. They were aiming to elect, or re-elect, the first black man as leader of the free world — a man whose vision for their country and for the world they passionately believed in. It was this grand calling that gave them both cohesion and momentum as a team.

And when we look at Facebook, Google, and Apple, we see teams that are driven by the same sense of a higher calling. All of these companies have articulated a bold and aggressive mission for their employees.

By comparison, most corporate mission and vision statements ring hollow. Many of them are constructed like matryoshka dolls — a succession of clichés inside banalities inside platitudes. They are usually cobbled together by senior management during a one-day offsite at a golf resort, led by an overly enthusiastic facilitator. They are far removed from the day-to-day reality of the work people do. The difference at companies like Google is how immediate and urgent and grand the goals feel.

Google's unofficial mission is "Don't be evil," penned by one of its earliest hires, Paul Buchheit, employee number twenty-three. Eric Schmidt relates the story of arriving at Google after being hired as its CEO and thinking that phrase was just a marketing ploy. But one day, in a meeting discussing the development of a new advertising product, an engineer objected by slamming his fist on the table and yelling, "That's evil!" The idea went no further.

Even when you consider Google's official mission statement — "To organize the world's information and make it universally accessible and useful" — it's not hard to see how any one of Google's more than 70,000 employees would feel that their work was intimately connected to this goal. But more important than this sense of connectedness to the corporate mission is the breathtaking ambition of the mission itself. From its very beginnings the company has displayed an instinct for setting lofty goals — digitizing all the world's books, for example. These visionary aims — on the same scale as John F. Kennedy's committing to putting a man on the moon in ten years — are what give these teams a sense of drive and purposefulness.

It's no different at Facebook, where the corporate mission, despite its many flaws, is no less ambitious: "To give people the power to share and make the world more open and connected." Here's how Sheryl Sandberg, in a television interview with Charlie Rose, described the decision to leave Google to work with Mark Zuckerberg at Facebook: "I could see from Mark that what he really wanted to build was something that was, you know, fundamentally going to change who we are and how we interact." If you're going to leave a company that's making the world's information more accessible and useful, it might as well be to join the one that is changing the way we all interact. Moving towards a lesser calling would have been a serious downgrade for Sandberg.

Long before Apple became the largest tech company in the world and before they could offer employees competitive wages, Steve Jobs would entice prospective hires with the pitch that coming to work at Apple would give them a chance to change the world. That audacious promise was made most famously (and disastrously) when he tempted John Sculley to leave PepsiCo and become Apple's CEO, with this challenge:

"Do you want to sell sugar water for the rest of your life, or do you want to come with me and change the world?" The desire to change the world is at the heart of Apple's corporate ethos, and captured most vividly in the closing line of the acclaimed "Think Different" television campaign: "Because the people who are crazy enough to think they can change the world are the ones who do."

The fact is, if you strip away the stock options, the lavish corporate headquarters, and the endless perks, what you're left with are two things: the diverse life experiences of the people who make up the successful teams and the inspiring mission they've been handed. And it is those things, perhaps less tangible and less visible and yet enormously powerful, that are the binding force in creating extraordinary teams. It's what helped to make the Obama analytics team a force to be reckoned with (absent stock options, lavish quarters, or perks). It's these qualities that separate the leading technology and Internet companies from the rest of the herd.

Companies seeking to emulate the success of these innovative teams are often dazzled by the superficialities of office design and employee perquisites. This is not an argument against those things; it's an argument for looking at the fundamentals first. Most important, companies need to ask themselves if the mission they've defined for their employees is sufficiently inspiring. Is the goal lofty enough to make the employees want to spend half their waking lives passionately pursuing it?

It's time to set aside the bland ambition and the vague phrases that populate vision statements and move towards a concrete and inspirational rallying cry. Among my clients is one of the world's leading renewable energy companies. After interviewing every senior executive in the organization, I was surprised at how passionately they believe the work they do every day has the power to transform people's lives for the better. In a multi-billion-dollar global company with a double-digit growth trajectory, I expected to find a bit more smugness and perhaps some cynicism, as I have often found elsewhere. But working to bring power to the one and a half billion people around the world who don't have it; launching rural electrification projects that allow individuals to start small businesses and earn a living; giving students light by which to study; and designing solar-powered water pumps that enable communities to irrigate the land and grow their own food feel immediate and meaningful and inspiring to each of these executives. As more than one of them said to me, "It's why I come into work every day."

Of course, not every company is working on large social problems like bringing solar power to remote parts of the world. But to create a motivated workforce requires some spark of inspiration in the mission, whatever that mission is. Too often that spark is merely a momentary pyrotechnic display that is quickly consumed by the heat of its own pretentiousness. Surprisingly, some of the worst offenders in this area are companies in the communications business. Here's how the world's largest public relations firm, Edelman, defines their corporate mission: "We recalibrate brands to broaden awareness, reframe global positions and re-connect with core customers. Our business is to help you form relationships and effectively engage." Edelman would have us believe that this relentless piling on of clichés is what passes for inspiration.

These words, we are told, are what led to "Thousands of talented employees connecting, informing and creating inspiring work around the globe." This strains the bounds of credulity just a notch.

Beyond being truly inspirational, a mission statement must also be credible. What's notable about the lofty mission statements from the most innovative companies today is not just that they aim high but that they're also grounded in truth. Apple technology *has* in fact changed the world, Facebook *is* changing the way we interact with each other, and Google *is* the first company in history that can actually claim to be organizing the world's information to be more useful and accessible.

Once organizations find the right balance between inspirational and credible goals and marry those up with talented people with diverse backgrounds and experiences, teams will start to coalesce. They'll start creating the rituals and inside jokes that help them forge a stronger bond. Even as Google has grown to over 70,000 employees, it manages to maintain the quirky rituals that became part of the culture early on. They've managed to create their own special internal language with words like Googlers, Nooglers, Nullplex, Googleplex, and Googley. They also have their own jokey traditions. Nooglers (new employees) have to wear propeller-topped beanies when they are introduced to the rest of the team at the weekly company-wide meeting (called TGIF even though it's now held on Thursdays). The company also has a long tradition of pulling ever more elaborate April Fool's Day pranks. All of this helps build cohesion, but none of it would matter if the company had not already assembled a highly driven team and given them all an inspiring mission.

I've seen companies struggle to build cohesive and motivated teams by starting at the tail end of the process, trying to create their own little rituals (beer and pizza on Fridays!). Too often there's a kind of forced jollity about these efforts, a false note that results in the exact opposite of the intended outcome. They can feel like the awkward office birthday party where a store-bought cake is brought out and everyone stands around for a few minutes with their paper plates and plastic forks and then slowly drifts back to their desks. At its best, team building grows organically out of a fertile environment. It comes from the ground up. It cannot be dictated from above. Attempts to do this always put me in mind of the gallows humour that used to fill the hallways at the very first advertising agency I worked at, where the most popular expression amongst the demoralized staff was "The floggings will continue until morale improves."

THE FIST IN THE FACE

The other thing Google does remarkably well for a large corporation is to instill a sense of the importance of winning. This brings us back to where we started this chapter, with the idea that in politics there is no room for second place. One of the core values at Google is "Great just isn't good enough." This is not a culture where "We're only No. 2. We try harder" would get much traction. Just as in politics, it's not always possible to win in business. But instilling in your team a powerful sense of wanting to beat the competition can improve their performance far beyond what might otherwise be expected. And encouraging a killer instinct can mean the difference between success and failure. As James Carville so colourfully put it, "It's hard for your opponent to say much when your fist is in his face." Sometimes the lofty ambition that can bring a team together and make them work harder than they imagined they could is simply a desire to beat the other guy.

About a year after our ill-fated bid for the Bell business, I was asked to head up another new business pitch. Our French-speaking sister agency in Montreal, Tam-Tam/TBWA, had been invited to bid for the global advertising assignment for Avid Technologies, based near Boston, Massachusetts. Avid produces software and hardware used in the production and editing of digital content, from movies to television shows to music recordings. Many of your favourite blockbusters and Top Ten hits have been produced using Avid's technology. It's also used in the production of television commercials. It was something of a coup that a Montreal ad agency, especially a small French agency, had been asked to pitch the global assignment for an American account. The management team at Tam-Tam/TBWA were pumped. There was only one problem. They weren't confident enough in their English-language skills to manage the pitch on their own. That's where I came in.

I assembled a small team of smart and aggressive people from our Toronto office — an account planner, a media planner, and the head of our digital department. Together with the talented creative team from Tam-Tam/TBWA, we worked over a period of a few weeks to pull together our pitch. I'd never worked with the members of our Montreal office before, and the fact that we were in two different cities, five hundred miles apart (and culturally even further apart), made coalescing as a team that much more difficult. We justifiably felt like the underdogs going into this battle, hampered as we were by our somewhat disjointed and very lean team and by our French connection. Our competitors included major agencies from both the U.S. and Canada. The human and financial resources they could put behind a pitch like this would outstrip our efforts by miles.

Our little troop flew from Toronto and Montreal to Boston the night before the pitch and met up in a hotel in the suburbs north of the city, close to the Avid offices. It was the first time everyone on the team had actually been together and the last chance we'd have to rehearse. That night, fuelled by hotel coffee and adrenalin, we assembled in my room and laid out the sixty-odd pages of our presentation on the floor, shuffling and reshuffling them until we felt they made sense, revising slides as we went. Someone was sitting at a laptop tapping the last-minute changes into PowerPoint.

The next morning, on a chilly and grey mid-December day, the six of us tumbled out of our rented minivan at the Avid offices along with computers, large presentation boards, and boxes of T-shirts we planned to leave behind for the client. We headed into the lobby and the first thing we heard was someone saying that one of our competitors had arrived for their pitch the day before in their corporate plane. I stared out the giant plate-glass window at our forlorn-looking minivan sitting in the parking lot and felt a sinking sensation in my stomach.

Nevertheless, I knew that what we had to say to Avid about revitalizing their brand was both powerful and original. Remarkably, the tension of the last-minute rehearsal, the anxiety of delivering a pitch, and, most important, the ambition to beat out our much bigger rivals made all of us suddenly feel connected as a team. Despite our differing accents we sounded like we were all singing from the same song sheet. We left the meeting on a high and headed into Boston to celebrate over a raucous lunch.

It was just days before Christmas when the call came. We'd won the business. Among the agencies that we'd beaten was Cossette Advertising. I was back in Toronto when I got the message, and that night my partner and I went out for a quiet celebratory dinner. With a nod and a wink to Frank Gehry and his grandmother's Shabbat dinners, I ordered the fish.

Our little David-and-Goliath battle had captured, on a small scale (and quite coincidentally), all the elements of effective political team building. We were driven to win, not just because this was a new business pitch but also because we were up against our archrival, Cossette, which had beaten us only months earlier in the Bell pitch. We were a diverse team — linguistically, culturally, geographically — and because of that we brought a unique perspective to the communications challenges Avid was facing. We were able to see the problem with fresh eyes. We even managed to recreate a cramped, intense mini war room experience the night before the pitch in a hotel room (and then carried it into our minivan). And last, we were on a mission. We wanted to prove that our little regional French-Canadian agency could stand up to the big guys and hold our own. It wasn't as noble a mission as electing the first black president, but in our little world it was every bit as important and every bit as powerfully motivating.

As marketers head into battle, with increasing demands for more innovation and more creativity, they must come to accept that riding the same horse and just flogging it harder will get you only so far. Sometimes you have to change steeds. As the boardroom planners plot their strategies for victory, they have some crucial lessons to learn from the war room on how to assemble an army in short order, make them function as a cohesive and resourceful team, and give them a goal that will inspire them to say, "Let us march."

CHAPTER 8

PLAN FOR FAILURE

IGNORING THE UNKNOWN

In 2003 the Plain English Campaign conferred its annual "Foot in Mouth" award to then U.S. Defense Secretary Donald Rumsfeld for this pronouncement: "There are known knowns. There are things we know that we know. There are known unknowns. That is to say, there are things that we now know we don't know. But there are also unknown unknowns. There are things we do not know we don't know." In his tortuous way, what Rumsfeld was saying is that stuff happens and sometimes we just have no way of anticipating what could go wrong. He was, in fact, missing the point, which is that stuff happens and we have to do everything in our power to anticipate what could go wrong.

Rumsfeld and his generals had confidently predicted that the U.S. invasion of Iraq would begin with shock and awe and end with flowers and candy as grateful Iraqis would flood onto the streets to greet their liberators. And so, less than two months after the first barrage of bombs rained down on Baghdad, President George W. Bush stood proudly on the deck of the aircraft carrier USS *Abraham Lincoln* beneath a banner that read "Mission Accomplished," cocked a thumb into the air, and declared, "In the Battle of Iraq, the United States and our allies have prevailed."

What the war planners hadn't predicted was that the candies and flowers would be replaced by roadside bombs and guerrilla raids in a war that would drag on for years, with hundreds of thousands of lives lost and trillions of dollars spent.

In an age of volatile and unpredictable social and political events, planning for victory is not enough. We must also plan for failure. What would happen if everything in your carefully devised plan went awry? Would you be ready to respond quickly and effectively? Like Rumsfeld's generals, many businesses today develop their plans based solely on a trajectory towards success. Sure, they might include different outcomes, based on reaching 100 percent of their goal or perhaps 80 percent or even just 60 percent, but the overall assumption is that the plan will succeed at some level. In a way this makes sense. It's necessary to define your goal and plan the best route for achieving it. But it makes no sense in a highly unstable socioeconomic environment not to plan also for failure.

Rumsfeld and his generals should have taken a page out of the political handbook, where disaster planning has been part of smart campaign planning for years. Political consultants do it because they know that disaster will inevitably strike. They assume the path to victory will not travel in a straight line and that it's necessary to handle the detours without losing momentum. A significant part of the campaign-planning process is taken up with scenario planning that tries to anticipate every conceivable thing that could go wrong and then puts in

253

place action plans for those things that are most likely to go wrong, the most plausible disasters. These plans might even include draft communication materials that can be used in the event of a crisis. These documents are then filed away, ready to be pulled out at a moment's notice should disaster present itself. Most of the time they're never needed.

Why do political strategists care so much about planning for failure? Because they live in a world of opposition, not just from other political parties but also from the media, special interest groups, and ordinary citizens who have an issue they feel zealous about. They have to consider all the negative things that others could say about them and be ready to counter those with ideas and arguments of their own. Historically, marketers haven't had to deal with the same problem. That's because most of the opposition they face is from their competitors. Sure, if you're an auto company, you might have the competition saying, "Our cars are better than your cars," but none of them are going to say that all cars are bad. They're not going to attack the category as a whole. Because there are so many outside groups attacking political parties, they often face the real dilemma of "a pox on all your houses."

Marketers can no longer live in this closed bubble. The digitally connected world has changed all that. The advent of social media means it's not only possible but also highly likely that brands will face attacks from all angles and any number of sources, not just from their category competitors. These days, brands need to be ready for whatever might happen. They have to anticipate the unknown unknowns.

The reason campaign strategists spend so much time on planning for failure is because it's incredibly liberating. If you've tried to anticipate all the things that could go wrong, it means that when the unexpected happens the team will not be struck by panic and paralysis. It means they can continue working towards their primary objective while dealing with the crisis in a calm and logical way, because they will have already thought through the issues and options and might even have responses at hand.

RUNNING THE WAR GAME

To see how this process works, I've come to a charming three-storey Georgian edifice on the eastern periphery of Toronto's downtown core, a few minutes away from the heart of the city's financial power centre. On the second floor of the building, which was Toronto's first post office and predates the incorporation of the city itself, are the offices of Crestview Strategy. Crestview is a Canadian public affairs agency whose slogan is "We make, change and mobilize opinion." Its three founding partners are all experienced political operatives, none more so than Chad Rogers, who pops his head out of the office door to greet me as I head up the short flight of stairs. Rogers is something of a contradiction. Although he's in his late thirties, his slightly formal way of speaking makes him seem older than his cherubic face suggests. From the waist up he's all yuppie conservatism, wearing preppy tortoiseshell glasses and dressed in a pink check button-down shirt. Below the waist he's rebel metrosexual in blue jeans, colourful striped socks, and tan brogues with bright blue rubber soles. But there's no contradiction in his political views, which skew firmly to the right.

Rogers has worked for Conservative Party senators and

members of the Canadian Parliament and has been an adviser and political strategist on numerous Tory election campaigns. In 2003 he advised Conservative leader John Hamm during the provincial election campaign in the Atlantic province of Nova Scotia, which saw the Conservatives win re-election despite facing massive voter unrest. He has also worked with governments and political leaders in emerging democracies from Iraq to Kyrgyzstan. Along with his partners at Crestview Strategy, he advises global companies like Coca-Cola, Facebook, and Target on how to manage their public affairs issues in Canada. Rogers is a passionate advocate for planning for failure. A big part of his job is trying to figure out all the unfortunate things that might happen, before they do.

"One of my favourite tools," says Rogers, "is to run a full war game." (The bellicose nature of political conflict seems to encourage jargon like "war room" and "war games.") No doubt the American generals who so rapidly took control of Iraq had war-gamed just such a forceful overthrow. What they clearly hadn't done was war-game the occupation that followed. For Rogers, war-gaming is a form of planning that allows you to play out all the scenarios of what could go wrong and all the things your opponents might do to undermine your campaign.

He prefers to start this process of planning at least two years before an election is called, usually at a two- or three-day retreat that brings together a group of campaign planners who will take on the roles of various opposition parties and groups and imagine how they might attack the campaign's message. He explains, "Teams will be assigned to play the various actors that will realistically exist in the space: Liberals, New Democrats, Greens, the press corps. They will have to spend time in advance understanding their positions, their biases, how they behave."

A proposition is then put in front of the group and the teams are given a couple of hours to develop their cases. "People come back into the room and present and then we debate. Is it realistic? Is it rigorous enough? Let's attack the person who's presenting. Were they robust enough in their thinking? Out of that debate would come further edits and then let's go again." This iterative process gets repeated until the group feels it has developed an optimal set of messages for the campaign, including a ballot question. "You're capturing everything over the weekend that could go into your master narrative. You're experimenting with all the smart things you could try," says Rogers. If that weekend effort doesn't produce the desired result, they'll do another and another until they finally get to where they need to be. Why go to this extreme effort to figure out all the scenarios of what might go wrong, when most of them will likely not happen? "Ultimately," he explains, "there's a big pitfall out there waiting for you that someone else is going to figure out." Better to figure it out yourself and be ready to deal with it.

One benefit of having run through a disaster scenario beforehand is that it saves time if and when disaster strikes. Political campaigning, Rogers notes, is about four things: time, people, money, and ideas. "Time is the variable you can control through good planning," he says. But there's a second benefit to planning for failure, a psychological one. "There is no decision-making time available to you in the midst of crisis. And if you haven't prepared for it, you're going to have both the emotional, psychological trauma that it's a crisis, along with real decisions to make. So the only way is to do it in advance." Imagining what could go wrong not only prevents you from being paralyzed during a crisis, it can actually be empowering for the team, Rogers says. "It becomes validating that the team has control. The team has actually spent time envisaging this might happen. And you can calm down your own folks, you can move on to your message."

The psychological benefit of imagining the worst (for example, the candidate is found to be engaged in infidelity) allows the team to remain focused in the midst of crisis. If you've already surfaced and given voice to everyone's anxieties and greatest fears, chances are you won't be left looking crippled or indecisive when the worst happens. The benefit is clear, says Rogers: "Crisis planning and war-gaming means you have a team that doesn't get spooked."

Plenty of corporations do crisis planning — or at least say they do. They have crisis management teams and PR agencies on standby in the event of disaster. But crisis planning isn't the same as scenario planning. Crisis planning is like a fire drill. Every department knows what to do when the alarm goes off: who are the team captains, what are the exit routes, where does everyone muster once they've left the building, how do we carry out a head count. Scenario planning is like trying to figure out what conditions are necessary for an actual fire to break out, how close you are to those conditions today, and how the organization might respond if fire does break out. Scenario planning is a more complex and nuanced exercise.

Scenario planning is also distinct from forecasting, which tends to be primarily a financial exercise. Forecasting has also become a devilishly difficult thing to do. In post–Second

World War America and Europe, thanks to steady and predictable growth, forecasting was as simple as plotting growth for the past few years, then placing a ruler on the page to project growth for the coming few years. But after the recessions of the seventies and eighties (both triggered by oil crises), business forecasting became about as accurate as political polling is today.

EMBRACING THE UNKNOWN

In the years leading up to the 1973 oil crisis, it was in fact an oil company that figured out that forecasting had its limitations and decided to replace it with scenario planning as a tool for long-term strategic planning. Royal Dutch Shell assigned some of its brightest business planners to the task. Among them was a Frenchman by the name of Pierre Wack. Almost fifteen years after the creation of the scenario-planning team, Wack would write a series of articles for the *Harvard Business Review*, outlining the work he and his team had done.

As described by Wack, the Shell planners began by defining which elements affecting their business were predetermined — that is, events that had already been set in motion, where one can predict the future consequences. For example, if a massive earthquake happens in the middle of the ocean near a coastline, a tsunami is almost certain to follow. One can predict the ripples of certain events. However, there are also uncertainties — events that might affect your business but that you can't accurately predict. These are Rumsfeld's unknown unknowns. Here's what Wack has to say on the issue of uncertainties: "It is essential to try to put as much light on critical uncertainties as on the predetermined elements. They should not be swept under the carpet."

Confronting the uncertainties, rather than dismissing them as being outside our capacity to predict, is what defines the difference between scenario planning and forecasting. Next, the planners separated out those elements that would happen from those that clearly could not. This further narrowed their options and allowed them to focus more fully on the most plausible scenarios. This process of embracing uncertainty and narrowing down the plausible options allowed the Shell planners to do something no other oil company, government, or corporation had done — anticipate the 1973 oil crisis, with its supply constraints and skyrocketing prices. In its own account of those events, Shell notes, "In 1973 the global economy was shocked by a major oil crisis. Shell wasn't." Even more impressively, the Shell planners were also able to anticipate when the opposite happened — an oversupply of oil and a dramatic drop in prices in the early 1980s. This allowed Shell to inoculate itself against these unprecedented upheavals in the oil industry and the global economy as a whole. Scenario planning had shown itself to be a powerful business tool.

This approach represented a radical shift in mindset. It moved away from the forecasting world view that believed the future is knowable and we should be able to predict it, and towards a scenario world view that believed the future was uncertain and we should embrace that uncertainty. It suggested that judgement and intuition have as much of a role to play in future planning as facts do. This is the opposite of the Rumsfeld doctrine, which holds that the unknown unknowns are beyond our contemplation.

Today, forty years after it was first introduced, scenario planning is an integral part of Shell's business-planning process. And it has given the company, time and again, significant strategic advantage over its competition. The Shell approach now includes a large and sophisticated "global energy model" that uses computer simulation to show the interactions across a complex matrix of energy, politics, and economics, and across geographies and industry segments. It's a daunting task. As Martin Haigh, one of the senior energy advisers on the current Shell scenarios team, says, "We have a very ambitious remit in the team, which is to try and cover the whole world, all countries, all the energy sources available — and the long term." The Shell process has become so widely admired that numerous other companies have embraced it, and countries from China to South Africa have turned to Shell to help them develop scenarios for their own futures.

The Shell scenario-planning approach is not about providing answers; it's about allowing the company's managers to imagine the future. It shakes off the business-as-usual impulse that is so easy to fall back on when managers engage in strategic planning. It challenges management's comfortable assumptions about the future and it uncovers the biases in their world view. But its greatest legacy might be that it has created a culture of forward thinking at Shell. The result is an environment in which future unseen events are factored into everyday decision-making and strategizing. What that means is, if disaster does strike, the chances are pretty good that the Shell management team has already contemplated the eventuality and hypothesized about possible solutions. And as with

Chad Rogers's campaign team, it breeds an atmosphere of confidence and calm in the face of crisis.

Given the success of Shell's pioneering work on scenario planning, it was not surprising that in 2013, when the consulting firm Bain & Company issued its annual "Management Tools & Trends" survey, it showed that 70 percent of companies intended to include scenario planning as part of their business-planning process. The Bain survey canvassed over 1,200 senior business executives from around the world, asking them which management tools they were most likely to use. But the surprise comes when you look at the answer to that question the year before. In 2012 that number was only 23 percent. In that year, less than a quarter of all companies surveyed planned to do any scenario planning at all. Scenario planning appears to be an optional extra. Sometimes companies think they need it, sometimes not.

A DARK RAIN BEGAN TO FALL

But what happens if companies sweep the uncertainties under the carpet, if they throw their hands up in the air when confronted by the unknown unknowns, if they fail to instill a forward-looking culture in their managers? To see the consequences, we must journey to the dark blue waters of the Gulf of Mexico, to a spot some forty-nine miles off the Louisiana coast. Here the ocean water is cold and deep. You would have to descend 5,000 feet below the surface, through darkness and into black, enduring near-freezing temperatures and deadly water pressure, before you touch the ocean floor.

Yet it was in this forbidding place that one of Shell's chief rivals, the British oil conglomerate BP, had come in 2010, and in a breathtaking feat of skillful engineering and brute force had punched a hole in the earth's surface 5,000 feet below the water, and then drilled an additional 13,000 feet below that to reach its pay zone, a black and viscous reservoir of oil and gas. The well was called Macondo, named for the fictional town in Gabriel García Márquez's seminal work of magical realism, *One Hundred Years of Solitude*. In the novel, Macondo is a place whose destiny is both tragic and inescapable. A city surrounded by water, it will eventually be ruined by a hurricane and fall into decline. BP's Macondo could have wished for a fate as serene as that.

Above the Macondo well, on the ocean surface, was a marvel of modern engineering, a 33,000-ton semi-submersible drilling rig designed for harsh environments, capable of withstanding forty-foot waves and winds of over a hundred knots. Floating on the water, unanchored to anything, the rig was powered by eight Rolls-Royce azimuth thrusters, each capable of generating 7,375 horsepower. These dynamic thrusters could, at the push of a button and with the aid of a satellite-guided system, hold the massive rig in a steady position above the drill hole thousands of feet below, even in rough water.

The Deepwater Horizon oil rig, owned by the world's largest offshore drilling contractor, Transocean, was valued at more than half a billion dollars and leased out at a cost of a million dollars a day. It made for an impressive sight. Resting on giant pontoons, four massive white supports held four decks above. The design appeared to have been inspired by a NASA launch pad. A large octagonal helipad occupied one corner of the top deck, and from the centre a grey and yellow oil derrick rose over 200 feet into the air.

April 20, 2010, was a good-news day for the workers on the Deepwater Horizon. After many delays — delays that had almost doubled the original seven-week schedule for drilling the well and had driven the project $60 million over budget — the last stages of securing what they called the "well from hell" were finally at hand. That morning, an engineer from Halliburton, the company responsible for cementing the well, had sent out an email announcing, "We have completed the job and it went well." It had gone so well, in fact, that a decision was made to forego testing of the cement seal. This would save both time and money. All that was left to do was some pressure tests and then the well could start doing what it was designed to do — release the oil and gas buried two and a half miles below the seabed, trapped there more than 10 million years ago and held under immense pressure at temperatures exceeding 200 degrees Fahrenheit.

By mid-morning the first of two pressure tests had been successfully completed. The second, a negative pressure test, showed some problematic readings. After repeating the test a couple of times, the crew decided the results were anomalous and declared the negative pressure test a success. By now it was dinnertime and shifts were changing in the drill shack. The only remaining task was to set a cement plug in the well. To do that, the crew first had to pump seawater into the steel shaft, or riser, to displace mud that had accumulated during the drilling process.

Shortly after 9:00 p.m., the workers on board the rig felt a vibration and heard a sharp hissing sound. Stepping out onto the decks, they were astonished to see a thick black rain falling. A slick, slippery substance had coated the decks, making it treacherous to walk. According to the official report on the event, one crew member thought to himself, "Why is all this snot on the deck?" Even more extraordinary, the supply ship *Bankston*, which lay at anchor nearby, was glistening with the same dark, wet downpour. It was drilling mud. And it was shooting through the crown of the derrick, hundreds of feet into the air.

And then it stopped. Silence. One of the crew held his breath and thought, "Oh, they got it under control."

The first explosion came only moments later, and with such violence that it knocked chief mechanic Douglas Brown through the control room floor and into the subfloor. The second explosion brought the ceiling down on him. The explosions kept coming, knocking out all the power and scattering the crew like pawns on an overturned chessboard. The only light now came from a roaring tower of flame that emerged from the legs of the derrick and shot straight up through the crown twenty storeys above, billowing thick black smoke as it went. The heat and noise were ferocious.

Ignited by methane gas, the well had blown. The blowout preventer, an elaborate four-storey-high valve installed underwater at the well head, had failed to stop the explosion.

There were 126 people aboard the rig at the time. Some scrambled to lifeboats and descended to the eerily calm water, where floating oil slicks blazed on the surface like some magic trick. The wounded had to be lowered on stretchers. Peering back up at the inferno and feeling its heat on their faces, the survivors saw men appearing out of the smoke and falling through the air. The remaining crew members were leaping from the burning rig, hurtling themselves 100 feet or more to the water below.

Just before midnight the last of the survivors had been taken aboard the supply ship *Bankston*. Helicopters started arriving to ferry sixteen seriously wounded people to hospitals on the mainland. When a final count was done, eleven men remained missing.

Because it was the only large ship in the vicinity, the *Bankston* was instructed to hold its position near the rig. It was not allowed to begin the long journey back to port with the remaining survivors until 8 a.m. the next morning. All through the night the surviving crew, some bandaged, some strapped into oxygen masks, sat silently on the crowded decks of the *Bankston* and watched, knowing that somewhere inside that terrible conflagration their friends lay dead or dying.

In its official report on the event, the National Commission on the BP Deepwater Horizon Oil Spill and Offshore Drilling quotes one of the crew, a seasoned veteran with decades of experience in offshore drilling: "To stay on location and watch the rig burn. Those guys that were on there were our family. It would be like seeing your children or your brothers or sisters perish in that manner. And that — that put some mental scarring in a lot of people's heads that will never go away."

Without power, the Deepwater Horizon drifted lifelessly in the water. With the powerful satellite-guided thrusters no longer functioning, the tide swung the rig a full 180 degrees and it drifted slowly away from the well. But the orange flames continued to hiss and burn, lighting up the dark waters of the Gulf and reaching high into the night sky. One of the world's most advanced offshore drilling rigs had become a funeral pyre.

In its report, the National Commission quoted the board that investigated the *Columbia* space shuttle accident, saying, "Complex systems fail in complex ways," and concluded that many factors contributed to the Deepwater Horizon tragedy.

FROM TOP KILL TO JUNK SHOT

Would Shell's scenario planning have helped BP to anticipate this disaster? No. Scenario planning is about long-term macro trends in energy, economics, and politics. But what it would have done is bred a more future-oriented culture at BP, a culture that believes anticipating and being prepared for disaster is important. If you're a major oil company engaged in the difficult and dangerous business of deep-sea drilling, you should expect serious accidents to happen. Instead, BP appeared to be fumbling about in the dark. In Chad Rogers's words, they were looking "spooked." It seemed that no one at BP had imagined the worst — they hadn't given voice to their greatest anxiety. So when it came to pass, the company was ill-prepared both tactically and, even worse, psychologically.

Here's what Pierre Wack had to say about accidents when he was preparing the Shell scenarios in the early 1970s: "Accidents, which included both political and internal and physical incidents, are events that any oil executive considers a matter of course. In the same way, a Filipino knows that a roof must be built carefully; even though the weather in the Philippines is usually balmy, typhoons are frequent enough that the only uncertainty is when the roof's strength will be tested."

If BP couldn't foresee this accident, then at least they would have been prepared for what to do after such an event happened. It should be "a matter of course" to know how to fix a blown wellhead. However, in the weeks following the blowout, it became clear to an increasingly astonished public that the BP engineers had no plan for dealing with this eventuality. As live video from remote underwater cameras showed thousands of gallons of oil billowing out of the breached well, the engineers struggled to find a solution. Never before had a blowout occurred at 5,000 feet under the sea.

Like doctors trying to treat a mystifying illness, the engineers desperately attempted one remedy after another. First they tried to drop a giant concrete containment dome over the leak. This failed. Next came a method called "top kill," which required pumping drilling mud (a specially formulated heavy mud) back down the well bore. At the same time they were doing this, they attempted a "junk shot," which literally involves dumping junk— shredded tires and golf balls — into the blowout preventer. After repeated attempts, this too failed. The mud and the junk came flying back out of the well and into the sea. The engineers were improvising on the fly, and they were demonstrating all the paralyzing panic that planning for failure is designed to prevent. The situation became so dire and the problem seemed so far beyond the capabilities of the BP engineers that InnoCentive, a crowdsourcing web site, posted the challenge of capping the well and invited ideas from the public. One suggestion was to explode a nuclear bomb underwater to choke off the well.

Realizing that stopping the flow in the short term was not going to work, the BP engineers moved on to their next option, the "top hat," which involved installing a collection device on top of the riser pipe that connected the well head to the rig. This allowed the engineers to direct the flow of oil into a vessel on the surface. While they hadn't stopped the flow, at least they were now capturing some of it. But the well was still not plugged and most of the oil was still leaking into the sea. So they tried installing a "capping stack" on top of the blowout preventer. This proved to be only a temporary and unstable solution. Eventually they attempted a "static kill." With the flow of oil temporarily halted, they once more pumped drilling mud into the well. It worked. The date was August 3, 2010, almost four months after the explosion aboard the Deepwater Horizon.

BP's initial estimate of 1,000 barrels of oil a day leaking into the Gulf proved to be wildly inaccurate. An engineering professor at Purdue University calculated the actual flow rate at closer to 70,000 barrels a day, which the National Commission ultimately concluded was a much more accurate figure. By the time it was all done, almost 5 million barrels of oil had spilled into the Gulf, creating a slick over 100 miles long that eventually started washing ashore along the Louisiana coastline. Along the way it played havoc with the livelihoods of many shrimpers and oystermen, some of whom had been fishing the abundant waters of the Gulf for generations.

Given all the time, money, innovation, and sheer audacity that had brought BP to the Macondo well and allowed them to pierce through to the treasure below, the remarkable thing about this story is how ill-prepared the company was for the eventuality of a deep-sea blowout. Unbelievably, the scenario planning for that eventuality started only after the well erupted. Like Rumsfeld's generals, BP had marched fearlessly into a hostile place and forcefully established their presence there, but they had no plan for what to do if the situation started to unravel. It's as if it had never occurred to anyone that anything could go wrong. And though the Deepwater Horizon was bristling with the latest technology, the solutions that were brought to bear on the oil leak seemed both crude and outmoded. The National Commission report noted as much: "The technology for deep water drilling has advanced enormously — but not the technology for cleaning up oil spills. That is still twenty years old." They were not only old but also ineffectual. "Twenty years after the *Exxon Valdez* spill in Alaska, the same blunt response technologies — booms, dispersants, and skimmers — were used, to limited effect."

If BP failed to foresee the Macondo disaster and if it then appeared unprepared to deal with the aftermath, then at the very least one would expect that a company of their size and sophistication would be prepared from a communications perspective to deal with the inevitable public relations fallout. But that, too, was not to be.

In an astonishing display of self-pity, just days after the spill, BP CEO Tony Hayward kicked off a series of PR blunders by saying to his fellow executives in London, "What the hell did we do to deserve this?" A month later, with oil still gushing into the waters off the Louisiana coast and gutting the fishing industry, Hayward, whose total compensation the year before was over $5 million, lamented, "There's no one who wants this over more than I do. I would like my life back." One wonders where the company's PR people were at this point. On the subject of the impact the largest oil spill in American history would have on the environment, Hayward told one news organization, "I think the environmental impact of this disaster is likely to have been very, very modest." And he explained to a British newspaper, "The Gulf of Mexico is a very big ocean. The amount of volume of oil and dispersant we are putting into it is tiny in relation to the total water volume."

As the company was preparing for the failed "top hat" solution, he told a television news crew, "We rate the probability of success [at] somewhere between 60 and 70 percent." Pat Campbell, the American expert brought in by BP as a key adviser during the crisis, watched in puzzlement as Hayward's statement played out on TV, and thought to himself, "Wow, that's very ambitious." His advice to BP had been that the "top hat" attempt had a very low probability of success.

Not to be outdone, BP chairman Carl-Henric Svanberg, after a meeting with President Obama at the White House to discuss the crisis, announced to the assembled press, "We care about the small people. I hear comments sometimes that large oil companies are greedy companies who don't care. But that is not the case. We care about the small people." He and his entourage then headed to their fleet of limousines idling nearby. Some attributed this gaffe to Svanberg's Swedish background and lack of facility in English. But whatever language this thought is expressed in, it remains shockingly tone-deaf and patronizing.

Focusing the company's message in a clear and consistent way and keeping the key spokespeople on that message are the most basic tasks of crisis communication. And in this case the most basic tasks weren't being attended to. By October, Hayward, the maladroit face of BP's response to the crisis, had been shunted out of his role as CEO and left the company.

All this was compounded by the fact that in 2000, under its former CEO John Browne, BP had undergone a $200 million rebranding initiative to reposition itself as a company committed to the environment. As part of the campaign, the initials BP, which for decades had stood for British Petroleum, were spun into a new slogan: Beyond Petroleum. And the company logo, which since the 1930s had consisted of the letters BP in yellow set inside a green shield, was transformed into a green and yellow circular design reminiscent of a sunflower. The company called this new logo the helios, after the Greek sun god, and said it represented dynamic energy in all its forms.

Landor, the international branding firm that handled the branding and identity of the makeover, had this to say about the new logo: "Bright and bold, the identity evokes natural forms and energy that represent, respectively, BP's position as an environmental leader and its goal of moving beyond the petroleum sector." As part of its internal strategic analysis, Landor created a mood board to explain the new brand to their client. It showed that if BP were an automobile, it would be an electric smart car, and if it were an animal, it would be a dolphin.

No doubt Landor and BP had done lots of consumer research in the process of developing the new brand identity. But like most marketers, they likely tested only the positive expression of the brand and not all the negative responses it might elicit once it went public.

Predictably, environmental groups ridiculed the change as an exercise in "greenwashing," accusing the company of trying to cloak itself in the consumer-friendly issue of environmentalism. A statement from Greenpeace sniffed that the change was "a triumph of style over substance." Greenpeace later awarded Browne an Earth Day "Oscar" for Best Impression of an Environmentalist.

For more than twenty years I've been working with clients, from detergent manufacturers to large energy companies, that have wanted to hitch a ride on the environmental bandwagon. My advice to them has always been the same. First, it's not enough to launch a few green products; you've got to be prepared to change everything about the way you do business, from what kind of energy you use to light your head office to how you dispose of waste in your plants and factories. And second, the minute you position yourself in the green space, be prepared for intense scrutiny from environmental groups and the media. Which is as it should be. Going green is not a marketing ploy; it's a serious commitment. People will be criticizing you and challenging you. By taking on the green mantle, a company is stepping into the volatile arena of political debate and action.

How, then, was it possible for a company engaged in one of the most environmentally risky businesses on the planet, and carrying it out in remote and hazardous places, to position itself as a green pioneer and not have a coherent communications plan in place to deal with the eventuality of environmental disaster? One might argue that perhaps BP had such a sterling safety record that it had never encountered a deadly crisis like this before, and that's why they weren't prepared to deal with it. But the National Commission report into the Deepwater Horizon oil spill says otherwise: "BP had a tarnished reputation for safety. Among other BP accidents,

15 workers died in a 2005 explosion at its Texas City, Texas, refinery; in 2006, there was a major oil spill from a badly corroded BP pipeline in Alaska."

No, the answer is that BP simply hadn't bothered to plan for it. When the inevitable disaster came, BP's green logo became an easy target for protesters. After the Gulf oil spill, Greenpeace ran a worldwide contest calling for a redesign of the BP logo. "BP's slick green logo doesn't suit a company that engages in dangerous offshore drilling," noted the environment group. "We're inviting you to design them a new logo that's more suitable for their dirty business." Many of the submissions showed the sunflower logo dripping with black oil. Several designs reworked the company's initials into a new slogan, ranging from "British Polluters" to "Black Plague."

The cycle was complete. BP had failed to anticipate a major blowout in its deep-sea drilling operations; it had failed to plan for adequate containment and recovery if a blowout did happen; and it had even failed to have in place an adequate communications game plan in the event of an environmental disaster — even as it was touting its green credentials to the world. On the one-year anniversary of the Deepwater Horizon tragedy, Moody's ratings agency estimated that the cleanup and compensation would cost BP somewhere between $40 billion and $60 billion.

Had BP war-gamed this tragedy they might possibly have prevented it and saved lives. At the very least they would have been able to work on a solution with greater speed and accuracy. And they would have saved everyone affected by this disaster from the distressing experience of seeing the culprit behave with such insensitivity and self-absorption.

It's tempting to think that BP was an isolated case, one company that had lost sight of the importance of forward thinking and planning. But what if an entire industry fell victim to the same lack of foresight? What would be the consequences?

Back in the early 1970s, when Pierre Wack and his colleagues were scenario-planning the coming oil crisis and preparing for its aftermath, another industry was blithely rolling along, totally unaware of what lay ahead. For decades the American auto industry had been cruising along a smooth and steady growth curve. From 1950 up to the early 1970s, auto sales had more than doubled, from roughly 6 million to over 14 million vehicles sold each year. Following the 1973 oil crisis, that number dropped by a staggering 3 million vehicles, a 20 percent decline in just one year. Not since 1933 had the industry experienced such a precipitous drop.

It took four long years, but auto sales eventually recovered to 1973 levels. However, for the Big Three American automakers, that recovery took place in an entirely altered landscape. As they were working their way out of that deep trough, they were joined by new competitors from Asia. From 1970 to 1980 the number of cars imported into the U.S. from Japan and Korea had quadrupled, from less than half a million to almost 2 million, and continued to increase steadily. The oil-price shock had jolted American consumers into noticing the smaller, more fuel-efficient, and surprisingly well-built Japanese vehicles. By comparison, the U.S. vehicles came to be seen by many as clunky and junky. "Ford" became a new acronym: Fix Or Repair Daily. The question of quality became such an issue that in 1981 Ford actually had to launch a multi-million-dollar global ad campaign to convince skeptical consumers that at Ford, "Quality is job one." The campaign would run for the next seventeen years.

Ford was not alone. All three major U.S. auto companies had failed to plan for a world in which smaller and more fuel-efficient cars would be in greater demand. They were further lulled into complacency by the dramatic drop in oil prices in the early 1980s. The result was ever bigger and more powerful vehicles coming to market, most notably the SUV.

Starting in the mid-1980s and for the next two decades, American consumers could reliably be depended upon to buy between 15 million and 17 million new vehicles almost every year. In that kind of environment, planning was a no-brainer. Superficial changes to styling and colour would be sufficient to keep things rolling along. In terms of market psychology, the U.S. auto industry was in the same headspace as the oil industry had been during the post-war years. They looked in the rear-view mirror and predicted that in the future it would be business as usual.

As Pierre Wack notes, in the decades following the Second World War, oil companies could rely on demand for oil to consistently outpace growth of gross national product in developed countries. It was a remarkably dependable indicator that could turn even the most inept planner into an oracle. The oil business was a growth industry. So what if you built too much refining capacity or overspent your exploration budget digging dry holes? A couple of years of growth would smooth out the problem.

It's not surprising perhaps that many of those managers thought they were riding a cable car to the top of the mountain.

It was the job of the Shell planners to let them know they were actually on a roller coaster. The message Wack and his colleagues delivered to Shell management was both stark and dramatic: "Prepare! You are about to become a low-growth industry." The roller coaster was creaking its way to the summit. And we all know what comes after that.

In 2007 the U.S. auto industry was winching itself into a similar position. The only problem was, there were no scenario planners issuing a warning about the looming precipice. When the 2008 financial crisis came, it triggered a heart-stopping plunge in vehicle sales. From 2007 to 2009, sales nose-dived from roughly 16 million to about 10 million vehicles, a drop of almost 40 percent in just two years. It made the 1973 downturn seem like a hiccup.

Some would argue that no one saw the financial collapse coming, but there were a few Cassandras foreshadowing danger. Not the least of these was Sir Andrew Large, deputy governor of the Bank of England, who in a 2004 speech at the London School of Economics laid out his concerns about several converging trends that could lead to a global financial crisis. He even identified the phenomenon of "too big to fail" financial institutions, giving them the more technical label of Large Complex Financial Institutions. Operating transnationally, these companies were difficult for any one government or regulatory agency to control, he argued. This, combined with the breakdown of the traditional barriers between banking, securities, and insurance; the rapid technological changes in the trading room; the spreading of risk, making risk assessment more difficult; and, perhaps most important, the opaque business of derivatives, had created a potentially unstable situation that could erode confidence in the financial markets.

What Sir Andrew was arguing was that "in times of instability or crisis that confidence — and with it liquidity — could evaporate." That's exactly what happened in 2008 with the sub-prime mortgage fiasco in the U.S., which packaged suspect loans into opaque instruments and then sold and resold them until nobody knew what they owned or how much risk they had assumed. When this house of cards finally collapsed, the result was that liquidity seized up.

Nowhere was this restrained liquidity felt more keenly than in the U.S. automotive industry. Having issued lousy house loans to people who should never have received them, financial institutions decided they shouldn't issue proper car loans to people who deserved them. The government had to step in with a "Clunkers for Cash" program just to start greasing the wheels again.

Could this crisis have been foreseen? The U.S. government's Financial Crisis Inquiry Commission, which looked into the subject, concluded: "This crisis was avoidable — the result of human actions, inactions, and misjudgments. Warnings were ignored." There were warning signs in the auto industry as well. The length of time Americans were holding on to their cars had started to climb dramatically in the years leading up to the economic crisis. In 2004 average car owners held on to their vehicles for about four years. By 2009 it was up to almost six years.

The problem for the auto industry was not a lack of foresight but a lack of imagination. They had failed to imagine a scenario in which credit would be so constrained that millions of Americans would hold on to their vehicles for two years longer and sales would plummet like never before. The Financial Crisis Inquiry Commission concluded, "The greatest tragedy would be to accept the refrain that no one could have seen this coming and thus nothing could have been done. If we accept this notion, it will happen again." Like BP, the auto industry had neglected to contemplate its worst-case scenario and to give voice to its greatest anxieties. The Big Three had planned what the next season's vehicles would look like. They had planned how to grow their market share. They had planned how to beat the competition. They had not planned for failure.

For the Big Three automakers the outcome of the crisis was devastating. Both GM and Chrysler filed for bankruptcy and had to be bailed out with billions in loans and investments from governments in the U.S. and Canada. Ford managed to secure long-term financing ahead of the collapse, staving off bankruptcy and saving it from the embarrassment of having to go to the government, hubcap in hand, begging for a bailout.

Despite the fact that the industry has rebounded in the years following the crisis, a heavy price was paid in lost jobs. And in 2013, in a final *coup de grâce*, the city of Detroit, once the heart of the auto industry, declared bankruptcy.

PLANNING TO PREVENT FAILURE

Planning for failure has two benefits. The first is that it allows a team in crisis to act with calmness and competence because they've already played out the scenario, or something like it. That's exactly what the BP team needed and didn't have. The second is that if you imagine what could go wrong, you can sometimes actually prevent it from happening. That's what the U.S. auto industry needed in the years leading up to the 2008 financial crisis: a strategy for averting crisis before it hit. But that takes long-term planning and foresight.

Back in Toronto at the offices of Crestview Strategy, Chad Rogers explained to me how the latter works, how planning for failure can help to change the course you're on. In 2001 Rogers was in Nova Scotia working for Conservative premier John Hamm, who was halfway through his four-year mandate. Two years earlier the Conservatives had won a remarkable upset victory. Starting the election campaign at the back of the pack, behind the New Democratic Party and the ruling Liberals, the Conservatives leapfrogged their way into a majority government.

But twenty-four months into the party's mandate, the electorate was deeply unhappy. Rogers was stunned by how dramatically the party's fortunes had fallen. Polls indicated the Conservatives were headed towards a catastrophic loss, one from which it would take decades to recover. "We realized two years in, when I started running the research, not only were we not going to get re-elected, we were going to get unelected for a generation," Rogers said.

The problem, as Rogers explains it, was that John Hamm, a small-town physician turned politician, had campaigned on fixing the healthcare system, but once he got into office he decided to focus first on balancing the budget. He managed to do that in 2002, the first time in decades the province had delivered a truly balanced budget. This was cold comfort to restive healthcare workers who were threatening a strike and to voters who were impatient for improvements to the health system. "We betrayed the people who elected us," says Rogers. "We got elected on a mandate to fix healthcare, we governed on a mandate to balance the budget."

The consequences of that betrayal were now making themselves known in the plummeting poll numbers. Equally disconcerting, the data showed that if the election were to be run on the issue of healthcare, there was literally nothing the government could say on the subject that would win back voter trust. The only way forward was to make sure the ballot question for the election had nothing to do with healthcare.

Hamm had also promised during the 1999 election to cut taxes by 10 percent. The Conservatives decided this was where the opportunity lay to shift the narrative. They proceeded to deliver a tax cut, but rather than doing it the conventional way, through the income tax system, they calculated the amount due to each taxpayer and sent them a personal cheque in the mail. Research indicated that more than 50 percent of voters did not prepare their own income tax returns, a situation that would make a straightforward tax cut less visible. A cheque in the mail, however, would be noticed by everyone. Predictably, the opposition parties rose up in fury, accusing the government of bribing the voters with their own money.

Having managed to steal the opposition's attention away from the most toxic issue, health care, the Tories then set about trying to find the best way to position themselves on the less toxic issue of a tax cut. Rogers set to work, scenario-playing various options the way he would in one of his war games. Only this time he did it through research with voters. He began with voter surveys, quantitatively testing hundreds of variations on messages relating to the tax cut. Those were then narrowed down to fifty variations that went into qualitative testing in focus groups. Finally they had whittled it all down to just a dozen messages.

But critically, just as he had done in the war-gaming scenarios, Rogers was testing not only the government's message but the likely opposition messages as well. He knew that the Conservative message would not be living in isolation; it needed to withstand attacks from the outside. Public discourse in politics is messy; lots of people want to have a say, not just the opposition political parties. In this atmosphere, Rogers insisted, "Unless you model the proposal you're going to put forward, in that more realistic, chaotic, asymmetric opinion environment, your testing isn't worth a damn."

This is where the political world diverges from the traditional marketing world. When developing their messages, marketers almost always test only their own messages and almost never test the likely conflicting messages that will come from others. Historically, they've never had to. When all you've had to face in the past is possibly the occasional competitive ad from one of your rivals in the category (that other car company, for instance), you needn't be too concerned. But today the world of marketers is just as chaotic and asymmetric as that of politicians. They have to contend with activist consumers who are adept at amplifying their voices through social media. This is the real world of public debate, and it affects marketers no less than politicians. "In real-world opinion," said Rogers, "the first thing you have to accommodate is adversaries."

Taking his real-world approach to the situation for the Tory party in Nova Scotia, Rogers found that the number-one argument against the very visible tax cut the government had handed out was that they were "bribing people with their own money." Sixty-five percent of people agreed with that view. However, the research also showed that simply presenting themselves as the party of tax cuts wasn't going to fly. The message that Conservatives were tax cutters was wearing thin. "As it turns out, cutting taxes has almost no power in it," said Rogers. "It's a double negative. 'Tax' is a bad word and 'cuts' is a bad word. They were tired of these words and were desensitized to them; politicians had used them for a long time."

But among the whittled-down statements, what Rogers found was that a whopping 93 percent of voters agreed that "lower taxes helped working families." In other words, this message would swamp the opposition claim that the Conservatives had merely bribed people with their own money. Two years away from the next election, with the polls predicting a massive defeat, the government had found the issue it wanted to fight the election on (tax cuts) and had developed a way to frame their message (helping working families) that would overcome the negative attacks.

They needed every day of those two years to play catch-up, but once they started to communicate their message, the Conservatives were able to slowly pull their way out of the trough they'd created. The poll results started to improve. "It took us two years to catch up and undo the damage, gaining a point a month over about fourteen months," Rogers said.

Had the opposition done their research they would have known that the way to defeat the Tories was to fight them on their broken promise of fixing healthcare. But Rogers pointed out, with just a hint of glee, "When we got to the campaign, every one of our opponents took the bait, and the whole election was about whether we should have bribed taxpayers with their own money. They should have run an election on us breaking our promise on healthcare and failing on healthcare. And they would have beaten us overwhelmingly if they'd run that campaign. We knew because that's what our numbers told us."

Instead, Hamm repeated his come-from-behind victory and the Conservatives won re-election, but with a reduced number of seats. "We were one seat shy of a majority," said Rogers, "but we should have lost by twenty seats if any of the polling from the previous two years had held true."

When I asked Rogers what lessons marketers can take away from his war-gaming and planning-for-failure strategies, he replied without hesitation: "It's okay if people hate you; it's okay if people disagree with you. You don't have to change their minds. You can't spend your time arguing with them or trying to change their minds." This is also where we started this book, acknowledging that pissing some people off is inevitable and trying to please everyone is the quickest road to mediocrity.

But there's more to it than that. Planning for failure is also a means for marketers to open up their minds to the possibility that those people who hate you might be putting out their own messages about your products and brands, and you owe it to yourself to figure out what those could be and how to deal with them. Brand managers still frequently use SWOT analysis as part of their planning process to identify strengths, weaknesses, opportunities, and threats. But this is frequently a superficial analysis of what outsiders might say about you.

Political strategists often use a different approach, called the Leesburg Diagram. It's also a four-box figure, but what it lays out are the following elements: what I want to say about me, what my opponents want to say about me, what my opponents want to say about themselves, and what I want to say about my opponents.

This approach takes into account the full spectrum of positive to negative messages, and it more accurately reflects the real-world situation in which brands will need to survive. It forces consideration of all the voices in the public square, not just one's own.

In addition to opening up brands to a wider view of the world, planning for failure is liberating and empowering for the team. It allows them to operate with confidence and fluency in the middle of a crisis and, in some cases, can even help stave off disaster.

But what all of this requires is the right mindset, one that says, *I'm going to take out an insurance policy on the future in the event that disaster comes my way.* It's hedging your bets against the unknown unknowns. It's an attitude that some people factor naturally into their thinking; others don't. Donald Rumsfeld was content to take the Scarlett O'Hara fiddle-dee-dee approach to planning. "I can't think about that right now. If I do, I'll go crazy. I'll think about that tomorrow," says Scarlett. After all, tomorrow is another day.

In 2011, Tony Hayward, no longer with BP, was called upon to testify in a suit brought against the company by several plaintiffs in the Deepwater Horizon tragedy. Dressed in a blue suit and purple tie and speaking barely above a whisper, he was questioned about BP's approach to insuring itself against potential environmental disasters. He stated that the company was "self-insured" against such incidents. The lawyer asked, "What did self-insurance mean to you?"

Looking weary, Hayward removed his frameless glasses and impatiently explained, "It meant the company didn't have an insurance policy against the risks it was undertaking, in essence. As it says here, we self-insured and took those risks onto our balance sheet."

"Is self-insured another way of saying no insurance?"

"Yes."

CONCLUSION

JOINING THE DEBATE

Politics is a frequently cynical business. It seems to attract more than its fair share of charlatans, tricksters, and toadies. But it isn't always that way. At its noblest, politics asks and answers the critical question "What kind of society do you want to live in?" That's not a question marketers have traditionally been concerned with. They prefer to keep the discourse on the level of "What kind of breakfast cereal do you want to eat?" That's why it was noteworthy when, just over a month after Cadillac started airing its controversial "Poolside" television commercial, with its unabashed celebration of American hard work and consumerism, Ford responded with an ad of its own that directly challenged Cadillac's world view.

The Ford commercial, a parody of Cadillac's macho chest-thumping, offered up a contrasting view of why Americans work so hard and what they care about. Mimicking the set-up of the Cadillac spot shot for shot, Ford shows a spokesperson talking directly to the camera, asking and answering a series of questions, starting with "Why do I work so hard? For this?" Only this time the scene is not a sun-drenched California pool but a giant pile of dirt. And the spokesperson is not an aggressive white male with swagger; it's an African-American woman with self-satisfied confidence and a bit of sass. She is not an actor but a real-life social activist, Pashon Murray, founder of Detroit Dirt, an organization that promotes composting and community farms. Its aim is to revitalize the blighted urban landscape of Detroit by reconnecting its citizens to the land.

Not coincidentally, the Ford commercial is for its environmentally friendly C-MAX hybrid vehicle. In a contrapuntal riff on the original commercial, Ford challenges the Cadillac ethos point by point. Cadillac sniffs, "Other countries, they work, they stroll home, they stop by the café, they take August off. Off." Ford counters that: "Other countries, they work, they stroll to the market and buy locally grown food. Locally."

"Why aren't we like that?" asks Cadillac. "Because we're crazy, driven, hard-working believers, that's why."

"Why aren't we like that?" responds Ford. "Well, more and more of us are like that, because we're crazy entrepreneurs trying to make the world better."

We're not like those Europeans; we should be more like those Europeans. That's a political debate that's been going on for some time in America. Donald Rumsfeld famously dismissed Germany and France as "Old Europe" in answering a question about why they weren't supporting the Iraq war. Not to be outdone, the cafeterias in the U.S. House of Representatives replaced the name "French Fries" with "Freedom Fries" on all their menus. Now this debate was making it into two sixty-second ads for American automobiles where there was

288

absolutely no mention of the vehicles being advertised and just a brief shot of them at the end.

The Ford ad goes on to question Cadillac's view of personal gain by countering with an appeal to social responsibility. Caddy's champion of individualism says, "It's pretty simple. You work hard, you create your own luck, and you gotta believe anything's possible." Ford's champion of the people answers, "It's pretty simple. You work hard, you believe that anything is possible, and you try to make the world better."

The upside of all the hard work? For Cadillac, it's more cool stuff. For Ford, it's helping the city grow more vegetables. The Ford commercial ends exactly the same way as the Cadillac spot, with Murray unplugging her Ford C-MAX from its charging station, hopping into the driver's seat, and turning to the viewer to deliver a smug "*N'est-ce pas?*"

The contrast between these two commercials could not be more black and white. They bookend the competing views of the American Dream: a society where individuals strive to better themselves and to seize the personal rewards that come with that striving versus a society where communities work together to lift everyone to a higher place. One celebrates the egalitarian American work ethic, where if you work hard enough you can achieve anything. The other celebrates the *e pluribus unum* spirit of social unity, where it takes a village to raise a child, or a community farm.

The question is, what are marketers doing engaging in a polemical debate on the kind of society America should be and the kind of values it should celebrate? They're doing what they've always done, adapting to the evolving environment around them. In the democratized world of public opinion, where divergent views are being shouted across the public square, marketers are finding that there isn't a no man's land of neutrality. They're being obliged to pick sides. It means tackling some big questions; it means taking a stand; and it means running the risk of antagonizing some people. Ford and Cadillac decided to plant their flags at the outer edges of the bell curve rather than struggle to find a safe middle ground. They will not be alone in this. Every day marketers are having to make decisions about what their advertising says, not just about their products or brands but also about the kind of corporate citizen they want to be.

In the summer of 2013, I was working with a large multinational packaged goods company as they were developing a new television ad for a leading food brand. The idea was that kids can be picky eaters but this product was so good it could win over even the pickiest eater in the family. Long before we got to the point of seeing advertising ideas from the agency, the president of the business unit took me aside and said, "I've been asking repeatedly that the agency not show me the same old thing when it comes to families: white mom, white dad, and two kids. The American family is changing and we should be reflecting that in our advertising."

The agency came up with an ad that involved a young boy dancing into the kitchen each day to reject whatever meal his mother had prepared. He is finally stopped in his tracks by the food he can't reject. As they had so many times before, the agency had scripted this spot with the traditional mom and dad and two kids. It was a vivid demonstration of how clients are pushing past their ad agencies in trying to keep up with the changing demographics of the American family, where more than a quarter of family households are headed by a single parent and where close to 40 percent of the population is non-white. That ratio is expected to flip by the year 2060, with whites accounting for only 40 percent of the population.

However, when we settled on this creative idea, we knew that the first character we'd have to cast was the little boy. We were looking for someone who could dance in a way that was natural, not professional, but would still be fun to watch, plus he had to be able to act. We had to find the best young double threat available. That meant a casting call from New York to L.A. and no restrictions on what ethnicity the kid would be. If the best talent we discovered turned out to be Korean, then so be it; the rest of the family would be Korean. As it happened, after screening 350 young actors we did not find the next Psy or "Gangnam Style" superstar; we found a charming and talented young boy from New York who was half African-American and half Hispanic.

Even as we were debating the issue of how to cast the rest of the family, a television spot for Cheerios hit the airwaves, and then it hit the fan. The ad featured an interracial family: white mom, black dad, and little girl. The spot is a delightful demonstration of Cheerios' heart-healthy message. The little girl asks her mom if Cheerios are good for your heart. Mom says they can remove some cholesterol, so that makes them heart healthy. The little girl runs off with the box of cereal. Next we cut to Dad napping on the sofa. He wakes to find a pile of Cheerios poured over the left side of his chest. The spot ends with the simple word "Love."

When Cheerios posted the ad to its YouTube channel, it garnered a lot of attention and a rash of surprisingly hostile comments. Some people were outraged that Cheerios was showing an interracial couple in one of their commercials. The online messages became so odious that Cheerios was forced to disable the comments section on their video channel. This might seem surprising given the range of non-traditional families seen on American television over the years, from *Modern Family* to *This Is Us*. But as Tim Nudd, writing in *Adweek* magazine, noted, "The problem is that TV ads have always lagged TV programming in this regard, as so many brands are clearly scared of being perceived as making a political statement with the casting of their commercials."

What the Cheerios, Ford, and Cadillac spots demonstrate is that brands are increasingly willing to step into territory where they have traditionally feared to tread. There can be little doubt that Cheerios debated at length the question of how to cast the commercial before it went to air, just as my client was doing at the time. (We ultimately opted for a single-parent family: mom and two kids, all non-white.) They must have anticipated that some people would react negatively. Like my client, the management at General Mills, the makers of Cheerios, made a conscious decision to reflect the changing face of the American family, regardless of the consequences. In fact, they might even have done it in expectation of provoking a reaction, in the well-established political tradition of wedge politics.

If so, it worked. The negative responses to the ad only served to inspire those who loved it to love it more. According to Ace Metrix, an analytics firm that evaluates video advertising, the Cheerios spot was the second highest rated of all cereal commercials in 2013. The dominant word people used to describe the spot was "cute." Of the over 5 million people who watched it on YouTube, the number of likes outweighed dislikes by a margin of more than twenty-five to one. The haters were a small minority but their voices were shrill and extreme.

The fact that this commercial should have inspired such vitriol for showing something so innocuous as an interracial couple is a sign of just how rare it has been for advertisers to do so. It's also a reflection of Cheerios' status as an iconic American brand with strong family associations. It's a product virtually every American parent feeds to their kids at some point. To take such a family-focused brand from a company like General Mills (whose stable of characters includes Betty Crocker, the Jolly Green Giant, and the Pillsbury Doughboy) and have it take a stand on an issue that was settled by the United States Supreme Court back in the 1960s seems like a no-brainer. But it provoked a certain fringe segment of American society precisely because it's such an unfamiliar sight in the risk-averse world of consumer marketing.

It was the very wholesomeness of Cheerios that seemed to inspire such a negative reaction. A year after the Cheerios ad appeared, another wholesome, all-American brand took to the airwaves with their own vision of the modern family that seemed to raise the stakes even further. The spot was for Honey Maid, makers of, among other things, that staple of the American pantry, graham crackers. The video opens on a close-up of a contented baby being fed its bottle. The camera pans out to reveal that Dad is doing the feeding. Then, in a surprising twist, a second dad leans in to kiss the baby. Because the camera is so close on these characters there's an intimacy to this scene that is almost as startling as the unexpected coupling itself. It is designed to arrest the viewer's attention. We then cut to two dads pushing a stroller. Then we see a series of "modern families," including single parents and interracial couples happily playing with their kids.

The voice-over that accompanies these images says simply, "No matter how things change, what makes us wholesome never will. Honey Maid, everyday wholesome snacks for every wholesome family. This is wholesome." Honey Maid is owned by food giant Mondelēz, the same folks who so cleverly exploited social media to raise awareness of the Oreo brand during the Super Bowl. Understanding the power of social media, and perhaps taking a lesson from the success of Cheerios the year before, Honey Maid produced an ad that is as much a statement about what makes a modern family as it is about what makes a wholesome snack. Gay dads — that too is wholesome.

Honey Maid was taking a word that it usually applied to its products and exporting it into a larger political and social context. It was taking a deliberate stand on one of the most divisive issues of the day. The debate over gay marriage had been swinging back and forth in states all over the U.S. Laws and ballot initiatives, pro and con, had been introduced in state legislatures from one end of the country to the other. The issue finally came to a head when Obama, after years of saying his views on the issue were evolving, finally came out on the side of gay marriage in a television interview with ABC's Robin Roberts in 2012, during the run-up to the election. As it turned out, Obama need not have waited. His declaration did nothing to diminish his re-election bid. It might even have boosted his support among younger voters.

Honey Maid, it seems, was on the right side of history, and of public opinion. It might appear cynical and self-serving for a brand to co-opt such important social issues, but the reality is that every day marketers have to make numerous decisions that touch on potentially controversial questions. Today, when an ad agency hands its client a script that calls for a family sitting around the kitchen table, someone will be asking, "What does that family look like?" In the 1950s, and for most of the decades that followed, this question was pretty easy to answer, and that answer was reflected in the homogeneity of countless advertising images over the years.

Much as companies might want to avoid stepping into these debates, it is becoming increasingly difficult to avoid them. For marketers, like politicians on the campaign trail, not taking a stand is taking a stand. And the relentless pressures of social media will force your hand one way or the other. Honey Maid doubtless anticipated the negative blowback their ad would receive. The group One Million Moms was reliably outraged, threatening a boycott and accusing Honey Maid of normalizing sin. But like a good political campaign strategist, the folks at Honey Maid were ready to respond quickly to all the anticipated hostility. Within weeks of airing its commercial, the company released a follow-up video that featured two artists from Chicago transforming all the negative comments, by taking printouts of the angry outbursts and rolling them into tubes that are then stood on end and glued together. Seen from above they look like giant bubbles. The camera pulls out to reveal that the tubes spell the word "Love."

As this action unfolds, the voice-over notes that the company received many negative responses to its Honey Maid commercial, an ad that "celebrates all families." It then goes on to say, "So we asked two artists to take the negative comments and turn them into something else." It is a clever and touching response. But just when you think the point has been made, the voice-over continues, "But the best part was all the positive messages we received. Over ten times as many." Now we pull back further to see the bubbles expanding all around the word "Love" and surrounding it with the overwhelming number of positive responses.

Just as Cheerios ended its commercial featuring the inter-racial couple with the word "love," so Honey Maid focused on the same idea in its follow-up to the ad with the gay couple. Both brands were boldly declaring, *This is what we believe love is; this is what we believe family is; this is the kind of society we want to live in.* It is the new voice of marketing.

Stepping into the spotlight at Chicago's Grant Park back in 2008, the Obamas had made concrete, at the apex of American society, the changing face of the American family. A little more than four years later, following his re-election and standing in Washington to deliver his second inaugural address, President Obama would solidify that change by making a statement about gay marriage that no other president had made before: "Our journey is not complete until our gay brothers and sisters are treated like anyone else under the law. For if we are truly created equal, then surely the love we commit to one another must be equal as well."

No doubt the President's message outraged many. But it was welcomed by many others. The gulf between red state and blue state may seem wider than ever, but the debate on what kind of society we want to live in is moving past the political sphere and has entered the world of marketing. And marketers, like their political counterparts, will have to declare their allegiances. Maybe that's not a bad thing. Maybe the elusive common ground politicians have been searching for has actually been there all along. Maybe it can be found in the grocery aisle.

NOTES

INTRODUCTION TO THE NEW EDITION

FAST FORWARD

CTV *News Special: America's Choice 2016*, broadcast November 8, 2016.

C-SPAN, "Donald Trump Presidential Campaign Announcement Full Speech," published on YouTube June 16, 2015. https://www.youtube.com/watch?v=apjNfkysjbM.

CTV *News Special: America's Choice 2016.*

AMERICAN FRANKENSTEIN

"Against Trump," Editorial, *National Review*, January 22, 2016. https://www.nationalreview.com/2016/01/donald-trump-conservative-movement-menace/.

Justin Caruso, "MSNBC Analyst: America Has Never Had Someone So 'Intellectually, Morally, Temperamentally' Unfit As President," *The Daily Caller*, accessed May 1, 2018. http://dailycaller.com/2018/02/13/msnbc-schmidt-trump-unfit/.

MY IGNORANCE IS AS GOOD AS YOUR KNOWLEDGE

Carol E. Lee, Courtney Kube, Kristen Welker, and Stephanie Ruhle, "Kelly Thinks He's Saving U.S. from Disaster, Calls Trump 'Idiot,' Say White House Staffers," NBC News website, accessed May 1, 2018. https://www.nbcnews.com/politics/white-house/kelly-thinks-he-s-saving-u-s-disaster-calls-trump-n868961. John Kelly, the White House Chief of Staff, has denied calling Trump "an idiot." Former Secretary of State Rex Tillerson also denied reports that he had called Trump "a moron"; he was dismissed a few months after the story broke.

Old Spice "Rocket Car" commercial, *AdForum*, released January 2016. https://www.adforum.com/creative-work/ad/player/34523835/rocket-car/old-spice.

Ronald Reagan Presidential Library, "'A Time for Choosing' by Ronald Reagan," video of a speech given on October 27, 1964; published on YouTube April 2, 2009. https://www.youtube.com/watch?v=qXBswFfh6AY.

Kimberly French, "Adlai Stevenson, the original egghead," *UU World*, Winter 2008. https://www.uuworld.org/articles/adlai-stevenson-original-egghead.

Isaac Asimov, "A Cult of Ignorance," *Newsweek*, January 21, 1980, p. 19. All subsequent quotations are from this one-page opinion piece.

TRIBAL LOGIC

"Gove: 'Britons Have Had Enough of Experts,'" portion of the EU Referendum Debate between Faisal Islam and Michael Gove on Sky News, June 3, 2016; published on YouTube June 21, 2016. https://www.youtube.com/watch?v=GGgiGtJk7MA.

Jonathan Chait, "Why Republicans Love Dumb Presidents," *New York* magazine, published January 10, 2018. http://nymag.com/daily/intelligencer/2018/01/why-conservatives-love-dumb-presidents.html.

Andrew Potter, "Steven Pinker, and Is Enlightenment Enough?: Why a New Age of Reason Won't Save Us," *Literary Review of Canada*, February 2018. http://reviewcanada.ca/magazine/2018/02/steven-pinker-and-is-enlightenment-enough/.

Paul Moloney, "Doug Ford Blasts Margaret Atwood over Libraries, Says 'I Don't Even Know Her,'" *Toronto Star*, July 26, 2011. https://www.thestar.com/news/gta/2011/07/26/doug_ford_blasts_margaret_atwood_over_libraries_says_i_dont_even_know_her.html.

Greg McArthur and Shannon Kari, "*Globe* Investigation: The Ford Family's History with Drug Dealing," *Globe and Mail*, May 25, 2013; updated April 17, 2018. https://www.theglobeandmail.com/news/toronto/globe-investigation-the-ford-familys-history-with-drug-dealing/article12153014/.

David Shum, "Doug Ford Booed at Mayoral Debate Over Comments on Jewish Community," Global News, October 6, 2014. https://globalnews.ca/video/1600047/doug-ford-booed-at-mayoral-debate-over-comments-on-jewish-community.

FIELD GUIDE TO THE FUTURE

Glenn Kessler, Salvador Rizzo, and Meg Kelly, "President Trump Has Made 3,001 False or Misleading Claims So Far," *Washington Post*, May 1, 2018. https://www.washingtonpost.com/news/fact-checker/wp/2018/05/01/president-trump-has-made-3001-false-or-misleading-claims-so-far/?utm_term=.f7f03515d38f.

Robert P. Jones, "White Evangelical Support for Donald Trump at All-Time High," Public Religion Research Institute (PRRI) website, April 18, 2018. https://www.prri.org/spotlight/white-evangelical-support-for-donald-trump-at-all-time-high/.

"Brexit is a Golden Chance to Throw Some EU Regulations on a Bonfire," Editorial, *The Telegraph*, March 28, 2017. https://www.telegraph.co.uk/opinion/2017/03/28/brexit-golden-chance-throw-eu-regulations-bonfire/.

INTRODUCTION: TILT SHIFT

Lyndon B. Johnson presidential campaign, "Daisy Girl," television commercial. https://www.youtube.com/watch?v=ouw1CAcr7xI.

"The Nuclear Issue," *Time*, September 25, 1964.

Carl Sandburg, "Chicago," *Poetry*, March 1914.

Jeffrey M. Jones, "Obama Ratings Historically Polarized," Gallup, January 27, 2012.

CHAPTER 1: THE POWER OF THE PASSIONATE FEW

THE BELOW-AVERAGE WINNER

"TEDxBOULDER — Jake Nickell — Never Stop Making," YouTube video, uploaded October 11, 2011. https://www.youtube.com/watch?v=mB2e4f1YhYw.

Rob Walker, "Threadlines," *New York Times*, July 8, 2007.

"Herman Cain Talks to Piers Morgan About Abortion," YouTube video, uploaded October 20, 2011. https://www.youtube.com/watch?v=LgKpZV39AKE.

"Herman Cain on Fox News — Responds to Abortion Comments Controversy," YouTube video, uploaded October 21, 2011. https://www.youtube.com/watch?v=STouYrf3bvQ.

"Romney on Abortion — 1994," YouTube video, uploaded May 3, 2011. https://www.youtube.com/watch?v=UeQGObiGGqY.

"Mitt Romney on Abortion Throughout the Years," YouTube video, uploaded November 1, 2011. https://www.youtube.com/watch?v=lNDsyKnQIes.

CNN/ORC Poll, September 9–11, 2011.

THE MAN WHO ATE FIFTY ORANGES A DAY

Peter Arnell with Steve Kettman, *Shift: How to Reinvent Your Business, Your Career, and Your Personal Brand* (New York: Broadway Books, 2010).

"Peter Arnell Explains Failed Tropicana Package Design," YouTube video, uploaded February 26, 2009. https://www.youtube.com/watch?v=WJ4yF4F74vc.

Daniel Lyons, "The Crazy Genius of Brand Guru Peter Arnell," *Newsweek*, March 27, 2009.

Linda Tischler, "Never Mind! Pepsi Pulls Much-Loathed Tropicana Packaging," *Fast Company*, February 23, 2009.

Stuart Elliott, "Tropicana Discovers Some Buyers Are Passionate About Packaging," *New York Times*, February 22, 2009.

Susan Fournier, "Introducing New Coke," Harvard Business School, October 31, 2001.

"Don Keough Speech Classic Coke," YouTube video, uploaded April 22, 2010. https://www.youtube.com/watch?v=t_djFC9Uhuw.

CHAPTER 2: PISSING PEOPLE OFF WORKS

THEY WILL BE TERMINATED

"Remarks and Q & A with Reporters on the Air Traffic Controllers (PATCO) Strike," YouTube video, uploaded December 1, 2009. https://www.youtube.com/watch?v=j3ZTCPJ39LA.

"President Reagan's Address to the Nation About Christmas and the Situation in Poland," YouTube video, uploaded December 10, 2012. https://www.youtube.com/watch?v=9kiFK6xxE08.

GOVERNING IN POETRY

Chris Harris, "Tom Morello Talks Obama, Not Rage Against the Machine, on Set of Anti-Flag Video," MTV News, April 7, 2008.

"Tom Morello on Bill Maher (Part 4)," YouTube video, uploaded November 19, 2011. https://www.youtube.com/watch?v=i_hthRZ_xto.

THE MOST OFFENSIVE AD OF 2000

Tammy Theis, "Tom Ford Departs World's Leading Luxury Label," *Dallas Morning News,* March 9, 2004.

Lauren Goldstein, "A Naked Bid for Attention," *Time,* October 27, 2002.

Laura M. Holson, "Tom Ford: Design Director," *New York Times,* December 2, 2009.

"I CAN'T WAIT TO GET MY MOUTH AROUND THESE BALLS"

"Schweddy Balls," YouTube video, uploaded January 3, 2014. https://www.youtube.com/watch?v=tJlofntR7f8.

Sarah Anne Hughes, "Ben & Jerry's Schweddy Balls Ice Cream Upsets One Million Moms," *Washington Post,* September 22, 2011.

Mark Memmott, "Stop 'Schweddy Balls' Effort Begins," NPR, September 21, 2011.

CHAPTER 3: ALL POLITICS IS INDIVIDUAL

NOT TOO BIG TO FAIL

Charles Duhigg, "How Companies Learn Your Secrets," *New York Times*, February 16, 2012.

Carole Cadwalladr, "Are the Robots About to Rise? Google's New Director of Engineering Thinks So . . . ," *Observer*, February 22, 2014.

Carlos Diuk, "The Formation of Love," *Facebook Data Science*, February 14, 2014.

DISOWNING THE MEANS OF PRODUCTION

Stanley B. Greenberg, *Dispatches from the War Room* (New York: Thomas Dunne Books, 2009).

Alan Barnard and Chris Parker, *Campaign It! Achieving Success Through Communication* (London: Kogan Page, 2011).

OUT OF THE CAVE AND INTO THE SUNLIGHT

"Obama Campaign Manager Jim Messina Talks Big Data at the Milken Institute's 2013 Global Conference," YouTube video, uploaded May 23, 2013. https://www.youtube.com/watch?v=mZmcyHpG31A.

"David Axelrod, Former Counsel to President Obama," Vimeo video. http://vimeo.com/66405527.

"A Conversation with David Axelrod," YouTube video, uploaded November 29, 2012. https://www.youtube.com/watch?v=h20IzYkwdR4.

Michael Scherer, "Friended: How the Obama Campaign Connected with Young Voters," *Time*, November 20, 2012.

Joshua Green, "Google's Eric Schmidt Invests in Obama's Big Data Brains," *Businessweek*, May 30, 2013.

CHAPTER 4: THE AGE OF THE OPEN BRAND

MAKE MINE COLOURLESS, ODOURLESS, AND TASTELESS

Richard W. Lewis, *Absolut Book: The Absolut Vodka Advertising Story* (North Clarendon, VT: Journey Editions, 1996).

THE BOXER BRIEF AS CORPORATE UNIFORM

Benoit Denizet-Lewis, "The Man Behind Abercrombie & Fitch," *Salon*, January 24, 2006.

Ashley Lutz, "Abercrombie & Fitch Refuses to Make Clothes for Large Women," *Business Insider*, May 3, 2013.

THE STREISAND EFFECT

Mike Masnick, "Since When Is It Illegal to Just Mention a Trademark Online?" *Techdirt*, January 5, 2005.

CHAPTER 5: THE BALLOT QUESTION

START THE CONVERSATION WITH A QUESTION

"1980 Presidential Candidate Debate: Governor Ronald Reagan and President Jimmy Carter," YouTube video, uploaded April 23, 2009. https://www.youtube.com/watch?v=_8YxFc_1b_0.

"Challenges — Obama for America TV Ad," YouTube video, uploaded October 13, 2012. https://www.youtube.com/watch?v=4nUDg-O93GU.

YOU CAN'T BE THE ANSWER IF YOU DON'T KNOW THE QUESTION

Beth Snyder Bulik, "Marketer of the Decade: Apple," *Advertising Age*, October 18, 2010.

SPENDING LESS TO GET MORE

James Poniewozik, "And the Grammy for Best Animated Pig in a Burrito Ad Goes to . . ." *Time*, February 13, 2012.

THE QUESTION IS HARDER THAN THE ANSWER

Ed Behr, "The Lost Taste of Pork," *The Art of Eating*, no. 51, January 17, 2013.

CHANGING THE TARGET AND THE MESSAGE

Carolyn Gregoire, "Cadillac Made a Commercial about the American Dream, and It's a Nightmare," *Huffington Post*, February 28, 2014.

Mike Colias, "Caddy CMO Subbed in Electric Car to Make Ad 'More Socially Palatable,'" *Advertising Age*, March 6, 2014.

Transcript, "Liberals Outraged by Cadillac Ad," *The Rush Limbaugh Show*, March 6, 2014.

CHAPTER 6: SPEED KILLS

HOGS IN THE WAR ROOM

Chris Hegedus and D. A. Pennebaker, directors, *The War Room*, 1993.

THE TEN-MINUTE AD

Angela Watercutter, "How Oreo Won the Marketing Super Bowl with a Timely Blackout Ad on Twitter," *Wired*, February 4, 2013.

CHAPTER 7: THE IMPROBABLE TEAM

WHEN YOU REACH FOR THE STARS

Patti Summerfield, "Executive Decision?" *Strategy*, August 3, 1998.

Susan Krashinsky, "Vision7's Claude Lessard: An Ad Man Reflects on Stiffer Competition," *Globe and Mail*, August 2, 2013.

FINDING THE PATTERNS IN THE DATA

"Everybody Has a Story with Obama for America Deputy Chief Analytics Officer Andrew Claster," YouTube video, uploaded April 22, 2013. https://www.youtube.com/watch?v=XhnnjdONZEI.

"Steve Jobs — Speech to the Academy of Achievement June 1982," YouTube video, uploaded October 7, 2011. https://www.youtube.com/watch?v=ymbD_a-G1IQ.

THE DAILY DISCO

"Wagner on Obama Campaign, Schmidt Investment, Cave," Bloomberg TV, May 31, 2013. http://www.bloomberg.com/video/wagner-on-obama-campaign-schmidt-investment-cave-TdZx1FTJTfeFmaFVPD35Vg.html.

A HIGHER CALLING

"Wagner on Obama Campaign, Schmidt Investment, Cave," Bloomberg TV, May 31, 2013. http://www.bloomberg.com/video/wagner-on-obama-campaign-schmidt-investment-cave-TdZx1FTJTfeFmaFVPD35Vg.html.

CHAPTER 8: PLAN FOR FAILURE

EMBRACING THE UNKNOWN

Pierre Wack, "Scenarios: Uncharted Waters Ahead," *Harvard Business Review*, September–October 1985.

Pierre Wack, "Scenarios: Shooting the Rapids," *Harvard Business Review*, November–December 1985.

A DARK RAIN BEGAN TO FALL

National Commission on the BP Deepwater Horizon Oil Spill and Offshore Drilling, "Deep Water: The Gulf Oil Disaster and the Future of Offshore Drilling. Report to the President," January 2011.

Tim Webb, "BP Boss Tony Hayward Admits Job Is on the Line over Deepwater Oil Spill," *Guardian*, May 14, 2010.

Clifford Krauss, "Oil Spill's Blow to BP's Image May Eclipse Costs," *New York Times*, April 29, 2010.

HUBCAP IN HAND

Andrew Large, "Financial Stability Oversight, Past & Present," London School of Economics, January 22, 2004.

CONCLUSION: JOINING THE DEBATE

Tim Nudd, "It's 2013, and People Are Still Getting Worked Up About Interracial Couples in Ads," *Adweek*, May 30, 2013.

ACKNOWLEDGEMENTS

As a first-time author I undertook the writing of this book with a kind of blithe naïveté. Thanks go to my publisher, Sarah MacLachlan, and my editor, Janie Yoon, for shaking me out of that mood and putting me to work in the most charmingly assertive way. Janie displayed the rare ability to crack a smile and crack the whip with equal alacrity.

I also owe a great debt to those who agreed to be interviewed for this book and who shared their wisdom and experiences so openly: Lord David Triesman and Alan Barnard in London, Steve Ells and Mark Crumpacker in New York, and Chad Rogers in Toronto. I owe an even greater debt to Barry Stringer and Kathy Doherty, the smartest and funniest people I have ever worked with, from whom I've cribbed all my best jokes and with whom I've shared some of the most exciting adventures of my career.

I am grateful also to Dorian Jabri and Michael Allen, whose friendship, intelligence, and discernment I value greatly. Both of them read early excerpts of the manuscript and, for better or worse, made enough encouraging noises to keep me going.

My thanks to Heidi Rubin and Frank Addario for their incisive legal counsel, without which this project would never have made it off the ground.

While most of this book was written in the cluttered confines of my office in Toronto, I did have occasion to do some writing in more congenial surroundings, provided by my generous friends Daniel Sigaud and Aurelie Giraud, in Marrakech, and Daisy Helman, in Martha's Vineyard. Thank you for welcoming me, and my laptop, into your homes.

And last, thank you to my many clients who have offered me so much encouragement and support over the years. You have taught me more than you know.

INDEX

A/B testing, 111–12, 116
Abercrombie & Fitch, 143–46; brand
    control attempts by, 144–46, 148, 157;
    corporate jet do's/don'ts of, 145–46;
    exclusion of large women by, 144–45
abortion issue, 28–32
Absolut vodka, 135–43; art
    commissioned for, 140–42, 156–57;
    initial branding of/ad campaign
    for, 138–40, 156; and simplicity of
    name/bottle design, 138, 140, 141–42;
    Swedish origins of, 137–38; Warhol's
    painting of, 140–41, 156
Academy of Achievement, 233
Ace Metrix, 292
actionable insights, as gleaned from
    data analysis, 86–87; by Obama
    re-election campaign, 103–4, 108–9,
    111–12
Adele: 21 (album), 177
Adobe products: Edge, 75; Flash, 73–77;
    Photoshop, 23, 128
advertising, in post-mass marketing
    era, 1–13, 15–17; and ballot question,
    160–90; and brand control, 124–25,
    127–28, 133–35, 143–52, 158; as
    capturing nascent trends, xxii–xxiv,
    xxv; and crowdsourcing, 148–52, 155,
    157; as exclusionary, 143–46; and family
    demographics, 290–97; and family

values, 64–65, 67, 70–71, 79, 81, 295;
    and importance of message, 123–25;
    and open branding, 10, 127–59; and
    ordinary consumer/citizen, 6–8, 10,
    127–28, 252; and "passionate few,"
    19–44; polarization in, 9–10, 45–79;
    and rebranding, 32, 35–44, 158–59,
    272–74; and speed of message, 10, 123,
    124, 191–219; team dynamics of, 10–11,
    221–23, 225–51; war room approach
    to, 10–11, 210–12, 216–18, 221–23,
    240, 248–51. See also specific topics;
    marketing, in post-mass marketing era
advertising, and social media. See
    Facebook; social media; Twitter;
    YouTube, postings on
Advertising Age, 167, 187
Advertising Standards Authority (ASA),
    64–65, 66, 67, 74
Adweek, 167, 292
AFL-CIO, 59
Aglukkaq, Leona, 56
air traffic controllers, 58–60, 72, 78
Albany Club (Toronto), ix–x
Ali, Muhammad, 186, 189, 190
Allstate Super Bowl ad ("Mayhem"),
    216–18
Amazon.com, 109
American Crossroads, 119
American Idol, 25, 106

and Russia collusion investigation,
xxxi, xxxvi; slogan of, 162, 188; tribal
politics under, xvi, xxviii; as Twitter
president, xxxiv–xxxv
Turner, Ted: and CNN, 191–92
Twitter, 51, 83, 116; and Abercrombie
& Fitch backlash, 144; and Israel's
assassination of Hamas leader, 192;
and #NeverAgain movement, 132;
and Obama re-election campaign,
109; ordinary citizens as broadcasters
on, 121, 132; Oreo Super Bowl ad on,
210–16, 219; and reaction to Chipotle
film, 177; and "Schweddy Balls" ice
cream, 71; Trump's excessive use of,
xxxiv–xxxv

Unilever, 72
union employees, as impacted by
Reagan: actors, 59; air traffic
controllers, 58–60, 72, 78; auto
workers, 93
United Auto Workers, 93
U.S. Civil War, 191
U.S. Financial Crisis Inquiry
Commission, 278–79
U.S. Olympic Committee (USOC), 133–35
U.S. Supreme Court, 229, 293

Vin & Spirit (V&S), 137. See also Absolut
vodka
vodka, 135–43; early market for, 137–38.
See also Absolut vodka
Vogue (French edition), 66
Volkswagen ad, 5
Vonnegut, Kurt, 141

Wack, Pierre, 259–60, 267, 275, 276–77.
See also Royal Dutch Shell, scenario
planning by
Wagner, Dan, 116, 231, 234, 237–38, 241
Wainberg, Mark, 54
Wallace, Chris, 118
Wanamaker, John, 87
Warhol, Andy: and Absolut vodka
painting, 140–41, 156
war room: of British Labour Party, 102;
of Clinton campaigns, 92–93, 194,

196–99, 211, 218, 238; at Facebook
headquarters, 240; as marketing
necessity, 216–18, 221–23, 240, 248–51;
as non-hierarchical, 194, 211–12, 238;
pollsters/researchers in, 85–86, 92–93;
as replicated by Oreo team, 210–16;
as replicated by TBWA teams, 248–51;
sharp minds of, 222–23; team dynamics
of, 10–11, 194, 211–12, 221–23, 238. See
also Clinton war room; "Cave"
The War Room (documentary), 196–99
Washington Post, xxxi
Weber, Bruce, 143
wedge politics, in Canada, 46–48, 54–58,
72, 78
Welles, Orson, 33, 35
Wendy's "Where's the beef?" ad, 165,
166, 167
Wieden + Kennedy, 210, 215
will.i.am, 129
Willis, Paul, 184
Winfrey, Oprah, 2
Winters, Dean, 216–17
work environments: of high-tech
companies, 238–41; political (Cave),
237–38
World Wildlife Fund (WWF), 46, 47
Wright, Orville and Wilbur, 186, 190
Wylie, Christopher, xxxii

Yelp, 116
"Yes, Pecan!" (Ben & Jerry's ice cream), 71
"Yes We Can" (Obama concession
speech video), 129–31
Young & Rubicam, 136
YouTube, postings on: Cheerios ad,
291–93; Chipotle film, 176–79;
comments on Cadillac ELR ad, 188;
"Fitch the Homeless" video, 144–45;
"Hillary and the Band" video, 128–31;
iPhone ad parody, 74–75; "Yes We
Can" video, 129–31
Yves Saint Laurent (YSL): Gucci's
acquisition of, 65; M7 ad created for,
65–66; Opium ad created for, 64–65

Zuckerberg, Mark, 240, 241, 243
Zune products (Microsoft), 237

© Maxime Bocken

CLIVE VERONI is a leading marketing strategist and political commentator. He is a consultant on branding, marketing, and advertising to a wide variety of blue-chip clients across North America. He is also a sought-after public speaker and a frequent political analyst on radio and television, and in print. His writing has appeared in the *Globe and Mail*, the *Hill Times*, and the *Literary Review of Canada*. Born in Cape Town, South Africa, he now lives in Toronto, Canada.